Food Governance in India

This book offers insights into the issues around food security, public health, equity and global governance. With a focus on India, it highlights the complex networks of sociopolitical, economic and agricultural challenges to ensure self-sufficiency in food production.

Based on field research conducted across India and an in-depth study on government agencies and multilateral fora, this book connects and juxtaposes global, national and local narratives on food security and policy. It analyses issues ranging from climate change to gaps in the nation-wide public food distribution systems. Through interdisciplinary narratives on food insecurity and poverty, the book exposes the underlying problems within policy frameworks and offers solutions for greater accessibility and distribution of food supplies while combating climate variability and agrarian distress.

The volume explores global food governance norms and India's role in further shaping them. It will be of interest to students and researchers of public policy and governance, development studies, sociology, agriculture studies, public health and nutrition and economics.

Anjoo Sharan Upadhyaya has served as a professor of political science at Banaras Hindu University since 1997. Her research interests are women and peace, human security, digital technologies and governance. She has edited several books, including *Nepal in Transition to Democracy* (2013), is the co-editor of the biannual journal, *Peace Works* and is the co-author of *Peace and Conflict Resolution in the Twenty-first Century* (forthcoming).

Åshild Kolås is a social anthropologist and research professor at the Peace Research Institute, Oslo (PRIO). Her core areas of expertise are governance, identity politics and peacebuilding. She is the editor of several anthologies, including *Women, Peace and Security in Myanmar: Between Feminism and Ethnopolitics* (2019) and *Sovereignty Revisited: The Basque Case* (2017, co-edited with Pedro Ibarra Güell).

Ruchita Beri is a senior research associate and centre coordinator for the Africa, Latin America, Caribbean and United Nations Centre at the Manohar Parrikar Institute for Defence Studies and Analyses (MP-IDSA), New Delhi. She has edited several books including *India and Africa: Common Security Challenges for the Next Decade* (2016).

Food Governance in India

Rights, Security and Challenges in the Global Sphere

Edited by Anjoo Sharan Upadhyaya,
Åshild Kolås and Ruchita Beri

Routledge
Taylor & Francis Group
LONDON AND NEW YORK

First published 2022
by Routledge
4 Park Square, Milton Park, Abingdon, Oxon OX14 4RN

and by Routledge
605 Third Avenue, New York, NY 10158

Routledge is an imprint of the Taylor & Francis Group, an informa business

British Library Cataloguing-in-Publication Data
A catalogue record for this book is available from the British Library

Library of Congress Cataloging-in-Publication Data
A catalog record has been requested for this book

ISBN: 978-1-138-34713-7 (hbk)
ISBN: 978-1-032-22459-6 (pbk)
ISBN: 978-1-003-27265-6 (ebk)

DOI: 10.4324/9781003272656

Typeset in Sabon
by Deanta Global Publishing Services, Chennai, India

Contents

List of tables vii
List of contributors viii
Foreword xiii
Acknowledgements xix
Introduction: Food for a growing India xx
ÅSHILD KOLÅS, ANJOO SHARAN UPADHYAYA AND RUCHITA BERI

1 **India's National Food Security Act (NFSA): Early experiences** 1
RAGHAV PURI

2 **The eco-system of India's food security regime** 19
SANJEEV CHOPRA

3 **Addressing nutritional challenges for India** 37
T.P. RAJENDRAN

4 **Challenges of the Targeted Public Distribution System in Eastern Uttar Pradesh** 54
ANJOO SHARAN UPADHYAYA

5 **Entitlements for the deprived: An empirical study of household food security in Karnataka and Bihar** 67
ARNE DULSRUD AND UNNI KJÆRNES

6 **Food entitlements: Political will versus preparedness of the state in Odisha** 86
NITA MISHRA AND EDWARD LAHIFF

7 **Global governance and India's food governance and security** 102
SHALINI KALA

8 The role of Israel in India's food security 118
MANJARI SINGH AND P.R. KUMARASWAMY

9 The G20 and India's food security concerns 133
ARPITA ANANT

10 Climate change and food security in India: Domestic and global solutions 155
MALANCHA CHAKRABARTY

Index 173

Tables

1.1 Important NFSA-related dates 7
1.2 Timeline of NFSA Implementation 7
1.3 Allocations for NFSA-related programmes, 2011–2012 to 2017–2018 (in INR millions) 9
2.1 Outlay/production of cereals, pulses and oilseeds (2007–2017) 22
2.2 Salient features of the NFSA 23
2.3 Evolution of the NFSA 25
2.4 Production of cereals, pulses and oilseeds (2010–2017) 28
2.5 Procurement status (2012–2013 to 2017–2018) 29
2.6 Performance of MGNREGA (2008–2018) 31
5.1 The number of times staple food (rice, wheat, other) and dhal were served yesterday 73
5.2 How main food items consumed in the household yesterday were procured (from own production, a PDS shop, other shop or being a gift or sharing with neighbours/relatives) 75
5.3 Access to land among rural households (in per cent) Multiple answers 77
5.4 Employment and access to the labour market 77
5.5 Holders of Below Poverty Line (BPL) and Antyodaya (AAY) ration cards (in per cent) 79
7.1 Government of India food security initiatives 104
7.2 Selected international institutions relevant to food security 107
8.1 List of CoEs in India 125
10.1 Cereal yields (kg per ha, 2016) 157
10.2 Growth rate of yield per hectare grain (per cent) 157
10.3 Change in nutrient content at elevated CO_2 compared with ambient CO_2 161

Contributors

Anjoo Sharan Upadhyaya has served as a professor of political science at Banaras Hindu University since 1997. She was the Indian Council of Cultural Relations (ICCR) Chair Professor at Dublin City University (2016–2017), ICCR Chair Professor at Tribhuvan University (2011–2013), guest professor at Karlstad University (2015–2016) and Fulbright visiting lecturer at Wellesley College (2010). She has been visiting professor at various academic institutions of the world including the London School of Economics, Concordia University, Wellesley College, University of Magdeburg, PRIO, Stanford University and Woodrow Wilson International Centre for Scholars, Washington DC. Her research interests are gender and human security, digital technologies and governance, and conflict transformation. She has published widely and has edited several books, including *Nepal in Transition to Democracy* (2013), is the co-editor of the biannual journal, *Peace Works* and is the co-author of *Peace and Conflict Resolution in the Twenty-first Century*, from Sage (forthcoming).

Arne Dulsrud is a senior researcher and research director at Consumption Research Norway, Oslo Metropolitan University, Norway. He has his PhD in sociology from the University of Oslo. His research interest and expertise are on economic sociology, food consumption, food security and consumer policy, the digital economy and consumer empowerment. He is currently the principal investigator and coordinator of two large research projects on food security: a project that explores the interconnection between food security and conflict in the context of Cauca, Colombia, and the "Platforms" project, which investigates the role of digital platforms on sustainable consumption (funded by the EU's Horizon 2020 programme).

Arpita Anant is associate fellow at Manohar Parrikar Institute for Defence Studies and Analyses (MP-IDSA), New Delhi, India. Her current area of research is India's multilateralism at the United Nations, with a focus on peacekeeping, terrorism and sustainable development. She was awarded the ICSSR Doctoral Fellowship and held a Commonwealth Visiting Fellowship (Canada) in 2001–2002. She holds a PhD in international politics from the School of International Studies, Jawaharlal Nehru University, New Delhi. Her doctoral thesis was on *Group Rights in the Indian and International Discourses*. She is associate editor of *Africa Trends: A Quarterly News Magazine*.

Åshild Kolås is a social anthropologist and research professor at the Peace Research Institute Oslo (PRIO). Her core areas of expertise are governance, identity politics and peacebuilding. She has conducted long-term fieldwork in multi-ethnic communities in India and China, and has written on Tibet, Nepal, Inner Mongolia and Northeast India. She is the editor of several anthologies, including *Women, Peace and Security in Myanmar: Between Feminism and Ethnopolitics* (2019) and *Sovereignty Revisited: The Basque Case* (2017, co-edited with Pedro Ibarra Güell), and the author of *Tourism and Tibetan Culture in Transition: A Place Called Shangrila* (2008) and *On the Margins of Tibet: Cultural Survival on the Sino-Tibetan Frontier* (2005; 2015, with Monika P. Thowsen). From 2006 to 2018, she coordinated an institutional cooperation between PRIO and the Institute for Defence Studies and Analyses (IDSA) in New Delhi. She currently leads the research project "e-Topia: China, India and Biometric Borders" at PRIO and serves as associate editor of the *Journal of International Development*.

Bishow Parajuli is the World Food Programme (WFP) Representative and Country Director in India. Prior to his current assignment, beginning in September 2019, he served as UN Resident Coordinator and UNDP Resident Representative in Zimbabwe; WFP Representative and Country Director in Yemen; Chief of Staff, WFP headquarters (Rome); Director, Executive Director's Office, WFP headquarters; Director of Government Donor Relations, WFP headquarters; UN Resident and Humanitarian Coordinator, Myanmar; and UNDP Resident Representative, Myanmar. He has also held various positions in the World Food Programme in Indonesia, Bangladesh, Mozambique and Botswana. He holds a master's degree in Agricultural Development and Business Administration and an honours degree in agricultural science. He has 35 years of experience in development, humanitarian affairs, diplomacy, fund-raising and management in Asia, the Middle East, Africa and WFP headquarters in Rome.

Edward Lahiff is a lecturer in international development at University College Cork and former director of the Bachelor of Science. Programme in International Development and Food Policy. He spent ten years in southern Africa working with rural NGOs and as senior lecturer in land and agrarian studies at the University of the Western Cape. In 2009–2010, he served as the coordinator of the International Doctoral School in Global

Health at the Centre for Global Health, Trinity College Dublin. His current research focuses on links between small-scale farming and nutrition, particularly in Ethiopia, and on the experience of rural-urban migrants in Vietnam. He has published widely on matters of food, land, rural and urban livelihoods, and natural resources.

Malancha Chakrabarty holds a PhD in Economics from the Centre for Economic Studies and Planning, Jawaharlal Nehru University. She is a Fellow with the Climate Change and Development Initiative at Observer Research Foundation in Delhi. Her research interests encompass issues related to economic and social development in Africa and India, and the links between climate change, agriculture, and food security. She is currently working on a project that explores India's trade, investment and development cooperation with African countries. Dr. Chakrabarty has published widely in international journals such as the *Review of African Political Economy* and *World Review of Political Economy*. She is also a regular contributor to newspapers such as *Asian Age* and *DNA*.

Manjari Singh is associate fellow at the Centre for Land Warfare Studies (CLAWS), New Delhi. Dr Singh is a Ryoichi Sasakawa Young Leaders Fellowship Fund (SYLFF) Fellow and holds a doctoral degree in West Asian/Middle Eastern Studies from Jawaharlal Nehru University. She has co-authored the book *Persian Gulf 2018: India's Relations with the Region* and co-edited the volume *Islamic Movements in the Middle East: Ideologies, Practices and Political Participation*. Her research papers have appeared in many national and international journals such as *Mediterranean Quarterly*, *Migration and Development* and *Contemporary Review of the Middle East*. Dr Singh has served as an assistant editor of *Contemporary Review of the Middle East* and managing editor of *CLAWS Journal*.

Nita Mishra is a researcher in international development in the Department of Food Business and Development at University College Cork, Ireland. She has lectured on theories of development, gender and rights-based approaches to development, the right to food, research methodologies, and non-government organisations in universities across Ireland, India and Vietnam. In India, she worked in research projects with the National Council of Applied Economic Research, Ford Foundation, Indian Social Institute, Nehru Memorial Museum Library, among others. She has published widely in peer-reviewed journals. Her current research focuses on social inclusion of rural migrants.

P.R. Kumaraswamy is a professor at Jawaharlal Nehru University (JNU) and an expert on the Middle East. From 1992 to 1999, he was a research fellow at the Harry S. Truman Research Institute for the Advancement of Peace, Jerusalem. At JNU, he has been researching, teaching and writing on various aspects of the Middle East. He also served as the director of the Gulf Studies Programme (2013–2015). His books include *India's Israel Policy* and *Historical Dictionary of the Arab Israeli Conflict*. In 2009, he set up the virtual Middle East Institute, where he continues to serve as honorary director. He is the editor of *Contemporary Review of the Middle East* and the series editor of Persian Gulf: India's Relations with the Region.

Raghav Puri is a postdoctoral associate at the Tata-Cornell Institute for Agriculture and Nutrition at Cornell University (USA). His research examines the implementation and impact of health and nutrition programmes in India. He received his PhD in public administration from the Maxwell School of Citizenship and Public Affairs, Syracuse University (USA), and a master's in public policy from the Lee Kuan Yew School of Public Policy, National University of Singapore. Before starting his PhD, he worked with the Social Protection and Labour Global Practice of the World Bank.

Ruchita Beri is a senior research associate and centre coordinator for the Africa, Latin America, Caribbean and United Nations Centre at the Manohar Parrikar Institute for Defence Studies and Analyses (MP-IDSA), New Delhi. She researches on political and security issues in sub-Saharan Africa, India–Africa relations and emerging powers in Africa. She is currently the president of the African Studies Association of India, a member of the Africa Committee of the Confederation of Indian Industry (CII) and serves on the executive board of the Forum for Indian Development Cooperation (FIDC). She is the editor of *Africa Trends*, a quarterly magazine published by MP-IDSA, and is on the editorial board of *Austral: Brazilian Journal of Strategy & International Relations*. She is also a member of the editorial advisory board of *Development Cooperation Review*. She has edited several books including *India and Africa: Common Security Challenges for the Next Decade* (2016).

Sanjeev Chopra is a historian, public policy expert and director of the literary festival, Valley of Words, an international literary festival, held annually in Dehradun, India. He was a member of the Indian Administrative Services (IAS) from 1985. His last IAS appointment was as the director of the Lal Bahadur Shastri National Academy of Administration. He writes extensively in various publications on public policy, development interventions, agribusiness, and rural economy. His chapter in the book was written while he served as the additional chief secretary to the Government of West Bengal, India.

T.P. Rajendran is a national expert on agriculture with a special interest in biosecurity and biodiversity. He is the author of over 128 research papers, book chapters and books in the areas of international policy perspectives on India–Africa cooperation, seed sector collaboration, improved farm efficiency in the Asia–Africa growth corridor and the framework in India for implementing Sustainable Development Goal 2 – Zero Hunger. He has been a consultant for many of India's farmer-based foundations on the development of products and technologies for improved agricultural efficiency.

Shalini Kala's areas of expertise are food security, smallholder agriculture and rural development. She has worked on agriculture policy and practice and developed and managed smallholder initiatives aimed at reducing poverty through better access to market, information, credit and other resources. She has explored the use of food as a tool for development in a food-surplus country like India in her work, while also examining ways to improve the effectiveness of food security and governance policies. An economist by training, she has worked across the Asia-Pacific region and advised initiatives in Africa, the Middle East and Latin America.

Unni Kjærnes holds an MSc degree in nutrition and a PhD in sociology. She works as research professor at Consumer Research Norway, Oslo Metropolitan University. Her work has concentrated on consumer perspectives on food policies in Norway, Russia and India, as well as comparative studies in Scandinavia and Europe. She has studied how patterns of consumption, public opinions and trust are influenced by provisioning systems and public policies, as well as how people as consumers influence these systems. Her areas of expertise are food safety, nutrition, sustainability, animal welfare and food security.

Foreword

It is a privilege to introduce *Food Governance in India: Rights, Security and Challenges in the Global Sphere* as an important body of work on food security by some of the leading academics, policy experts, researchers and practitioners.

I see this as an opportunity to highlight a strong convergence between issues, challenges and opportunities delineated in this book and the mandate of the United Nations World Food Programme (WFP).

This work comes at a watershed moment in a world disrupted by the COVID-19 pandemic. Two years into the global health crisis that has spawned social and economic disruption, we are witnessing the emergence of a major food security and livelihood threat to millions. The pandemic has led to a serious setback to the developmental gains we have collectively made over decades, towards ending poverty and hunger.

Globally, some 690 million people do not get enough to eat. Over half of this population lives in Asia. About 10 million people are added each year to the total number of hungry people. The World Food Programme estimates that, due to this ongoing crisis, the number of acute food-insecure people across the globe will double, to reach 270 million by the end of 2021.

The themes and issues covered in this book underline food security as the centerpiece of human rights, with "food governance" – based on equity, access, inclusion, and transparency – being the most important aspect of ensuring and guaranteeing this entitlement.

The overarching importance of this work also comes from the fact that it provides actionable insights and analysis for exploring solutions and discussion towards addressing some of the most pressing challenges that we face in our time.

Food security, and its governance, in a global and interconnected world, need collective engagement. While several chapters in this book look at the national and state-level experiences, a few of them draw on experiences from other countries and global examples.

India's journey towards attaining self-sufficiency in food production and evolving one of the world's largest food-based net is inspirational and replete with learnings on food governance. Food security discussion in India is not limited to the Right to Food but extends to the availability, safety, affordability and nutritional value of food products. However, we must equally and, perhaps even more strongly, underline the aspects of equity, inclusion, and access by addressing the exclusion and vulnerabilities of marginalised groups.

The World Food Programme in India has been a co-traveler in the journey from the Green Revolution to the Right-to-Food milestone since its operations started in 1961. Its work in this country has evolved with the changing landscape of hunger and food security, aligning with the policies and initiatives of successive governments. The fifty-year trajectory has seen the World Food Programme, the world's largest humanitarian food assistance agency, engage in most of the aspects covered in this book.

Drawing on this common ground, I would like to stress upon selected areas of importance related to addressing malnutrition and hunger in India, and globally.

However, before plunging into these issues, it is important to reiterate that hunger and food insecurity are key drivers of conflict and instability across the world. We often use "Food is peace" as a catchphrase to highlight how hunger and conflict feed on each other. We must continue to focus on food security and access to nutrition also as an important foundation for peace and social cohesion.

In 2020, when the pandemic was manifesting its global sweep, locking down economies, disrupting supply chains and livelihoods, the World Food Programme was conferred the Nobel Peace Prize, with the citation specifically highlighting the importance of food in reducing and addressing conflicts.

Created in 1961 as an experiment to provide food aid through the UN system, the World Food Programme (WFP) was to be reassessed within three years, to see if it was needed. Crises spill over the years, revealing hunger's deadly prevalence, marking the conscience of humanity. Subsequent decades consolidated the Programme's role as a humanitarian agency. In 2020, the Programme assisted 115.5 million people – the largest number since 2012 – in 84 countries.

In emergencies, the World Food Programme is often first on the scene, providing food assistance to the victims of war, civil conflict, drought, floods, earthquakes, hurricanes, crop failures and natural disasters. When the emergency subsides, the Programme helps communities rebuild shattered lives and livelihoods. We also work to strengthen the resilience of people and communities affected by protracted crises by applying a development lens in our humanitarian response.

In 2020, the World Food Programme provided 4.2 million metric tons of food and US$2.1 billion of cash and vouchers. By buying food as close as possible to where it is needed, we can save time and money on transport costs, and help sustain local economies. Increasingly, the WFP meets people's food needs through cash-based transfers that allow the people we serve to choose and shop for their food locally.

The World Food Programme also provides services to the entire humanitarian community, including passenger air transportation through the UN Humanitarian Air Service, which flies to more than 280 locations worldwide. Funded entirely by voluntary donations, WFP raised a record-breaking US$8 billion in 2019. The Programme has a staff of 20,000 worldwide, of whom over 90% are based in the countries where the agency provides aid.

There is a need to continue highlighting the role that the World Food Programme continues to play through humanitarian food response – non-stop and around the year – reaching some of the worst impacted and least accessible areas of the globe, as a collective resource for the UN, governments and communities.

First, we need to embed the principle of "leaving no one behind" when it comes to food security safety nets and entitlements. The "stubborn persistence of malnutrition" in India despite its phenomenal economic success needs, among other things, a razor-sharp focus on making sure that we are driven by context and deep understanding of pathways that create barriers to accessing the Right to Food.

Food insecurity and hunger are systemic as well as dynamic. Hence there is a need to constantly review and assess how various factors are impacting citizens and communities. An engaged and persistent assessment of needs and gaps is essential for ensuring that food support systems work and reach those they are meant to serve. Several aspects need to be considered for this, such as availability, transportation, economic and social access, systemic accountability, procurement and distribution. Targeting at-risk groups, such as people with disabilities, the elderly, single women-led households, transgender people, HIV-affected people and orphan children must be at the heart of any need-based safety net. Built around the broader value of equity and inclusion, food security schemes must ensure that the government system and process are transparent and accountable.

Second, to achieve the goal of "Zero Hunger", adequate food production is not enough. Providing food assistance in an emergency can save lives, but the right nutrition at the right time can also help change lives and break the cycle of poverty. Malnutrition is a matter of life and death, and in the long term, widespread malnutrition can hold back entire nations and countries, undermining economies, and development. As we focus on providing food assistance to those in need, we must prioritize nutrition for pregnant and lactating women, and for children.

Despite significant progress over recent decades, poor nutrition remains a massive and universal problem, with one in three people on the planet affected by some form of malnutrition. Undernutrition – inadequate energy or nutrients – continues to affect more than 150 million children worldwide, while rates of overweight and obesity are also rising in all countries. The Government of India has robust schemes and programmes in place to address food insecurity and malnutrition, such as the Targeted Public Distribution System (TPDS), the Mid-Day Meal (MDM) Scheme and the Integrated Child Development Services (ICDS), all covered under the National Food Security (NFS) Act, 2013. The Mid-Day Meal Scheme represents predictable support, constitutes a lifeline for millions of school children in the country and has a significant impact on children's daily diet, reaching close to 100 million school-aged children with hot-cooked meals.

In National Family Health Survey-5, data for only 22 states and union territories have been released so far. Ten of these 22 states and union territories have recorded an increase in stunted growth among children, while 4 of the 22 have a decrease in stunting in children. Likewise, 11 of 22 states and union territories have an increase in the prevalence of wasting among children, while seven of 22 see a decrease. Regarding the prevalence of anaemia in children, 18 of 22 states and union territories reflect an increase, and 4 of 22 have a decrease.

In the current context of the pandemic, I would like to suggest the following: Safeguard and promote access to nutritious, safe and affordable diets; invest in improving maternal and child nutrition through pregnancy, infancy and early childhood; re-activate and scale up services for the early detection and treatment of child wasting; maintain the provision of nutritious and safe school meals for vulnerable children; expand social protection to safeguard access to nutritious diets and essential services.

Micronutrient deficiency continues to affect sizeable sections of the global population in India and this "hidden hunger" extracts a substantial toll in terms of morbidity, mortality, reduced economic productivity and poor quality of life from those who are affected. Fortification has proven to be an effective strategy for addressing micronutrient deficiency.

Third, we need to prioritize a progressive and sustainable approach to Food Systems. The basic concept of food security globally is to ensure that all people, at all times, have physical, social and economic access to sufficient, safe and nutritious food for their active and healthy life, and is characterized by availability, access, utilization and stability of food. The fact that almost 700 million people are chronically hungry across the world suggests that food systems – the networks that are needed to produce and transform food, and ensure that it reaches consumers – are not meeting the needs of large sections of society.

The systems should be resilient to shocks such as the coronavirus pandemic, which has made life difficult for people at large, but caused serious distress for the vulnerable, those living with hunger and those living with food insecurity.

Fourth, climate change is fundamentally linked to and impacts Food Systems. The number of people affected by hunger in the world continues to increase. This trend started in 2014 and extends into 2019. There are nearly 60 million more undernourished people now than in 2014. The reason for this growth in hunger is primarily associated with climate shocks. This disturbing trend, and now the COVID-19 impact, challenges the achievement of Sustainable Development Goal 2 (SDG 2) on "Zero Hunger" by 2030, as documented by a 2019 report by the Global Centre on Adaptation.

Food systems, which encompass actors such as farmers, and credit lenders and processes such as production, processing, distribution, consumption and disposal, contribute to nearly 30%t of the global anthropogenic greenhouse gas emissions. Agricultural production, including indirect emissions associated with land-cover change, contributes nearly 86% of total food system emissions. Greening the Food Systems in addition to creating environmental sustainability and reducing the carbon footprint by investing in sustainable livelihoods, ensuring the availability of safe, nutritious, affordable food to everyone, improving efficiencies, reducing inequalities and strengthening climate resilience are key to achieving zero hunger and a sustainable environment simultaneously.

A third of all food produced is lost or wasted, which not only fails to contribute to food security and nutrition, but also increases the burden on natural resources. Lost or wasted energy used for food production accounts for about 10% of the world's total energy consumption, and annual greenhouse gas emissions associated with food losses and food waste reach 3.5 gigatons of CO_2 equivalent, according to the Food and Agriculture Organization.

Fifth, it is with utmost urgency that we must emphasize the importance of integrating a gender perspective and focus on women in the design and delivery of food security initiatives and programmes. Of the 690 million people who are food insecure in the world right now, 60% are women and girls. Because of the pandemic, hunger levels are expected to double – and the heaviest burden will again fall on women and girls. It is important to focus on the disproportionate impact that the rising hunger levels are expected to have on women. But what is equally important is to highlight that women are also part of the solution, and giving them access to food, tools and resources can make all the difference.

We are at the intersection of exceptional circumstances facing the triple crises of COVID-19, a global pandemic that has disrupted the world for close to two years now; a looming global hunger crisis fuelled by the pandemic and conflict; and a tipping point in the ongoing climate crisis. We must act collectively and with great urgency.

UN Secretary-General António Guterres will convene a Food Systems Summit as part of the Decade of Action to achieve the Sustainable Development Goals (SDGs) by 2030. The Summit seeks to launch bold new actions to deliver progress on all 17 SDGs, each of which relies to some degree on healthier, more sustainable and equitable food systems.

The Summit aspires to awaken the world to the fact that we all must work together to transform the way the world produces, consumes and thinks about food. At a time when Food Systems are under unprecedented stress, facing a crisis of equity, sustainability and resilience, we must seize this as an opportunity to add food security and food governance as fundamental aspects of revamping and reimagining a better future with Zero Hunger.

By addressing some of these vital issues, I am confident that this title will be welcomed and relished by a wide range of audiences, from media to policymakers, and from academics to practitioners.

Bishow Parajuli

UN World Food Programme Representative and Country Director, India

Acknowledgements

We would like to acknowledge and extend our gratitude to a number of individuals and institutions towards the making of this volume. Special thanks go to Dr Uttam Kumar Sinha, Dr Elida Kristine Undrum Jacobsen and Professor Priyankar Upadhyaya for supporting the project all through. The faculty, students and staff of the Malaviya Centre for Peace Research and the Department of Political Science, BHU, and Peace Research Institute Oslo (PRIO) for helping us organize conferences on Food Security at Varanasi (India) and Oslo (Norway); to the various participants who shared their time and insights during these significant events; to the civil supplies officials of Uttar Pradesh and to Manohar Parrikar Institute for Defence Studies and Analyses (MP-IDSA) for partnering with PRIO on this important project.

Introduction

Food for a growing India

Åshild Kolås, Anjoo Sharan Upadhyaya and Ruchita Beri

India has become the world's sixth-largest economy and is on a trajectory of rapid economic growth. Yet, a large part of its population suffers from malnutrition and the lack of food. As per latest data, the overall rate of inflation in India is around 6%, but in food items, it is closer to 10%. More than a quarter of the Indian population under the age of five suffers from wasting due to malnourishment (Global Hunger Index, 2020). There is a widespread lack of adequate protein intake among pregnant women and mothers of breastfeeding infants. These are crucial issues related to gender equality as well as maternal and child health, which highlight the need to understand food security and insecurity as a complex sociopolitical phenomenon (Vir, 2016), and to recognize the interrelated nature of hunger, deprivation and entitlement (Sen, 1981).

Indian perspectives on food security and governance are multifaceted, and there are manifold views and experiences following the institution of the Right to Food as a legal entitlement under the National Food Security Act, 2013. Based on field research in a number of Indian states, government agencies and multilateral fora, this book connects and juxtaposes global, national and local narratives on issues ranging from global food security challenges such as climate change and nation-wide governance mechanisms such as the Public Distribution System (PDS) to concerns about household-level and individual nutrition, food safety and access to food. Bringing all these issues together, this volume investigates India's role as a key actor on the global food governance scene.

The Right to Food (enshrined in Indian law in 2013) gave legal entitlement to subsidized grain through the PDS. Nevertheless, food insecurity and malnutrition are still an everyday battle for millions of Indian citizens, coexisting with India's emergence as a global power, and regardless of the rapid growth of its economy (Banik, 2007). Indian researchers have raised concerns about leakages from the PDS system (see, for instance, Sen et al., 2015), as well as the system's effectiveness and transparency (Drèze et al., 2015). Civil society organizations in India are calling for more efficient implementation, and measures to safeguard the Right to Food, recognizing the urgent need to address the prevalent inequity and the disparities that continue to produce poverty and malnourishment. Vital to the food security of India's citizens is not only the Right to Food, but also the availability, safety, affordability and nutritional value of food products.

From the Green Revolution to the Right to Food

In the 1960s, India was faced with serious food shortages and had to receive aid from the USA under the Public Law (P.L.) 480 Scheme. India subsequently called on international agencies for further support. The Philippines, Taiwan and the USA assisted India with high-yield varieties of seeds, including IR8 rice, through the collaborative efforts of the International Crops Research Institute for the Semi-Arid Tropics (ICRISAT) and the Indian International Rice Research Institute (IRRI) (Modgal, 2016). New efforts to boost agricultural production comprised the development of seed industries, fertilizer industries, various extension services and many other measures. India's food production increased as a result of these efforts, and in the mid-1960s, the success story became known as the "Green Revolution". By 1997, the agricultural production of India had reached 200 million tonnes, which was four times that of 1947.

Self-sufficiency in food production has been a central policy agenda since India gained its independence, as reflected in the consecutive Five-Year Plans of the Government of India. After receiving high-yielding seeds from abroad, the government launched a series of programmes to produce high-quality seeds, suitable for all the geographical conditions on the subcontinent. However, high-yielding varieties of seeds need proper irrigation and other input requirements so as to maintain the higher productivity over time. As demands on India's agricultural production increased, water for irrigation and other inputs created new bottlenecks (Singh and Singh, 2018).

As of 1991, the Indian government started liberalizing the country's economic policies. This was a big boost to industry and business, but food production suffered, due to loss of cropland to industry, mining and urbanization and agricultural land alienation. In the period from 1996 to 2006, agricultural productivity started to decelerate. While the agricultural growth rate decreased, there was an increase in the number of Indians living below the poverty line (Thivet, 2013).

The Minimum Support Price (MSP) was introduced by the Government of India to insure agricultural producers against sharp falls in crop prices. Various schemes were subsequently introduced to address other aspects of food security as well, such as the Bharat Nirman Scheme, the National Food Security Mission, the horticulture policy and others. A number of individual food security measures were also introduced, such as the Public Distribution System (PDS), the Mid-Day Meal Scheme, the Mahatma Gandhi National

Rural Employment Guarantee Act (MGNREGA), the Fair Price Scheme and the system of ration cards.

The National Food Security Bill was tabled in late 2011 and subsequently referred to the Standing Committee on Food, Consumer Affairs and Public Distribution. The recommendations of the Committee were presented in January 2013, covering issues such as the categorization of beneficiaries, cash transfers and cost-sharing between the union and state governments. A revised version of the Bill was introduced to the Parliament in March 2013, giving legal entitlement to subsidized grains under the PDS to 67% of the population, 75% of the rural population and 50% of the urban population (Thivet, 2013). In August 2013, the Food Security Bill was passed in the Lok Sabha. The successful implementation of this policy depends not only on the production of grain, which stood at around 253 million tonnes as of 2015, but also on universal access to a nutritionally balanced diet, including milk products, vegetables and fruits, pulses and a variety of other foods (Modgal, 2016).

The goal of the MGNREGA, initially enacted as National Rural Employment Guarantee Act (NREGA 2006), is to ensure that everybody in India has a very basic income and purchasing power. However, there have been enormous irregularities and exclusions (Shekhar, 2014). Large leakages of resources have been observed. Even with the introduction of biometric unique IDs (Aadhaar) and the issuing of Aadhaar cards to all MGNREGA recipients, critical questions have been raised about the replacement of food supplies to recipients with cash transfers to beneficiary accounts. The matching of IDs with actual recipients and the lack of Internet facilities and infrastructure continue to pose serious challenges.

The sheer size of India's population and the scale and complexity of its governance structures are daunting. As contributors to this volume have described, Indian policymakers and civil servants struggle to ensure the Right to Food and face difficulties in the day-to-day management of food security measures and schemes. Another major challenge is to reconcile India's policy of self-sufficiency in food production and its need to protect the nation's agricultural sector with the equally important need to integrate the country with global markets.

The Indian government has repeatedly stressed the need to place food security on the agenda of international trade negotiations under the World Trade Organization (WTO), reflecting the government's concern for basic food security and food safety (Purohit, 2015). India has taken a cautious view as regards open international pricing systems, as this would leave Indian farmers in a vulnerable position. Agricultural producers' unions are actively involved in multilateral negotiations on agricultural trade, as key stakeholders in India's agricultural development and agrarian economy.

India has taken a leading role in broader debates on North-South divides in multilateral fora, especially with regard to intellectual property rights in agriculture. India has its own Patenting Act, 1970, prohibiting the patenting of agricultural and horticultural plants, and Indian organizations have strongly criticized the Trade-Related Aspects of Intellectual Property Rights (TRIPS) agreement for opening up for the patenting and private ownership of "global commons" such as seeds and plants. India also hosts a number of powerful movements, civil society groups and small landholders who promote food sovereignty and seed sovereignty, nationally as well as internationally. From their perspective, food sovereignty implies a holistic approach to food, including the right to grow food, and the right to have secure access to healthy and affordable food, resources and entitlements (Gosh, 2009; Shiva, 2000). The food sovereignty movement further advocates the right of peoples and countries to democratically determine their own agricultural and food policies. Seed sovereignty, which involves the cultivation, storage and exchange of home-grown seeds, is promoted for the sake of crop diversity, sustainability and self-reliance. Supporters of seed sovereignty view pressure from global markets as a key cause of increased reliance on pesticides and genetically modified seeds, and a reduction in the variety of crops produced.

There has been growing debate in India on the use of seeds from genetically modified organisms (GMOs) as a way to boost crop yields. Critics disagree with the promotion of GMO seeds by experts who envisage the high technology of GMOs as a crucial element of India's "second Green Revolution". Across India, extension workers continue to promote high-yield seeds, including seeds from GMOs, to local farmers. According to the critics, reliance on non-local, expensive seeds creates economic dependency. Small farmers still know how to store their own seeds, but they are led to believe that expensive inputs such as pesticides, fertilizers and seeds from GMOs and high-yielding varieties of crops produced by multinational companies are necessary to produce high yields (Gosh, 2009). The seed sovereignty movement in India has championed the protection of global crop diversity and raised awareness about the need to protect indigenous seeds, and the advantages of growing indigenous crops, the right to grow food, and the significance of secure access to healthy and affordable food (Shiva, 2009). Importantly, Indian supporters of seed sovereignty have warned against multinational pressures to use seeds from GMOs, and the risks associated with loss of crop biodiversity as climate variability increases.

Scientists agree that the protection of crop diversity becomes increasingly important with greater climate variability. In 2004, the Global Crop Diversity Trust was established to provide financial support to the world's biodiversity gene banks. Together with the Nordic Genetic Resource Center (NordGen), the Trust established the Global Seed Vault in Svalbard to provide the world's crop seed depositories with safe storage space for crop seeds, so as to conserve crop biodiversity further and help prevent the extinction of valuable strains of edible plants. The Global Seed Vault was opened in 2008, and in 2014, India made its first seed deposit, consisting of one box of 25 accessions of pigeon pea (Jacobsen et al., 2017). The pigeon pea is an important crop for farmers in India's semi-arid environments and is considered a valuable crop for global food security. The pigeon pea is also a high-priority research topic at the International Crop Research Institute for the Semi-Arid Tropics in Hyderabad, as a crop that is particularly resistant to drought and other climate challenges.

Researching food governance

Research on food governance and food security was once limited to the domains of agriculture and economy. However, researchers have increasingly turned their attention to the wider implications of food scarcity and insecurity, investigating in greater depth the concerns and experiences of the producers, providers and distributors, as well as the consumers of food and the meaning of "food security" in the wider context (Drèze et al., 2015). The research spotlight has thus been turned to the despair of Indian small farmers who commit suicide, the struggles of extension workers and civil servants charged with the implementation of government policies, and the legal and institutional challenges faced by bureaucrats responsible for procuring safe food for public distribution. The nexus between officials and politicians, large food production companies and mining corporations competing for water and land and the uprooting of farmers from their land, turning them into urban poor, are issues of vital importance to food security for the individual, the household, the community and society at large.

Policymakers need a more comprehensive understanding of the causes of malnourishment in India. There is an urgent need for medical research on nutrition and livelihood among the urban poor. Another important research topic is indigenous knowledge of forest foods and traditional methods of subsistence farming. Local knowledge of farming and indigenous seeds should be preserved, not devalued. Communal property rights and the governance of communal resources should also be studied more carefully.

Food security has been a topic of academic debate in several disciplines, including economy, law, agronomy and political science. Regardless of disciplinary boundaries and perspectives, the vital issues are the same. Disciplinary debates become insignificant in light of everyday experiences of scarcity of food, hunger and insecurity. No matter who we are, and regardless of our views and perspectives, we all rely on food for our everyday life. With this volume, we want to bridge disciplinary boundaries, leave viewpoints from capital cities behind, and try to gain a deeper understanding of vitally important issues and concerns about food governance, and how healthy and nutritional food can be produced and distributed to cover the needs of every individual in a rapidly growing population. We aim to examine these issues and concerns, bringing global perspectives together with experiences of everyday life on the Indian subcontinent.

The first chapters of this volume lay out the concepts, issues and frameworks of India's food governance. In Chapter 1, Raghav Puri covers the legal frameworks of food security in India after the Indian parliament passed the National Food Security Act (NFSA), making the Right to Food a legal entitlement for three quarters of the rural population and half of the urban population of India. Besides ensuring access to highly subsidized food grain, the NFSA also made maternity benefits and nutrition for children aged six months to 14 years a legal entitlement. While it is too early to provide a comprehensive evaluation of the impact of the NFSA, Puri documents the roll-out of the Right to Food, discussing important innovations and challenges emerging from the early experiences of the NFSA in different states and union territories. The NFSA provides an important example of a policy to ensure food security as a legal entitlement. The varied experiences of NFSA implementation at the subnational level can offer valuable lessons for other countries facing similar challenges in ensuring food security.

Equally critical are the "eco-systems" of India's food security regime. Sanjeev Chopra in Chapter 2 takes a holistic view of India's quest for food security in recent years, covering food production gains under the National Food Security Mission (NFSM) and the National Agricultural Development Program (NADP) with the help of new technologies, financial support and extension outreach, and the entitlement and access to food guaranteed by the NFSA. Chopra takes a closer look at the roll-out of the program in West Bengal, examining the links between procurement policies and prices of agricultural produce. The author also examines the acceptance of the "Right to Food" and "Right to Work" across the political spectrum, and the role of technology in weeding out corruption in the procurement and distribution system. Finally, Chopra discusses the issuance of identity cards under the Aadhaar programme, and its impact on the entitlements of farmers and resource-poor consumers.

Nutritional security challenges in India are critically evaluated in the next chapter. T.P. Rajendran addresses India's development aspirations, and how the government has pinned these aspirations on the provision of food and nutritional security in this chapter. The social protection network that has been created over the past five decades involves an elaborate administrative strategy and infrastructure that attends to the national goal of food security for all. The integrated development of Indian agriculture has substantially enhanced the production and productivity of agricultural commodities. Despite the enhanced food production system, a large section of the Indian population continues to suffer from poor nutrition. This could partly be explained by early marriages, lack of medical attention during pregnancy and, of course, the quality of food intake. Rajendran examines what it would require for India to attain United Nations (UN) Sustainable

Development Goal 2, to "End hunger, achieve food security and improved nutrition and promote sustainable agriculture" by 2030.

Moving from the concepts and issues of food governance, the second section of this volume offers insights from the grassroots. Anjoo Sharan Upadhyaya deals with food security in Uttar Pradesh in Chapter 4, as it is implemented in the Targeted Public Distribution System (TPDS). Upadhyaya contextualizes recent efforts and innovative practices to rearrange and fine-tune the TPDS to carry out the core predicates of the National Food Security Act, 2013. It looks at the problematic of implementing the ambitious Act at the grassroots, through the hitherto worn-out systems of public distribution. The chapter examines some of the critical challenges of governance that continue to beleaguer the TPDS, and how the implementation of the Act intends to redress them. To this end, the chapter examines the recent initiatives in Uttar Pradesh to rectify the long-drawn inertia in the TPDS, as also the challenges of implementation in everyday practices in India's most populous state. Drawing on the inputs from poor beneficiaries, PDS officials, local civil society organizations, local politicians, fair price shop allottees and common people, this chapter highlights several less traversed constraints in ensuring food security. The study also elicits fieldwork-based insights from the innovative model of PDS through multiple actions to build household food security, as in the state of Chhattisgarh. The overall aim is to critically evaluate the innovative trajectories of rebuilding the PDS, and suggest fresh policy perspectives in the emerging policy discourse on food security.

Food entitlements in Bihar and Karnataka are described by Arne Dulsrud and Unni Kjærnes in Chapter 5. Starting out with Amartya Sen's idea that the law stands between the food and the eater, this chapter investigates entitlements to food in poor villages and urban slums in the two states. The authors discuss how entitlements are understood and enacted in India's approach to food governance, and how this differs across states. With a household survey and key informant interviews, the chapter searches for the actual entitlements among poor households: access to land, waged employment and social rights such as subsidized food and food services, identifying the dominant patterns in the two states, and what characterizes the individuals who have the fewest entitlements. The chapter also discusses the degree to which social rights to food in effect compensate for the lack of other types of entitlements originating in socio-economic inequalities. Finally, the authors discuss the extent to which actual access to social rights is influenced by the regulatory setup in the two states.

How to implement rights-based policies such as the National Food Security Act, 2013 (NFSA) without tackling existing realities in terms of policy implementation at the village level comprises the subject matter of Chapter 6, authored by Nita Mishra and Edward Lahiff, who take up the case of food security and governance in Odisha. Mishra and Lahiff analyze the importance of state preparedness in executing food-related provisions, with special reference to Odisha. While acknowledging that the NFSA was rights-based, and largely the result of public activism, the authors contend that policymakers must take into cognizance the practical and experiential knowledge of block-level and village-level duty-bearers in the day-to-day implementation of food-related entitlement provisions. Such duty-bearers are state government officials and members of civil society, especially campaigners, experts and trade union activists. Drawing upon interviews and group discussions with duty-bearers across three districts in Odisha, the authors conclude that, unless the government addresses the concerns raised by the duty-bearers, the preparedness of the state in realizing food entitlements for the poor will be a distant dream.

During the last two decades, global food governance has become more complex, as a consequence of increasing challenges due to environmental degradation, globalization and privatization of agricultural markets and associated international price volatility, and concomitant civil society activism in support of the rights of the hungry. In Chapter 7, Shalini Kala covers global governance and India's food governance and security. While a slew of government schemes provides food support, approximately 200 million Indian citizens are still undernourished, comprising about a quarter of the world's 815 million undernourished. India continues to toil at improving the effectiveness of its food policies to eliminate hunger, canvassing for international policies friendly to its own interests in particular, and to those of developing nations in general. Kala argues that the Indian government should improve the implementation of domestic policies while taking a proactive role in global trade discussions to ensure food security at home, while also supporting it globally.

Israel has a long history of assisting India in the agricultural sector, including the provision of water supply systems, climate risk management techniques and Agri-Tech solutions. The Government of India seeks to utilize the new technology to address its food security problems. In Chapter 8, Manjari Singh and P.R. Kumaraswamy describe how India is seeking technological assistance from Israel to achieve greater accessibility, utilization and stability of food supplies by the application of new technology that promises to maximize output and minimize input requirements. The authors discuss the opportunities as well as challenges of Indo-Israeli cooperation in boosting India's food security.

The Group of Twenty (G20) has emerged as an important forum for dealing with global financial issues. However, its development agenda is a work in progress. Food security is one of the nine pillars of development of the Multi-Year Plan for Development agreed to at the Seoul Summit of the G20 in 2010. Arpita Anant discusses this important issue pertaining to India's food security in Chapter 9. Though much has been attempted through the UN-related bodies that were created to deal with food-related issues, the uneven position of the developed and developing countries when it comes to agriculture and food continues to stall fundamental changes that will ease food security issues for the latter. In this context, the G20 makes for an interesting forum to study as it brings together countries that have historically been on the opposite sides of the food debate. Developing country concerns that required global policy changes and were hitherto not amenable to discussion in the UN-related fora, have been sequentially brought on the agenda of the G20. The chapter also compares the Indian narrative with what has been attempted normatively and put in place concretely by the G20 thus far. The two focus areas of the G20 pillar are to increase agricultural production and stabilize the volatility of prices of food products. Amidst calls for reorienting the focus of the G20 towards availability of food, some progress has been made on achieving greater transparency on food stocks with the setting up of the Agricultural Market Information System (AMIS) and the Excessive Food Price Variability Early Warning System. Chapter 9 studies the position of the G20 countries on the issue of food security and suggests how India's food security concerns could best be addressed through the forum.

Addressing the climate change and food security nexus, Malancha Chakrabarty discusses the role of global governance in Chapter 10 of this volume. A major impact of climate change is the increasing risk of food insecurity. As a large developing country, India is particularly vulnerable. Chakrabarty discusses the impact of climate change on three aspects of food security: availability, access, and utilization, and finds that climate change is set to create serious challenges for India's long-term food security. Climate change is essentially a collective action problem, and in a globalized world, a country's food security is not only affected by its own policies. Global governance hence has an important role to play in boosting India's food security. Chakrabarty concludes with the following recommendations: firstly, there is a need for greater integration of climate change and food security concerns. Secondly, a well-functioning international trade system is an important strategy to increase food security. Thirdly, developing countries like India will need more agricultural aid to ensure future food security. Finally, better policymaking for food governance will require more research, with a particular focus on the climate change and food security nexus.

Balancing the local and global significance of food governance

In recent years, multilateral agencies have been calling for a strengthening of global governance, with food security as one of the key issues at stake (Page, 2013; World Health Organization, 2014). In 2008, the UN set up a High-Level Task Force on the Global Food Security Crisis (HLTF). Since the 2008 food price crisis, food security has also become a main item of consultations at G8/G20 summits. In 2011, the BRIC countries adopted an action plan on "Making Joint Efforts for World Food Security". Similarly, the India Brazil South Africa (IBSA) dialogue forum has been investigating global food security solutions.

Recent research on climate change has highlighted the risks associated with increased climate variability: more frequent extreme weather events, rising temperatures and a greater propensity for drought, resulting in water shortages and forest fires. Greater climate variability presents an additional set of challenges to food security, in India and worldwide. When we understand the close linkages between food security and climate change, it becomes abundantly clear why food security is an issue of international relations and global politics, as well as national policymaking.

While food governance gains prominence as a topic of international debate, we should not forget to consider the unique social, cultural and economic contexts of food production and consumption, bearing in mind that farming is a lifestyle, an ancient heritage and a repository of cultural traditions and knowledge. We hope that the present volume will move the research frontier another small step towards a more holistic view of India's food governance challenges and prospects.

References

Banik, Dan, 2007. *Starvation and India's Democracy*. New York: Routledge.

Drèze, Jean, Jessica Pudussery and Reetika Khera, 2015. 'Food Security–Bihar on the Move', *Economic & Political Weekly* 50(34): 44–52, 22 August 2015.

Ghosh, B.N., 2009. 'Globalization and Food Policy Dilemmas in Developing Countries: Contextualizing the Indian Scenario', *Journal of Third World Studies* 26(2): 107–120.

Global Hunger Index, 2020. 'India'. Online at: https://www.globalhungerindex.org/india.html (accessed 23 May 2021).

Jacobsen, Elida Kristin Undrum, Åshild Kolås and Anjoo Sharan Upadhyaya, 2017. 'Food for a Growing India: Seed Sovereignty or GMOs?', PRIO Policy Brief no. 2017.

Modgal, Suresh C., 2016. Inaugural Lecture Delivered at the International Symposium on "Food Security Debates in India: Experiences from the Grassroots", Banaras Hindu University, 28–29 September 2016.

Page, Hans, 2013. 'Global Governance and Food security as a Global Public Good', Centre on International Cooperation. New York University. Online at: http://cic.nyu.edu/sites/default/files/page_global_governance_public_good.pdf (accessed 12 November 2020).

Purohit, Ketaki, 2015. 'The Political Trilemma and India at the WTO', *Asian Journal of Public Affairs* 8(1): 100–105.

Sen, Abhijeet, Himanshu, Jean Drèze and Reetika Khera, 2015. 'Clarification on PDS Leakages', *Economic & Political Weekly* 50(39): 39–42, 26 September 2015.

Sen, Amartya, 1981. *Poverty and Famines. An Essay on Entitlement and Deprivation*. Oxford: Clarendon Press.

Singh, Nandita and Singh, O.P., 2018. 'Green Revolution in India and its Impact on Water Resources', *Millennium Water Story*. January 15. Online at: http://www.millenniumwaterstory.org/Green%20Revolution%20and%20its%20Impact%20on%20Water%20Resources.html (accessed 26 November 2020).

Shekhar, Shreyes, 2014. *MNREGA—Programme Details, Critical Analysis, and Alternatives*. New Delhi: Centre for Civil Societies.

Shiva, Vandana, 2000. *Stolen Harvest: The Hi-jacking of the Global Food Supply*. New Delhi: South End Press.

Shiva, Vandana, 2009. 'Earth Democracy, Living Democracy', in Rajesh Chakrabarti, ed., *The Other India. Realities of an Emerging Power*. New Delhi: Sage Publications, pp. 123–143.

Thivet, Delphine, 2013. 'A Nation without Hunger? Threats to Food Security in Contemporary India', in Jason Miklian and Åshild Kolås, eds, *India's Human Security: Lost Debates, Forgotten People, Intractable Challenges*. London: Routledge, pp. 15–32.

Vir, Sheila C., 2016. 'Maternal Nutrition. Breaking the Intergenerational Cycle of Malnutrition: Significance, Challenges and Opportunities', in Sonalde Desai, Lawrence Haddad, Deepta Chopra, and Amit Thorat, eds, *Undernutrition and Public Policy in India: Investing in the Future*. New Delhi: Routledge, pp. 151–179.

World Health Organization, 2014. *Global Nutrition Targets 2025. Stunting Policy Brief*. Department of Nutrition for Health and Development, World Health Organization.

Chapter 1

India's National Food Security Act (NFSA)

Early experiences

Raghav Puri

In her article "Food Security in India: The Imperative and Its Challenges", Narayanan (2015) highlights the "stubborn persistence of malnutrition" in India despite the rapid economic growth over the past three decades. According to her, the "crux of India's food problem today pertains not so much on increasing food availability or production but with the distribution of food". The World Food Programme (WFP) defines food security as the "availability and adequate access at all times to sufficient, safe, nutritious food to maintain a healthy and active life". As Narayanan points out, it is access to food that is of concern to many low-income households in India.

Despite that Article 42 of the Constitution of India states that the State must "raise the level of nutrition ... to improve public health", the right to food remained unaddressed for over seven decades. However, a sustained campaign by civil society for a rights-based approach to food (or the right to food movement) led to the enactment of the National Food Security Act (NFSA) by the Indian Parliament in 2013. The NFSA aims to provide "food and nutritional security in human life cycle approach, by ensuring access to adequate quantity of quality food at affordable prices to people to live a life with dignity" (Government of India, 2013). It does so by increasing coverage (i.e. the number of eligible beneficiaries) and improving the implementation of existing social programmes to provide food security for all citizens at different stages of life (the *human life cycle approach*). These include maternity benefits through the Pradhan Mantri Matru Vandana Yojana (PMMVY, previously known as Indira Gandhi Matritva Sahyog Yojana, or Indira Gandhi Motherhood Support Programme), child nutrition through the Integrated Child Development Services (ICDS), school meals through the Mid-Day Meal (MDM) programme and subsidized food grain distribution through the Targeted Public Distribution System (TPDS). While the PMMVY provides a maternity benefit of Rs 5,000 for the first birth to all women, the ICDS and MDM programmes ensure that all children aged six months to 14 years get a free meal at their *Anganwadi* (childcare centre) or school. The TPDS provides highly subsidized food grain to approximately 813.4 million Indians under the NFSA. As the

DOI: 10.4324/9781003272656-1

NFSA converts all four welfare benefits into entitlements, the government is legally required to provide resources for the implementation of these programmes. This chapter aims to document the important innovations and challenges emerging from different states and union territories (UTs) in the early years of NFSA rollout.

On 1 November 2016 – three and a half years after the Act came into effect – all states and UTs in India had either implemented or started the process of implementing the NFSA. This chapter reviews the early experiences of different states and UTs in rolling out the NFSA. The first section provides a brief overview of the important provisions of the NFSA. The second section highlights three important obstacles to the effective implementation of the NFSA. The third section discusses three issues emerging from early experiences of NFSA implementation: first, issues in identification of beneficiaries; second, use of technology; and third, the experience of using cash transfers instead of in-kind food transfers.

The National Food Security Act: a brief introduction

The National Food Security Act (NFSA) aims to ensure food and nutritional security by introducing a maternity benefit for all pregnant women and building on three existing programmes (maternal and child nutrition through the ICDS, school meals through the MDM scheme and subsidized food through the PDS). By converting the existing programmes to legal entitlements, the NFSA aims to increase coverage and improve the implementation of nutrition-related interventions in India.

Maternity benefits

Under Section 4 of the NFSA, all pregnant and lactating women are entitled to a maternity benefit of "not less than rupees six thousand" and a free meal at their *Anganwadi* (government-run childcare centre) during pregnancy and six months after childbirth. While free meals at *Anganwadis* were available to all women before the enactment of the NFSA, maternity benefits were only accessible to women covered under the Indira Gandhi Matritva Sahyog Yojana (IGMSY), which provided a benefit of Rs 4,000 as partial wage compensation for wage loss during childbirth and childcare. However, IGMSY was rolled out in only 52 of India's 640 districts and was limited to the first two live births. In 2013, the government increased the maternity benefit under IGMSY to Rs 6,000 per live birth as mandated under the NFSA, but the coverage remained limited to 52 districts (Falcao and Khanuja, 2016). In 2017, the government renamed IGMSY the Pradhan Mantri Matru Vandana Yojana (PMMVY) and expanded its coverage to all districts of India. However, the benefit was limited to the first child only.

Nutrition for children

Section 5 of the NFSA entitles all children within the age group of six months to 14 years to an age-appropriate, free of charge, daily meal. Children aged six months to six years receive this meal at their *Anganwadi* through the ICDS programme, while those between 6 and 14 years receive the meal at their school, through the MDM programme.

Subsidized food grain

The TPDS, which provides subsidized food grain to more than 800 million people, is the main pillar of the NFSA. Most provisions of the NFSA aim to increase food security through TPDS reforms that focus on increasing coverage and improving the implementation of the subsidized food distribution system. The TPDS was introduced in 1997 when it replaced the Revamped Public Distribution System (RPDS). While the RPDS was targeted based on location (drought-prone, tribal, hilly and remote areas), the TPDS used income (household poverty) to identify those eligible for food subsidies. Before the NFSA, the central government provided 25–35 kilograms of subsidized food grain through the TPDS to households living "below the poverty line (BPL)". Over the years, the TPDS in most states became synonymous with corruption (see Bhattacharya et al., 2017; Drèze and Khera, 2015a), due to high levels of diversion of food grain (i.e. subsidized food grain from the TPDS was sold in the open market) and poor targeting (i.e. erroneous exclusion of poor households and inclusion of non-poor households). Khera (2011) uses data from the National Sample Surveys (NSS) between 1999 and 2008 to estimate the trends in the diversion of TPDS grains at the state level. Using these estimates, she classifies states into three categories: (a) "functioning" (Andhra Pradesh, Himachal Pradesh, Jammu and Kashmir, Karnataka, Kerala, Maharashtra and Tamil Nadu); (b) "reviving" (Chhattisgarh, Madhya Pradesh, Odisha, Uttarakhand and Uttar Pradesh); and (c) "languishing" (Assam, Bihar, Gujarat, Haryana, Jharkhand, Punjab, Rajasthan and West Bengal). States designated as "functioning" were those where per capita purchase of food grain remained above 1 kg per month during the study period. States designated as "reviving" were those where the per capita purchase of food grain was below one kg per month in the beginning of the study period but rose above 1 kg per month by the end of the period. States designated as "languishing" were states where per capita purchase of food grain remained above 1 kg per month during the study period. This study raises three important points about TPDS performance: first, there is significant variation at the state level; second, there is variation over time; and third, many states experiencing a "revival" are low-income states. Over the past decade, various studies have highlighted the success of state-level TPDS reforms in low-income states such as Chhattisgarh (Puri,

2012), Odisha (Aggarwal, 2015) and Bihar (Drèze et al., 2015). The NFSA incorporates many of these lessons from the reviving states. Important changes proposed to the TPDS under the NFSA are discussed below.

Increased coverage of the TPDS

Section 3(2) of the NFSA extends TPDS coverage to 75% of the rural population and 50% of the urban population. This is a large increase from the pre-NFSA coverage of the TPDS, which was limited to households living below the poverty line (BPL). According to a report for the Planning Commission (Rangarajan, 2014), in 2014–2015, a person earning Rs 47 per day in urban areas and Rs 32 per day in rural areas was considered living below the poverty line. Approximately, 29.5% of the Indian population was hence in the BPL category. It is important to note that many states and UTs had expanded TPDS coverage before the NFSA was enacted, by introducing a "state-BPL" category that covered households that were poor but did not meet the central government's BPL "cut-off" (see Karat, 2011). For example, in Chhattisgarh, only 1.3 million households were receiving TPDS food grain subsidized by the central government in 2012 (Puri, 2012). The state government created a "state-BPL" category to expand the coverage of the TPDS to an additional 1.9 million households (not considered BPL by the central government). The NFSA also simplifies the different categories of beneficiaries from three categories in the pre-NFSA TPDS to two categories, by merging the Above Poverty Line (APL) and BPL categories into a single "priority" category and retaining the Antyodaya Anna Yojana (AAY) category. The AAY category was introduced in 2000 to target additional food subsidies to the "poorest of poor" households. Merging the APL and BPL categories was an important PDS reform, as one of the major criticisms of the pre-NFSA TPDS was the high diversion of food grain in the APL category (Drèze and Khera, 2015b).

Uniform entitlement of 5 kilograms of food grain per person

Under Section 3(1) of the NFSA, every person belonging to a priority household is entitled to receive 5 kilograms of rice per person per month from the TPDS. In the pre-NFSA period, all BPL households would receive 25–35 kilograms of food grain, irrespective of the number of members in each household. The NFSA accounts for the differences in the number of members in each household by providing "per person" rather than "per household" entitlements. However, the NFSA retains pre-NFSA entitlements for AAY households that continue to receive 35 kilograms of food grain per household. This provision ensures that AAY households do not see a reduction in their pre-NFSA entitlements, as many AAY households have less than seven members.

Reduction in prices of food grain

In the pre-NFSA period, the central government set "central issue prices (CIP)" for subsidized food grain distributed through the TPDS. The prices were Rs 5.65, 4.15 and 3 per kilogram for rice, wheat and coarse grains, respectively. However, many state governments provided state subsidies to further reduce prices (for example, Chhattisgarh reduced the price of TPDS rice from Rs 5.65/kg to Rs 3/kg in 2007 and Rs 2/kg in 2012). According to Schedule I of the NFSA, all eligible households shall be entitled to food grain at subsidized prices not exceeding Rs 3, 2 and 1 per kilogram for rice, wheat and coarse grains, respectively, for the first three years since the commencement of the Act. Subsequently, the central government may set prices that should not exceed the minimum support prices of each of the three food grains.

Identification of eligible households by state governments

Under Section 10(1a and 1b) of the NFSA, state governments are required to identify the households to be covered under AAY and priority categories, within a year of the commencement of the Act. Once households have been identified, the list of eligible households is made available to the public. This provision addresses the high prevalence of inclusion and exclusion errors that were synonymous with the pre-NFSA TPDS due to its reliance on the 2002 BPL survey for rural areas and the 2007 BPL survey for urban areas (as mentioned earlier, some states expanded the coverage of their TPDS to non-BPL households through state subsidies).

Reforms of the TPDS

Besides increasing coverage, reducing prices and streamlining entitlements, the NFSA places major emphasis on increasing the effectiveness of the TPDS by improving "last-mile" delivery. Section 12 of the NFSA makes it the responsibility of central and state governments to "progressively undertake necessary reforms of the TPDS". These include "doorstep delivery" of food grain from warehouses to TPDS fair price shops (FPSs), application of information and communication technologies (ICTs) with the aim of end-to-end computerization of the TPDS, transparency of records, shifting management of FPSs from private owners to public bodies such as women's cooperatives, diversification of commodities distributed (selling pulses and cooking oil at the FPS), leveraging Aadhaar (unique biometric ID) for identification of beneficiaries, and introducing programmes such as cash transfers and food coupons. "Doorstep delivery" of food grain involves transporting food grain from central government warehouses to TPDS shops. This replaced the practice of FPS managers being responsible for transporting food grain, which would often result in the diversion of grain (Puri, 2012).

The NFSA also makes provision for a food security allowance (to be paid in case food entitlements are not provided), sets up grievance redress mechanisms (for monitoring the implementation of the NFSA) and requires the central government to provide financial assistance to state governments for intra-state movement of food grain.

These provisions of the NFSA aim to improve the performance of the TPDS by improving targeting, increasing coverage and reducing corruption. It should be noted that while the NFSA covers four social programmes (child nutrition, school meals, maternity benefits and subsidized food grain distribution), this chapter primarily focuses on the subsidized food grain distribution programme (TPDS) as it is the largest component of the NFSA.

Rollout of the NFSA

In this section, three important issues related to the rollout of the NFSA are discussed. These include the delay in the implementation of the Act, the lack of universal maternity benefits and the impact of fiscal devolution resulting from the recommendations of the 14th Finance Commission on NFSA-related programmes. Table 1.1 provides a detailed timeline of the major events relating to the rollout of the NFSA.

Delay in implementation

One of the first setbacks in the rollout of the NFSA was the delay in its implementation as state governments were unable to complete the identification process. According to Section 10(1b) of the NFSA, state governments are required to identify eligible households within a year of the commencement of the Act. Table 1.2 provides a timeline to indicate when states and UTs started NFSA implementation. Only 11 of the 36 states and UTs had started receiving an allocation of food grain under the NFSA (i.e. based on the number of eligible NFSA beneficiaries rather than the pre-NFSA TPDS households) from the central government by 4 July 2014. Of these, six states and UTs (Chhattisgarh, Haryana, Karnataka, Maharashtra, Punjab and Rajasthan) had completed the process of identifying beneficiaries while the remaining five (Bihar, Delhi, Himachal Pradesh, Madhya Pradesh and Chandigarh) were still in the process of identifying beneficiaries.

Despite three extensions, moving the deadline to implement the NFSA to 30 September 2015, only 18 states and UTs were able to meet the deadline (Comptroller and Auditor General of India, 2015). In the following nine months, 16 more states and UTs implemented the NFSA. It was not until November 2016 that all states and UTs were implementing the NFSA.

Table 1.1 Important NFSA-related dates

Date	*Event*
5 July 2013	National Food Security Ordinance (NFSO) promulgated.
20 August 2013	Haryana becomes first state to implement NFSA.
26 August 2013	National Food Security Act (NFSA) passed by Lok Sabha.
10 September 2013	NFSA receives assent from President of India.
11 February 2014	Press note issued by central government indicating that ICDS, MDM and PMMVY will deliver entitlements listed in Sections 4–6 of NFSA.
30 June 2014	First extension of NFSA deadline by three months to 4 October 2014.
28 November 2014	Second extension of NFSA deadline by six months to 4 April 2015.
25 January 2015	Food Security Allowance Rules, 2015 notified by government.
20 March 2015	Targeted Public Distribution System (Control) Order, 2015 published – Section 3 (3) stated that no new AAY households will be identified.
4 April 2015	Third extension of NFSA deadline by six months to 30 September 2015.
21 August 2015	Cash Transfer of Food Subsidy Rules, 2015 notified by central government.
28 October 2015	Targeted Public Distribution System (Control) Amendment Order, 2015 published – Section 3(3) limiting AAY removed.
1 November, 2015	All states/UTs implementing NFSA (as Kerala and Tamil Nadu agree to implement NFSA).
31 December 2016	Prime minister announces maternal entitlement of Rs 6,000 for all pregnant women under PMMVY.

Source: Compiled by author using information from the Government of India's Press Information Bureau (PIB)

Table 1.2 Timeline of NFSA Implementation

Month and Year	*State/UT*
September 2013	Haryana
October 2013	Delhi, Himachal Pradesh, Rajasthan
December 2013	Punjab
January 2014	Chhattisgarh, Karnataka
February 2014	Chandigarh, Maharashtra
March 2014	Bihar, Madhya Pradesh
August 2014	Lakshadweep
June 2015	West Bengal
September 2015	Puducherry, Tripura
October 2015	Jharkhand, Telangana, Uttarakhand
November 2015	Odisha, Daman & Diu
December 2015	Goa, Assam, Andhra Pradesh
January 2016	Sikkim
February 2016	Jammu & Kashmir, Andaman & Nicobar Islands
March 2016	Meghalaya, Mizoram, Uttar Pradesh, Dadra & Nagar Haveli
April 2016	Gujarat, Manipur, Arunachal Pradesh
July 2016	Nagaland
November 2016	Kerala, Tamil Nadu

Compiled by author from various sources

One of the major reasons for the delay was the lack of transparency in the release of Socio-Economic Caste Census (SECC) data. According to a writ petition filed in May 2015 (Peoples' Union of Civil Liberties, 2015), the central government was "grossly negligent in releasing this data". As the latest census data available, it could have played a pivotal role in identifying beneficiaries. According to PUCL, of the 640 districts in India, final SECC data was only available for 141 districts in February 2015. The NFSA provided states and UTs with an opportunity to address the high inclusion and exclusion errors, one of the most pressing concerns that had ailed the TPDS. However, given the delay in the availability of SECC data, many states and UTs had no option but to use old data.

The delay raises important questions regarding the inability of states and UTs to deliver food grain to all eligible beneficiaries under the NFSA within a year of its coming into effect. As highlighted in the public interest petition filed by PUCL, the validity of these extensions provided by the central government is questionable. Millions of eligible beneficiaries in the 25 states and UTs that did not implement the Act on time were denied their food grain entitlement for more than a year.

Lack of universal maternity benefits

Maternity benefits play a pivotal role in the NFSA's "human life cycle" approach to nutrition by ensuring that all women have access to nutrition when they are pregnant. Section 4 of the NFSA requires the central government to provide all pregnant and lactating (until six months after childbirth) women a hot meal at their local *Anganwadi* and a cash entitlement of no less than Rs 6,000. Though the Ministry of Women and Child Development (MoWCD), that had been implementing the Indira Gandhi Matritva Sahyog Yojana (IGMSY) before the NFSA was enacted, the cash-based maternity benefit only provided Rs 4,000 and was limited to 52 "pilot" districts. With the enactment of the NFSA, the MoWCD increased the maternity benefit to Rs 6,000 but did not expand its geographic coverage. By limiting the programme to 52 of India's 640 districts and only the first two live births, the central government failed to ensure universal maternity benefits under the NFSA.

In 2015, the government announced plans to expand the coverage of IGMSY to 200 "high burden" districts, but no additional budgetary allocations were made to fund this expansion (Falcao and Khanuja, 2016). Instead, the allocation for maternity benefits declined from Rs 2,334 million in 2015–2016 to Rs 754 million in 2016–2017 (see Table 1.3 for budgetary allocations for maternity benefits). It was not until December 2016 that the Government of India announced plans to universalize maternity benefits. Under the PMMVY, or the Prime Minister's Maternity Benefit Programme),

Table 1.3 Allocations for NFSA-related programmes, 2011–2012 to 2017–2018 (in INR millions)

Year	*Total Food Subsidy*	*ICDS Services*	*Maternity Benefit*	*Mid-Day Meal*
2011–2012	7,28,221	1,42,662	2,898	98,907
2012–2013	8,50,000	1,57,116	821	1,08,492
2013–2014	9,20,000	1,63,626	2,319	1,09,176
2014–2015	11,76,712	1,65,523	3,425	1,04,466
2015–2016	13,94,190	1,54,331	2,334	91,449
2016–2017	11,01,729	144,331	754	94,754
2017–2018	10,02,816	1,51,554	20,483	90,923
2018–2019	10,13,270	1,68,147	10,549	95,143
2019–2020 (RE)	10,86,885	1,77,045	23,000	9,91,221
2020–2021 (BE)	11,55,696	2,05,323	25,000	1,10,000

Source: Government of India, online at http://indiabudget.gov.in

a beneficiary is eligible for a cash incentive of Rs 5,000 for the "first living child of the family" and an additional Rs 1,000 from the *Janani Suraksha Yojana* (JSY) for institutional delivery. There are two major concerns regarding this programme, first, it limits maternity benefits to the first birth despite the NFSA requiring universal maternity benefits; and second, it does not provide the full amount required under the NFSA. If an individual does not have access to institutional healthcare, it would be impossible to claim the additional maternity benefit of Rs 1,000 under JSY.

Impact of fiscal devolution on NFSA implementation

Two years after the enactment of the NFSA, the central government accepted the 14th Finance Commission's recommendation to increase tax devolution to states from 32% to 42%. Accordingly, states started receiving a larger share of the divisible pool of taxes. This was followed by the central government accepting the recommendation of the Sub-Group of Chief Ministers on Rationalization of Centrally Sponsored Schemes (CSSs) to reduce the number of CSSs from 66 to 30. Centrally Sponsored Schemes are social programmes designed and funded by the central government and implemented by state governments. The Sub-Group further recommended grouping CSSs under three groups: "Core of Core" (programmes for "social protection and social inclusion"), "Core" (programmes where the centre and states can work together) and "Optional" (programmes that states can choose to implement). This classification had major financial implications as the "Core of Core" programs would follow the existing funding pattern and "Core" programs would require states to fund 40% of the expenditure (10% in the case of 11 mountainous states). Three important NFSA-related programmes – Mid-Day Meal (MDM), Integrated Child Development Services (ICDS) and Maternity Benefits – were classified as "Core" programmes, implying that states would have to fund two-fifth of the expenditures incurred in implementing these programmes. This move by the central government raises two important concerns: first, should the central government exclude "legally mandated" programmes from the "Core of Core" programmes and second, will the states be able to bear the additional costs with the extra 10% of taxes that devolve to them.

Table 1.3 provides details of budget allocations made for the four main NFSA-related programmes: TPDS (food subsidy), ICDS, Maternity Benefit and MDM. While the food subsidy has seen a considerable increase owing to NFSA implementation starting in 2014–2015, ICDS and MDM have seen a slight decline. Though it is too early to assess the impact of fiscal devolution on NFSA implementation, there are concerns regarding the ability of low-income states to finance these programmes, as they are now legal entitlements.

Innovations and challenges in NFSA implementation

With the rollout of the NFSA, state governments got a larger role in the design and implementation of the TPDS. This led to the emergence of state-level innovations and challenges during the implementation process. This section discusses three important issues: (a) identification of beneficiaries (which the NFSA delegates to state governments), (b) use of technology (a requirement under the NFSA) and (c) and an option to shift from in-kind food subsidy to cash transfers.

Identification of beneficiaries

One of the main objectives of the NFSA is to reduce the high inclusion errors that had become synonymous with the TPDS over the past two decades. As most states used BPL survey data from 2002 and 2007 to identify rural and urban beneficiaries, respectively, the list of TPDS beneficiaries was fraught with errors. The NFSA provided an opportunity to rectify this problem by allowing states to use more recent data and new eligibility criteria to identify beneficiaries. Commonly used identification methods included recently collected data (such as SECC and state social security databases), the self-declaration process and, in some cases, using the old TPDS database with new additions. In most cases, states created eligibility criteria and used one of these methods to identify eligible beneficiaries. Each of these methods is discussed below with the help of examples.

Using recently collected data

As most states used a combination of inclusion and exclusion criteria for determining eligibility for the NFSA, the SECC database provided the most updated and detailed information for this purpose. Bihar was one of the first states to use SECC for identifying NFSA beneficiaries. The government of Bihar used a set of exclusion criteria to determine NFSA eligibility (Drèze et al., 2015). For example, all households that had government employees or any members with a monthly income above Rs 10,000 were excluded from the NFSA. Similarly, households owning motorized vehicles or agricultural land above a certain limit were also excluded. Once identification of eligible households was completed, the state government printed NFSA ration cards for all households (with details of all beneficiaries) and distributed them to beneficiaries.

Unlike Bihar, many states were unable to use the SECC data due to delays in the processing of data. In Madhya Pradesh, the state government used a set of inclusion criteria to identify eligible beneficiaries from the Samagra Samajik Suraksha (comprehensive social security) mission database. The inclusion criteria included all old TPDS beneficiaries and all scheduled tribe/caste households. Again, there was no application process as the state government used the existing comprehensive social security mission database to print and distribute NFSA ration cards to eligible households.

Using a self-declaration process

A self-declaration process requires all eligible beneficiaries to apply for a new NFSA ration card if they meet the eligibility criteria set by their state government. The governments of Chhattisgarh and Odisha adopted this approach. In Odisha, the department of food supplies and consumer welfare published six inclusion (homeless, destitute, primitive tribal group, widow pensioner, disabled or transgender) and nine exclusion (income taxpayer, government employee, owner of a motorized vehicle, owner of house with more than three permanent rooms) criteria to determine the eligibility for the NFSA.

A self-declaration process, combined with a post-application verification procedure, helps circumvent the problem of high exclusion errors (as was the case with the old BPL survey data) by ensuring that all eligible beneficiaries have an opportunity to apply. The government of Odisha digitized and de-duplicated all applications using the National Population Register (NPR) database. To identify applicants who were not eligible, the state linked the applicant database to external databases with information on inclusion and exclusion criteria (Satpathy, 2016).

Using the old TPDS beneficiary database

The NFSA provided a great opportunity to rectify the inclusion and exclusion errors resulting from the use of old BPL lists. However, some states, such as Karnataka, Madhya Pradesh, Himachal Pradesh and Maharashtra included all old TPDS beneficiaries besides adding new beneficiaries due to increased coverage under the NFSA (Comptroller and Auditor General of India, 2015). This results in high inclusion errors due to two reasons: first, it includes non-poor households that were incorrectly included in the old BPL lists and second, it includes households that were poor during the BPL surveys conducted more than a decade ago but are not poor anymore.

Use of technology in the TPDS

The use of ICTs is pivotal to the success of TPDS reforms. The NFSA makes provisions for states and UTs to increase transparency and reduce the diversion of food grain by "end-to-end computerization" of the TPDS. End-to-end computerization of the TPDS involves modernization (moving from paper-based to electronic systems) of the four main processes involved in providing food grain to beneficiaries: procurement, storage, transportation and distribution of food grain. While most states have computerized their procurement, storage and transportation processes over the past decade, the distribution process remains manual. Distribution of food grain refers to the final transaction that takes place between the fair price shop (FPS) manager and the TPDS beneficiary. Most states rely on "sales registers" for recording this transaction (beneficiaries buy their food grain entitlement and sign in the register) and this makes it a major avenue for diversion of food grain. One of the main sources of "leakage" of TPDS food grain involves the forging of sales information by FPS managers. If beneficiaries do not purchase their food grain entitlement for the month, a practice common among APL households, FPS managers forge entries in the sales register and sell this excess food grain in the open market (Drèze and Khera, 2011). FPS managers can also forge sales information by using fake or "ghost" beneficiaries (these are beneficiaries who either do not exist or have died).

Chhattisgarh has emerged as a front-runner in solving this last-mile delivery problem. In 2011, the government of Chhattisgarh launched the Centralized Online Real-Time Electronic Public Distribution System (COREPDS) that uses point of sale (PoS) machines and chip-based smart cards to record transactions between FPSs and TPDS beneficiaries. Unlike a conventional FPS, where transactions are recorded in a sales register, COREPDS transactions are recorded online (Vaidya and Somashekhar, 2017). When the beneficiary arrives at the FPS with her COREPDS smart card, the FPS manager inserts the smart card into the PoS machine. The PoS machine retrieves the information of the beneficiary from the server (the PoS machines require internet) and allows the beneficiary to purchase NFSA entitlements. Once the transaction is complete, the beneficiary gets a receipt with details of the quantity purchased and the price paid for each item.

Other than ensuring that all transactions are captured by the TPDS information system, COREPDS provides two benefits that have the potential to improve the quality of food grain and reduce corruption. First, COREPDS allows "portability of benefits" as beneficiaries can choose which FPS they want to purchase their NFSA entitlements from. Not only does this provide beneficiaries with a choice, but also increases competition among various FPSs. One of the major criticisms of the TPDS is the monopoly that FPS managers have over beneficiaries that are "attached" to their nearest FPS. With COREPDS, this attachment ceases to exist as beneficiaries can choose to purchase their NFSA entitlements from any FPS using their smart cards.

Second, COREPDS provides real-time information of stock availability at each FPS to the State Food Corporation (the government agency responsible for transporting food grain to all the FPSs) which helps streamline the transportation process. In the conventional TPDS, the SFC provides TPDS food grain to all FPSs at the beginning of each month based on the number of TPDS beneficiaries attached to each FPS. This leads to two problems: first, limited storage at the FPS does not allow for proper storage of food grain and second, this incentivizes corruption as FPS managers make fake entries for the leftover food grain and sell it off in the open market. Under COREPDS, there is real-time allocation of food grain based on the availability of stock at each FPS. As and when each FPS sells half of its existing stock, the respective FPS managers get an alert to place an order for more food grain, based on the information on the COREPDS server. Once the order for more allocation is received, food grain is dispatched to the concerned FPS.

COREPDS is only operational in urban areas of Chhattisgarh. An evaluation by the World Bank (Bhattacharya et al., 2017) found that, while COREPDS had improved the functioning of the TPDS, there were issues that need to be addressed before a similar system could be scaled up to rural areas and other states. First, internet connectivity is crucial for the success of a COREPDS-like system. Second, extensive training of all stakeholders (especially government agencies and FPS managers) must be a prerequisite for the adoption of any new technology. Third, there is a need to carry out widespread awareness campaigns to ensure that all beneficiaries have the required information to be able to access and use new technologies. Finally, for a system like COREPDS to work, the government must invest in good quality PoS machines and smart cards.

While COREPDS shows how technology can be used to improve the food distribution system by providing a choice to TPDS beneficiaries, ensuring timely delivery of food grain to FPSs and increasing accountability of all stakeholders, it is important to ensure that new technologies do not create hurdles in the effective implementation of the NFSA. The adoption of Aadhaar-Based Biometric Authentication (ABBA) for the identification of beneficiaries in the Rajasthan TPDS illustrates the limitations of new technologies when adopted without the necessary infrastructure and administrative preparedness.

Beginning in November 2015, the government of Rajasthan installed PoS machines in FPSs across seven districts and made biometric authentication mandatory for all purchases of NFSA food grain. Anumeha Yadav (2017) recounts her experiences in Ajmer and Baran districts where she met many beneficiaries who were unable to purchase food grain due to technical glitches. These included four problems: poor network leading to low internet connectivity (delaying distribution of food grain); errors in capturing fingerprints during Aadhaar enrolment; changes in fingerprints due to abrasions; and problems during "seeding" (i.e. linking of Aadhaar to NFSA ration card). Yadav also quoted the Additional Director of UIDAI who said that fingerprints for 10 to 15% of beneficiaries do not match and they are in the process of introducing iris scanners to address this problem.

Similar experiences have also emerged from Jharkhand, where the department of food and public distribution introduced biometric authentication in all FPSs of Ranchi district in mid-2016. Data from July and August (2016) show that beneficiaries received only half of their NFSA food grain entitlements after the introduction of PoS machines (Bhatnagar, 2016). Once again, common problems included "faulty seeding" (errors in data entry making authentication impossible), "biometric failure" (failure to recognize beneficiaries' fingerprints) and incorrect quantities being displayed in the PoS device due to errors in data entry.

It is important to mention that, in principle, the use of Aadhaar-based authentication can be used for ensuring that the intended beneficiary benefits from the NFSA. However, new technology can help improve the existing system only if the required prerequisites for it to function exist. In the case of Aadhaar-enabled PoS machines, the basic requirements are high-speed internet, uninterrupted power supply, good quality PoS devices, training for all stakeholders involved in the TPDS process, careful seeding of data and, most importantly, an effective grievance redressal system. The experience in both states suggests that these basic prerequisites were not in place before the new system was introduced.

Cash vs. kind

Over the past decade, many academics and policymakers have suggested replacing in-kind food transfers with cash transfers to address the issues of leakage and poor quality of food grain from the TPDS (Saini and Gulati, 2015). Rather than going through the process of procurement, storage, transportation and distribution of food grain, which entails high costs, the government should transfer an equivalent amount of cash in all beneficiaries' bank accounts and let them buy the food grain themselves. Though this sounds very efficient in principle, many have raised concerns about the negative impacts of such a move on TPDS beneficiaries.

Khera (2016) presents findings from qualitative interviews across nine states that asked TPDS beneficiaries whether they preferred to buy food grain from the TPDS or a hypothetical cash transfer that allowed them to purchase the same quantity of food grain from the market. Approximately 67% preferred food over cash though the figure ranged from 91.3% in Andhra Pradesh (where the TPDS is functioning well) to 20.8% in Bihar (where TPDS was "languishing") when the survey was conducted in the summer of 2011. According to Khera, the respondents gave various reasons for preferring food over cash. These include food security (expenditure on non-food items), poorly developed rural markets (irregular supply of food grain), limited access to banks (costs involved in accessing faraway banks), experience with other cash transfers (delays in payment and hassles in accessing banks) and inflation (will the government be able to index the cash transfer to inflation).

This debate, as contentious as it is, relies heavily on hypothetical situations (or on the experience of other cash transfer programmes such as old age-, widow- and disability pensions) that makes it difficult to understand how cash transfers would work as a replacement for the TPDS. With Section 12(h) of the NFSA encouraging states and UTs to introduce "cash transfers and food coupons" as part of efforts to reform the TPDS and the Government of India notifying the "Cash Transfer of Food Subsidy Rules", states and UTs can now move from in-kind food transfers to cash (Khera, 2016; Government of India, 2015). However, despite notification of the cash transfer rules, no state has shown an interest in replacing the TPDS with cash transfers. As of early 2018, only three union territories (UTs) had implemented direct benefit transfers (DBT) of the food subsidy.

In September 2015, Chandigarh and Puducherry became the first state and UT to replace their TPDS with DBT. Six months later, Dadra and Nagar Haveli also introduced DBT. A study by the Jameel Poverty Action Lab (J-PAL) (Muralidharan et al., 2017) covering the first year of DBT implementation in the three UTs shows that in all three UTs, only two-thirds of the beneficiaries confirmed receiving the cash amount. Of the remaining, more than half reported not receiving any benefit. The report also mentions that on average, beneficiaries had to spend more time and money to purchase food grain and often spent more than the cash transfer amount, to purchase the same quantity of food grain that they would purchase from the TPDS. While any new programme experiences teething troubles, beneficiaries not receiving their full benefit amount one year after implementation is a major concern. More importantly, if cash transfers of food subsidies are not working in UTs, that are predominantly urban and have relatively well-functioning food grain markets, will they work in rural areas? The report goes on to recommend more pilots that test the feasibility of having a choice-based system that allows beneficiaries to opt for either in-kind transfers through the PDS or cash transfers through DBT.

Conclusion

The National Food Security Act provides the right to food as a legal entitlement to all Indians. It does so by making provisions for universal maternity benefits, nutrition for children and access to highly subsidized food grain. Whether the provisions of this law translate into increased food and nutritional security depends on its successful implementation. This chapter has provided an overview of the early experiences of the rollout and implementation of the NFSA. It has highlighted the hurdles in the effective rollout of the programme and focused on the significant variation in NFSA implementation across states and UTs. This varied experience at the subnational level has resulted in innovation and posed challenges during the NFSA implementation process, that offer important lessons for ensuring food security through legislation. Two of these lessons include the need to ensure laws are implemented in letter and spirit and that a one-size-fits-all approach can do more harm than good.

Implementing the law in letter and spirit is essential for its success. The NFSA's implementation experience shows that delays in the rollout of the NFSA left millions of individuals without their legal entitlements. More importantly, the central government's attempts to reduce its financial liability resulting from the NFSA hampers the main objective of ensuring all individuals have the right to food. For instance, the law makes provisions for universal maternity benefits, but the new maternity benefits programme only covers the first child. Similarly, the government's attempt to phase out the Antyodaya Anna Yojana (AAY, a subsidized food programme for the poorest of poor households) by curtailing any new intake into the programme, shows how it goes against the letter and spirit of the NFSA, which makes special provisions for ensuring that AAY beneficiaries do not lose their coverage.

The initial experience of the NFSA also reveals that reforms of NFSA-linked social programs need to consider the local context rather than rely on a one-size-fits-all approach. More importantly, it is essential to ensure that all the prerequisites for the success of reforms are in place before the reform is initiated. A case in point is the use of new technologies to modernize the TPDS. The use of biometric authentication and point of sale devices to increase transparency and reduce diversion of food grain, though helpful in principle, has caused major disruptions in the TPDS. The experience with cash transfers in UTs further corroborates this as it shows how a sudden shift in the method of delivery without creating the required infrastructure can create problems for beneficiaries.

While the NFSA has provided the legal framework to ensure food and nutritional security in India, only the successful implementation of all its provisions can help achieve this goal. Hopefully, the NFSA will help the "languishing" states to revive their food and nutrition programmes, so they can become "functioning" again.

Acknowledgements

The author would like to thank Dr Jean Drèze, Dr Reetika Khera and Dr Bhavani R.V. for their feedback on the chapter. This study is part of the research generated by the Leveraging Agriculture for Nutrition in South Asia (LANSA) research consortium funded by the UK government.

References

Aggarwal, Ankita, 2015. "The PDS in Orissa: Against the Grain?" *Economic and Political Weekly*, 46 (36): 21–23.

Bhatnagar, Gaurav, 2016. "Aadhaar-based PDS Means Denial of Rations for Many, Jharkhand Study Shows," *The Wire*, September 8, 2016. Online at: https://thewire.in/64756/jharkhand-aadhaar-pds-nfsa/ (accessed 25 October 2018).

Bhattacharya, Shrayana, Vanita Leah Falcao and Raghav Puri, 2017. "The Public Distribution System in India," in Alderman et al. (eds.), *The 1.5 Billion People Question: Food, Vouchers or Cash Transfers?* Washington, DC: The World Bank.

Comptroller and Auditor General of India, 2015. *Audit of the Preparedness for Implementation of National Food Security Act, 2013 for the Year Ended March 2015*, Report No. 54, Comptroller and Auditor General (CAG) of India.

Drèze, Jean and Reetika Khera, 2011. "PDS Leakages: The Plot Thickens", *The Hindu*, 11 August 2011. Online at: http://www.thehindu.com/opinion/lead/PDS-leakages-the-plot-thickens/article13651790.ece (accessed 25 October 2018).

Drèze, Jean and Reetika Khera, 2015a. "Understanding Leakages in the Public Distribution System," *Economic and Political Weekly*, 46 (21): 39–42.

Drèze, Jean and Reetika Khera, 2015b. "Ending the Above Poverty Line (APL) Scam," *Live Mint*, 2 March 2015. Online at: http://www.livemint.com/Opinion/i68dgwUiRCIGam9TBuhr2O/Ending-the-abovepoverty-line-scam.html (accessed 25 October 2018).

Drèze, Jean, Reetika Khera and Jessica Puduserry, 2015. "Food Security: Bihar on the Move", *Economic and Political Weekly*, 50 (34): 44–52.

Falcao, Vanita and Jasmeet Khanuja, 2016. "India's Unrealised Maternity Entitlements," *The Hindu*, 13 July 2016. Online at: http://www.thehindu.com/opinion/op-ed/indias-unrealised-maternity-entitlement/article7040790.ece (accessed 25 October 2018).

Government of India, 2013. "The National Food Security Act, 2013," *The Gazette of India: Extraordinary (Part II, Sec 1)*, September 2013. Online at: http://indiacode.nic.in/acts-in-pdf/202013.pdf (accessed 25 October 2018).

Government of India, 2015. "Cash Transfer of Food Subsidy Rules," *The Gazette of India: Extraordinary* (Part II, Sec 3(i), August 2015. Online at: http://dfpd.nic.in/writereaddata/images/cash.pdf (accessed 25 October 2018).

Karat, Brinda, 2011. "Planning Commission and Poverty Estimates," *The Hindu*, 9 June 2011. Online at: http://www.thehindu.com/todays-paper/tp-opinion/planning-commission-and-poverty-estimates/article3041638.ece (accessed 25 October 2018).

Khera, Reetika, 2011. "Trends in Diversion of Grain from the Public Distribution System," *Economic and Political Weekly*, 46 (21): 106–114.

Khera, Reetika, 2016. "Cash vs. In-Kind Transfers: Indian Data Meets Theory," *Food Policy*, (46), 2016: 116–128. Online at: http://www.sciencedirect.com/science/journal/03069192/46 (accessed 25 October 2018).

Muralidharan, K., Paul Niehaus and Sandip Sukhtankar, 2017. "Direct Benefits Transfer in Food: Results from One Year of Process Monitoring in Union Territories." University of California, San Diego. Online at: https://econweb.ucsd.edu/~kamurali/papers/Other%20Writing/20170905_UT_DBT_Report.pdf (accessed 25 October 2018).

Narayanan, Sudha, 2015. "Food Security in India: The Imperative and Its Challenges," *Asia and the Pacific Policy Studies*, 2(1), 2015, 197–209, Australian National University.

Peoples' Union of Civil Liberties, 2015. *Civil Original Jurisdiction Writ Petition (Civil) No. 277 of 2015*. Peoples' Union of Civil Liberties (PUCL), 16 May 2015.

Puri, Raghav, 2012. "Reforming the Public Distribution System: Lessons from Chhattisgarh," *Economic and Political Weekly*, 47 (5): 21–23. May 2012. Online at: http://www.epw.in/journal/2012/05/commentary/reforming-public-distribution-system-lessons-chhattisgarh.html (accessed 25 October 2018).

Rangarajan, C., 2014. *Report of the Expert Group to Review the Methodology for Measurement of Poverty*. New Delhi: Government of India, Planning Commission, June 2014. Online at http://planningcommission.nic.in/reports/genrep/pov_rep0707.pdf (accessed 25 October 2018).

Saini, Shweta and Ashok Gulati, 2015. "The National Food Security Act (NFSA) 2013 – Challenges, Buffer Stocking and the Way Forward," Indian Council for Research on International Economic Relations (ICRIER), Working Paper 297, March 2015. Online at: http://icrier.org/pdf/Working_Paper_297.pdf (accessed 25 October 2018).

Satpathy, Subhranshu Kumar, 2016. "Implementation of National Food Security Act (NFSA) in Odisha," *Odisha Review*, February-March 2016. Online at: http://odisha.gov.in/e-magazine/Orissareview/2016/Feb-Mar/engpdf/23-28.pdf (accessed 25 October 2018).

Vaidya, Omkarprasad and A.K. Somashekhar, 2017. *COREPDS: Empowering with Portability: Case Studies on e-Governance in India*. New Delhi: National Institute of Smart Governance (NISG).

Yadav, Anumeha, 2017. "Six Months after Rajasthan Introduced It, Only 45% Beneficiaries Used Aadhaar at Ration Shops," *Scroll*, January 3, 2017. Online at: https://scroll.in/article/809661/six-months-after-rajasthan-introduced-aadhaar-at-ration-shops-only-45-beneficiaries-accessed-food (accessed 25 October 2018).

Chapter 2

The eco-system of India's food security regime

Sanjeev Chopra

Food security is directly linked to agricultural development enabled by policies to ensure adequate domestic food supplies. From importing over 10 million tons of food grains (primarily wheat and rice) in 1966–1967, India became self-sufficient in these grains in 1985–1986 (Kumar, 2016). Although India overcame a critical phase of food insecurity and dependence on external assistance for food, the challenge of recurrent droughts and crop failures directed agricultural policymaking towards "abundant precaution". The focus was hence always on adequate food production, to ensure that particularly staple food prices remain stable and within the affordable range, and to avoid situations in which India might again become critically dependent on imported staple foods. Self-sufficiency is the primary goal of India's National Food Security Mission (NFSM), a key agency under the Union Agriculture Ministry. The success of India's food and agriculture policy not only ensures the transformation of the rural economy and livelihoods – it also gives India political clout and stature in the community of nations.

It is essential for India's continued self-sufficiency that food production keeps pace with population growth and increasing consumption. This includes not only food grains, but other important crops such as oilseeds and pulses, of which India cannot produce enough to sustain its own needs. There is also a need to rethink the food security ecosystem, and the notion of "food security" itself. As described by Nobel Laureate Amartya Sen, famine is not about lack of production, but rather, it occurs when a large number of people in a region lose the means or entitlement to access food. The National Food Security Act (NFSA) has become the entitlement that is meant to help every citizen, especially the most vulnerable, to access food, along with income from employment, which is ensured by the Mahatma Gandhi National Rural Employment Guarantee Act (MGNREGA). As Amartya Sen points out in his seminal book *Development as Freedom* (Sen, 1999), protection from abject poverty and unemployment are the freedoms that are necessary for the development of a country.

DOI: 10.4324/9781003272656-2

Drivers of agricultural policy

The Government of India drives the agriculture policy in at least five distinct ways. Firstly, the Department of Agriculture and Co-operation and Farmers' Welfare (DAC & FW) drives the NFSM and the Rashtriya Krishi Vikas Yojana (RKVY). It is under these two programmes that major funding for direct assistance to farmers, in terms of frontline demonstrations and the introduction of new technologies (farm equipment, newer seed varieties, plant protection), is made available to state governments. The financial resources available to the state government are no match for those of the centre, which can therefore set the agenda and the direction of the interventions.

Secondly, the agriculture research agenda is driven by the National Agriculture Research (NAR) system. Till 2014, the Planning Commission used to approve state plans. The Commission would advise departments of the states to relocate their research wings to the agricultural universities governed by the Indian Council for Agriculture Research (ICAR). West Bengal and Uttar Pradesh are perhaps the only two states that maintain their own independent research wings to study problems that are specific to their agriculture. West Bengal continues to maintain two important research stations, the Pulses and Oilseeds Research Station at Berhampore in Murshidabad and the Rice Research Institute at Chinsurah in Hooghly, both of which have many national and international research collaborations.

Thirdly, together with the Ministry of Commerce, the external trade regime is driven entirely by the Government of India. Whether it is the import of onions or the export of potatoes, both are directed by the Union Government. Of late, the Ministry of Consumer Affairs has also begun participating in the process to protect the interests of consumers. Thus, when prices of commodities such as onion and potato cross the politically accepted price threshold, executive orders like the Minimum Export Price are issued, and the parastatals are also advised to import the commodity in question.

Fourthly, financial inclusion for farmers – both in terms of credit and crop insurance is driven by institutions directly controlled by the Union Government. The Kisan Credit Card programme, as well as the National Farmers Insurance Programme (Pradhan Mantri Fasal Bima Yojana), depend substantially on the "institutional capacity" of the National Bank for Agriculture and Rural Development (NABARD) and the insurance division of the agriculture ministry. The Department of Fertilizer co-ordinates the supply of fertilizer, especially urea, to the states, based on their cropping patterns and landholdings.

The roll-out of programmes such as farmers' insurance and soil health cards require pan-Indian collaboration and co-operation. States have the option of running these on their own, but would then lose the funds that accrue to these programmes. The Constitution of India has clearly defined the powers of the Union and the state governments. While the Union Government of India has the lead in shaping the agricultural development of the country, the Constitution mandates implementation to the states. After the 73rd and 74th constitutional amendments, many powers and obligations were transferred to Zila Panchayats, including agriculture and allied sectors such as extension services for animal husbandry. Agriculture is the 14th entry in the state list. However, according to the concurrent list, the Union Government has the mandate to trade and commerce in foodstuff, raw cotton and raw jute, among others.

The Union Agriculture Ministry with its three departments – agriculture, co-operation and farmers welfare, agriculture research and extension and animal husbandry, dairying and fisheries – is one of the larger ministries of the Union Government. It operates out of Krishi Bhawan (KB). As such, many of the ministry's policies are colloquially termed "KB policies", and the ministry's view on the Minimum Support Price (MSP) and Minimum Export Price (MEP) is termed the "KB view", which favours higher MSP and lower MEP because these benefit the farmer. The consumer affairs and public distribution department always counter this view, because they would like consumers to pay reasonable prices.

The ministry has established "Missions" or Mission Mode programmes to deliver specific objectives with assured government funding for the implementation of a set of interventions as "national priorities". Thus, the Horticulture Mission was launched with the specific objective of raising horticulture production, and the Mission on Micro Irrigation was established to promote precision agriculture. However, as state governments were uncomfortable with the direct transfer of funds to these programmes outside of the state budgets, the missions eventually became subject to the same financial procedures as other government programmes, losing a fair bit of autonomy.

The actual groundwork of policy implementation is the mandate and the responsibility of state governments. States differ in their zeal, capacity and political will to implement the policy prescriptions laid down by the central government. However, in most states, the chief secretary heads the state-level sanctioning committees for the RKVY, and the agricultural secretary heads the NFSM. Likewise, the secretaries of horticulture and animal husbandry and dairying also head missions that focus on High-Value Agriculture (HVA). As the focus of this chapter is on food security, we will examine the NFSM in detail with some references to RKVY, which sets the overall direction of agriculture in the state.

The Green Revolution

India has come a long way since the food grains crisis of the 1960s. Thanks to the determined efforts of the government to give full thrust to the Green

Revolution, farmers have been able to use quality hybrid seeds, fertilizers and enhanced irrigation and many have also accessed credit for the agricultural sector. First implemented in the fertile and irrigated tracts of Punjab, the Green Revolution was extended to other irrigated tracts in North India. The success of the Green Revolution in Punjab and Haryana, and irrigated tracts elsewhere, gave the NFSM confidence to replicate this model in the eastern region, which is well endowed with water. With the objective of "Bringing the Green Revolution to Eastern India (BGREI)" the NFSM widened the food basket of the country while achieving its objective of vertical growth by raising productivity per unit of land, besides a tangible increase in production of cereals, pulses and oilseeds (see Table 2.1).

Besides quantitative improvements, the NFSM has emphasized the need for qualitative changes in the way agriculture is practised in India, promoting new farm practices such as SRI (System of Rice Intensification) and the cultivation of hybrid rice. Awareness-raising regarding the use of farm machinery, nutrients, quality seeds and good soil practices have yielded results in the form of increased sales of seeds and machinery components for the cultivation of rice, wheat and pulses from 2007–2008 to 2011–2012. This in turn has triggered a substantial increase in the production of food grains. Machines supported by the NFSM include water-saving devices such as irrigation pump sets and sprinkler sets, to help achieve the goal of "more crop per drop". Farmers' Field Schools (FFS) enable capacity-building and familiarize farmers with new agricultural technologies. Increased public and private investments in agriculture have also created direct and indirect employment opportunities, in the primary, secondary and tertiary sectors. Lastly, the National Food Security Mission works on the principle of convergence between various institutions that are responsible for the supply of

Table 2.1 Outlay/production of cereals, pulses and oilseeds (2007–2017)

Year	*Outlay (INR in crores)*	Production (in million tonnes)		
		Cereals	*Pulses*	*Oilseeds*
2007–2008	1,629	216.01	14.76	28.54
20082009	3,718	219.90	14.57	26.38
2009–2010	4,744	203.45	14.66	23.72
2010–2011	7,683	226.25	18.24	30.98
2011–2012	8,815	242.20	17.09	27.35
2012–2013	10,115	238.79	18.34	28.83
2013–2014	9,027	245.79	19.25	30.88
2014–2015	10,237	234.87	17.15	25.49
2015–2016	5,077	235.22	16.35	23.37
2016–2017	4,839	249.84	22.14	31.71

Sources: National Informatics Centre, Ministry of Electronics and Information Technology (MeitY); National Food Security Mission, Ministry of Agriculture and Farmers Welfare

agriculture inputs, such as power, water supply, credit and assured minimum price and procurement, so that farmers are not just left to the mercy of favourable monsoons.

The Public Distribution System

The Public Distribution System (PDS) was introduced in the 1940s to prevent speculative trade in commodities like wheat, rice and sugar. It was continued post-Independence but was marked by nepotism, inefficiency, complaints regarding rent-seeking by almost everyone in the value chain – from the ration dealer, who had to cut corners on account of very low margins, irregular supply and patronage pay-outs, to the political executive (Table 2.2).

The central and state governments jointly manage the PDS, with the centre being responsible for procurement, storage, transportation and allocation. The states are responsible for the distribution through Fair Price Shops (FPSs) as well as for identification of families Below Poverty Line (BPL), issuing cards, supervision and monitoring.

Table 2.2 Salient features of the NFSA

Coverage and entitlement	Guarantee of 5 kg per person per month, with the poorest of the poor (i.e. Antyodaya households) being entitled to 35 kg per household per month
Subsidised price under TDPS and their revision	Food grains under TDPS to be made available at subsidised prices of Rs.3/2/1 per kg for rice, wheat and coarse grains respectively for a period of three years from the date of commencement of the Act; thereafter prices will be suitably linked to Minimum Support Price (not implemented)
Nutritional support to women and children	Pregnant women, lactating mothers and children aged 6 months to 14 years entitled to meals as per prescribed nutritional norms under the Integrated Child Development Service (ICDS) and Mid-Day Meal (MDM) Schemes; higher nutritional norms prescribed for malnourished children up to 6 years of age
Maternity benefit	Pregnant women and lactating mothers to be entitled to receive maternity benefit of no less than INR 6,000 as per scheme formulated by the Central Government
Women's Empowerment	Eldest woman of the household aged 18 years or above to be designated head of household for the purpose of issuing of ration cards
Food Security Allowance	Provision for food security allowance to entitled beneficiaries in case of non-supply of entitled food grains or meals
Grievance Redressal Mechanism	States mandated to appoint Food Commissioners with powers to impose penalties on public servants for failure to comply with the provisions of the Act

Source: Compiled by author

India joined the World Trade Organization (WTO) on 31 December 1994. The WTO Agreement on Agriculture includes certain safeguards for developing countries, especially with regard to staples and small farmer-driven agriculture. Nevertheless, there was a lurking fear that, with India's membership of the WTO, the subsidization of food would come under observation and found non-compliant. However, WTO Agreement on Agriculture makes a special reference to staples with regard to the calculation of eligible subsidies that are exempt from the regime, wherein developing countries can claim exemption with regard to the subsidization of staples, or food commodities that form the main ingredient of the diet of a community.

From the mid-1990s, efforts were made to streamline the PDS, as leakages had touched unacceptable levels, and both administrative will and technology united to take corrective steps.

The Right to Food

Although the Right to Food was not explicitly mentioned in the Constitution of India, the Fundamental Right to Life as enshrined in Article 21 of the Constitution has been interpreted by the Supreme Court and National Human Rights Commission to include the "Right to Live with Human Dignity". This includes the right to food and other basic necessities. Article 47 of the Directive Principles of State Policy provides that the state shall regard the raising of the level of nutrition and the standard of living of its people and the improvement of public health as among its primary duties. Nevertheless, it was only with the enactment of the National Food Security Act, 2013, that the government's efforts to achieve food security achieved a legal backing, while citizens could demand it as a matter of right. Prior to this, even though there were a plethora of schemes, they were dependent upon the "grace" of the political executive.

How did the statutory backing for the Right to Food come about? Among a series of developments, the most pertinent was the Public Interest Litigation (PIL) filed by the PUCL People's Union for Civil Liberties (PUCL) – India's leading human rights advocacy and support organization – against the Union Government of India and all state governments. The PUCL moved the Supreme Court for recognizing the "Right to Food" as a right under Article 21 of the Constitution, after it observed that sections of the population could not access food grains for a variety of reasons, including the lack of financial resources. Other reasons included poor logistics, lack of monitoring, deliberate diversion of PDS stocks, and management issues within the Food Corporation of India (FCI) – the agency responsible for procurement of wheat and rice. Till such time as the responsibility for providing rice to the states was the exclusive preserve of the FCI, states were not really concerned about the logistical costs, as the financial burden was to be borne by the government.

From welfare to right

The National Food Security Act, 2013, marks a paradigm shift from a welfare approach to a rights-based approach, enabling 75% of the rural and 50% of the urban population (almost two-thirds of the population) to receive highly subsidized food grains. Some salient features of this Act are provided in Table 2.3.

Successful implementation of the NFSA depends on the seamless integration and clear division of responsibilities between the centre and the states. Figure 2.1 depicts the specific responsibilities of each tier.

Competitive politics, the ubiquitous nature of the media, and civil society activists are quick to highlight errors in the implementation of the NFSA. In fact, many states have taken proactive steps to enhance the scope of coverage beyond the statutory provisions of the Act. The Government of India extends its financial support only to the extent stipulated under the Act. Anything that the states may want to provide beyond this, has to be provided for by the state exchequer. Thus, Tamil Nadu follows the "zero exception" norm, in which the entire state is covered under the PDS with any extra costs being borne by the state itself. Similarly, the Khadya Sathi (Food Support) programme of West Bengal covers almost 90% of the state's population (United News of India, 2018). Launched in January 2016, the programme is a comprehensive measure to extend the reach of the PDS, providing 7.20 crore people rice or wheat at Rs 2 per kg and food grains at half the market price to another 1.39 crore. Punjab has introduced the *Atta-Dal* scheme, wherein pulses are also provided. The scheme provides 25 kg of wheat at Rs 1 per kg and 2.5 kg pulses at Rs 20 per kg per month to eligible beneficiaries, targeting households with an annual income of less than Rs 60,000 and landholdings of less than 2.5 acres in rural areas, or 100-yard plot holders in urban areas. States such as Chhattisgarh have introduced the GPS tracking of food trucks and issued food coupons to reduce pilferage and ensure that benefits actually accrue to the poor (Sinha, 2014).

Table 2.3 Evolution of the NFSA

Programme	*Year*	*Purpose*
Public Distribution System (PDS)	1940s	Launched as general entitlement scheme
Targeted Public Distribution System (TPDS)	1997	Targeted poor households
Antyodaya Anna Yojana	2000	Targeted "the poorest of the poor"
PDS Control Order	2001	Government notified order on TPDS
PUCL vs. Union of India	2001	Case contending that the right to food is a fundamental right
National Food Security Act	2013	Act to provide legal right to food

Source: Compiled by author

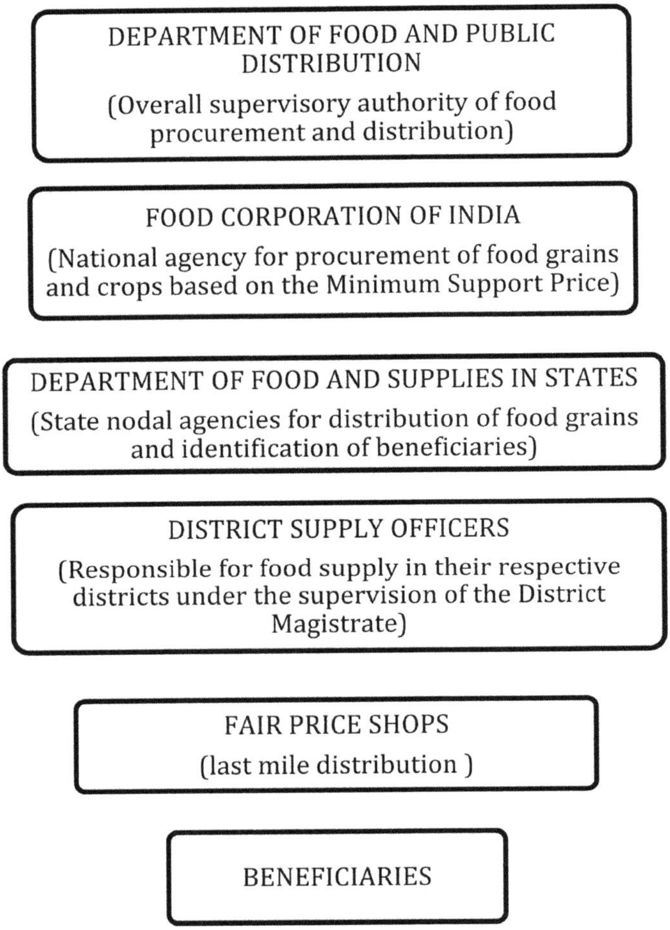

Figure 2.1 Structure of Public Distribution System.
Source: Author.

These efforts certainly seem to be yielding results, with the current debate encompassing food quality, mode of distribution and replication of best practices. A cursory scan of the literature shows that the focus of research is no longer on purposeful exclusions and significant diversions from the PDS, or discrimination against certain castes.

Importantly, the enactment of the NFSA has ensured adequate budgetary provision for its implementation. From 2014–2015 till now, food subsidy makes up a good 6–7% of India's total budget. The National Human Rights Commission (NHRC) recognizes the NFSA, 2013, as a comprehensive policy that ensures food security, primarily for the poor in normal circumstances, but *for all* during natural calamities, such as earthquakes, tsunamis and droughts, irrespective of the economic and social status of individuals. The Commission has also recognized the Act as being pivotal for achieving three Sustainable Development Goals (SDGs): to end poverty (SDG 1), to achieve zero hunger (SDG 2) and to move towards sustainable consumption and production (SDG 12).

Impacts on procurement and prices

One immediate and direct impact of the Right to Food has been that many state governments have taken proactive steps to reform the PDS system, procure food locally and ensure a higher price for their farmers, besides cutting down the cost of logistics. This has also reduced the asymmetry of information and power between thousands of marginal players on the one hand, and the large agribusiness aggregators on the other. When production goes up in the absence of a market or state procurement, the prices farmers can get for their produce tend to plummet. In order to prevent distress sales, the West Bengal government undertook a massive procurement operation with two distinct but clearly related objectives. The first was to provide rice at Rs 2 per kg to over 80 million citizens. Closely linked to this was the need to procure from within the state, to ensure that farmers got a fair price for their produce.

The starting point of food procurement in India is the purchase of food grains by the central or state government from farmers on the basis of the MSP Programme, under which food crops are procured by the FCI, or a state procurement agency at a minimum price determined annually by Commission for Agricultural Costs and Prices. The crops are stored in warehouses across the country, to be distributed to the beneficiaries of the PDS on the basis of the lists of BPL persons maintained and updated by the state governments. In this process, the state governments are the agencies for monitoring and identifying the beneficiaries. Food grains are transferred to FPS through a specified transport system and infrastructure. In the FPS, food is distributed on the basis of a digitized list, prepared on the basis of the issuance of ration cards. This allows for the online entry and verification of beneficiary data as well as the online accounting of the monthly entitlement of beneficiaries, the number of dependents as well as the off-take of food grains by beneficiaries from the FPS. Likewise, the computerization of FPS allocation ensures declaration of the stock balance, and the web-based monitoring of truck movements ensures quicker and more efficient tracking of transactions.

The case of West Bengal

West Bengal has taken full advantage of the NFSM interventions and its success is acknowledged by five successive awards that it has received for its contribution to National Food Security. In fact, West Bengal is the only state in the country to have won the Krishi Karman Award (Excellence and Accomplishment in Agriculture) five times in a row. These were for: record pulses production in 2011–2012; total food grain production in 2012–2013; coarse cereal production in 2013–2014; oilseed production in 201420–15 and pulses production in 2015–2016.

The Krishi Karman Awards was instituted in 2010–2011 to acknowledge efforts of the best performing states for the production of food grains and individual crops, such as rice, wheat, pulses and coarse cereals, to encourage and motivate the states. Later in 2013–2014, oilseeds were also included in the individual crop category. The production figures for West Bengal that led to this recognition, are given in Table 2.4.

The award amount is Rs 5 crore in the food grains category and Rs 2 crore for the individual crops category. The performance of the states is assessed on the basis of notified criteria such as production outcomes, implementation of crop production programmes, innovative approaches adopted for effective service delivery, post-harvest management, etc.

Further, the two best-performing progressive farmers, including one female farmer of the awardee states are awarded the agriculture minister's Krishi Karman Award for Progressive Farmers. This consists of a cash prize of Rs 2 lakh and a citation. The objective is to inculcate a sense of healthy competition and encourage the farmers to enhance the production and productivity of individual crops and thereby of food grains as a whole.

Prior to the concerted drive for procurement under the Khadya Sathi scheme, farmers in West Bengal were finding it difficult to offload their produce at the MSP and were often getting less than the MSP rate. Moreover, there were serious issues of delayed payments, lack of transparency and arbitrariness with regard to weight and quality. Traditionally, paddy procurement in West Bengal was undertaken on behalf of various Custom Milled Rice (CMR) agencies by respective co-operative societies, by organizing paddy purchase camps at the society premises or elsewhere, depending

Table 2.4 Production of cereals, pulses and oilseeds (2010–2017)

Year	Production (in thousand tonnes)			
	Total cereals	*Total pulses*	*Total food grains*	*Total oilseeds*
2010–2011	14,634.35	176.52	14,810.87	703.27
2011–2012	15,855.79	153.98	16,009.77	710.51
2012–2013	16,320.18	201.65	16,521.83	821.50
2013–2014	16,941.07	215.23	17,156.30	840.65
2014–2015	17,532.35	230.87	17,763.22	858.09
2015–2016	17,415.53	256.20	17,671.73	888.59
2016–2017	17,276.96	275.79	17,552.75	893.84

Source: Department of Food and Civil Supplies, Government of West Bengal

upon the need of local farmers. During the kharif marketing season (KMS) 2014–2015, 46 Kisan Mandis that had the required infrastructure were identified as Centralized Procurement Centres (CPCs). In order to incentivize the farmers to bring their paddy to those locations, Rs 15 per quintal of common paddy was allowed over and above the MSP of Rs 1360 per quintal. Encouraged by the positive response of farmers, 275 CPCs were opened at all major paddy producing blocks in KMS 2016–2017. In the 2017–2018 season, the total number of CPCs rose to 325 and the amount of incentive payable to farmers was increased to Rs 20 per quintal for common paddy. CMR agencies were also procuring paddy through 950 co-operative societies for the KMS 2017–2018. More than 300 SHGs participated during the 2017–2018 season, procuring 31,217 MT of paddy from 9,600 small and marginal farmers.

No distress sale of paddy has been reported during the past six years. Farmers are getting a higher MSP than the MSP in the open market. Dependence on the FCI for rice procurement has decreased during the past six years. Last but not least, with the introduction of e-procurement software, payments to farmers are being made through the National Electronic Fund Transfer (NEFT) within three days of purchase (Table 2.5).

The Right to Work

The Right to Work is enshrined in the Universal Declaration of Human Rights and the Indian Constitution, Article 41 (Directive Principles of State Policy). In 2005, the Indian Parliament passed the Right to Work Act, notified on 7 September 2005. Along with wage employment, the inherent idea was to provide income security to all resource-poor persons in the country. The MGNREGA is the largest work guarantee programme in the world. The Act provides a hundred days of wage employment to a household

Table 2.5 Procurement status (2012–2013 to 2017–2018)

Year	*Minimum Support Price (INR) per quintal*	*Procurement of paddy (in LMT)*	*Procurement of CMR (in LMT)*
KMS-2012–2013	1,250	25.93 (including levy)	17.63
KMS-2013–2014	1,310	19.99 (including levy)	13.59
KMS-2014–2015	1,360	30.36 (including levy)	20.64
KMS-2015–2016	1,410	38.53	26.20
KMS-2016–2017	1,470	39.59	26.92
KMS-2017–2018	1,550	28.38 (till date)	19.29

Source: Department of Food and Civil Supplies, Government of West Bengal

whose adult members are ready to do unskilled manual work. If employment is not provided within 15 days, the job-seeker is entitled to an unemployment allowance. The list of work is prepared by the concerned Gram Sabha, ensuring a general consensus about the kind of work that needs to be taken up with community assets, such as the construction of schools, shelters and roads, and management of water bodies. The active participation of the Gram Sabha has a two-fold benefit, reducing the role of middlemen and creating a sense of ownership in the local communities regarding the assets created. The funding is provided by the central government and the states according to fixed criteria. This makes the "entitlement to work" a matter of right, rather than an act of grace by the political dispensation. It also means that there is recourse to the judicial process in case of a denial of the Right to Work. Again, while the state government implements, the centre lays down the policy guidelines and provides much of the funding.

The Government of India and the government of West Bengal's share in the overall allocations and spending under the MGNREGA during Financial Year 2008–2009 to 2017–2018 are shown in Table 2.6.

MGNREGA has direct implications for the rural economy, as the MGNREGA wage sets the floor rate for rural wages, and the work is demand-driven. Wage employment can therefore be created during economic shocks or agricultural off-seasons. Men and women get equal wages in rural areas, unlike private jobs, which pay women far less for the same kind of work. During the Eleventh Five Year Plan (2011–2012), the nominal farm wage in India increased by 17.5% annually, while real farm wages increased by 6.8%, registering the fastest growth since economic reforms began in 1991 (Virmani, 2001). This has primarily benefited the scheduled castes, scheduled tribes and daily wage labourers. Wage rates are revised periodically to factor in inflationary trends. The programme is environmentally beneficial, as it involves the creation of durable rural assets which augment land and water resources, thereby strengthening the resource base.

For example, Burdwan district in West Bengal turned around 1,445 acres of land that was either fallow, barren or prone to floods and droughts into productive farmland. This created huge social forestry assets, as well as increasing the paddy production. The district has been given the National Award for Effective Initiative in Social Inclusion by the Union Ministry of Rural Development.

Identity and entitlement

The Aadhaar card is a unique identity document that facilitates access to a host of benefits and entitlements for Indian citizens. It is important to note that many state governments, including West Bengal, have taken the view that benefits and entitlements cannot be denied in the absence of the Aadhaar card. This view has been upheld in a recent judgement of the

Table 2.6 Performance of MGNREGA (2008–2018)

	2008–2009	*2009–2010*	*2010–2011*	*2011–2012*	*2012–2013(as per audit)*	*2013–2014 (as per audit)*	*2014–2015 (as per audit)*	*2015–2016 (as per MIS)*	*2016–2017 (as per MIS)*	*2017–2018 (as on 31.08.17)*
Person days generated (in lakhs)	786	1,551	1,553	1,504	2,012	2,315	1,714	2,865	2,356	1,305
Wage rate (INR)	75/81	81/87	100/130	130	136	151	169	174	176	180
Funds received from the central government (INR in crores)	932	1,787	2,117	2,597	3,395	2,894	3,744	4,711	5,383	3,218
Funds received from states (INR in crores)	64	136	271	222	497	656	506	1,023	942	350
Expenditure (INR in crores)	940	2,110	2,533	2,927	3,894	3,777	4,085	4,853	7,264	4,200

Source: Compiled from MGNREGA reports (www.nrega.nic.in)

Supreme Court Justice (Retd) K.S. Puttaswamy vs Union of India, wherein the nine-judge bench unanimously upheld that privacy is a constitutionally protected right, emanating from the guarantee of life and personal liberty under Article 21 of the Constitution. However, most government schemes and programmes insist on, or at least seek Aadhaar card details. The fact that it is useful for getting benefits under government programmes is clearly mentioned on the Aadhaar card itself.

Several departments of the Government of India – from agriculture to social welfare, health and fertilizers have requested states and UTs to seed the Aadhaar numbers in the database of ration card/health card/Kisan Credit Card/farmers' insurance/fertilizer distribution. With specific reference to the National Food Security Act, the scheme will enable the weeding out of bogus/ineligible ration cards and better targeting of food subsidies. It will also facilitate the availability of food grains to intended beneficiaries at Fair Price Shops, and check leakages and diversions. As per the information given in response to a question in the Parliament, 100% digitization of ration cards and approximately 73% seeding of Aadhaar was achieved by January 2017, while approximately 1.78 lakh e-PoS were operational at FPS/PDS outlets. From 2013 to 2016, 23.3 million ration cards were deleted due to detection of "ghost" beneficiaries, or beneficiaries that are ineligible due to having passed away, having duplicate residency or other issues.

The Aadhaar saturation level (88.7%) indicates an easy enrolment procedure with fairly easy access. The states with a high scheduled caste population as per the 2011 Census, that is, Uttar Pradesh (Aadhaar saturation: 86.6%) and West Bengal (Aadhaar saturation: 93.2%) as well as the states with a large scheduled tribal population as per the 2011 Census, that is, Madhya Pradesh (Aadhaar saturation: 88.9%) and Orissa (Aadhaar saturation: 92.4%) suggests that the most vulnerable sections that is, SC/ST population find it easy to get an Aadhaar card. There are concerns regarding some of the north-eastern states, as well as Jammu and Kashmir, where the saturation is below 80%. The factors responsible for this variation may include gaps in infrastructure and a disturbed law and order situation. However, the Aadhaar enrolment procedure does not appear to be a hindrance for the SC/ST population in these states.

Thus, we note that the Aadhaar card has the potential for weeding out fake ration cards and plugging economic leakages that would help ensure implementation of the Right to Food. This would not only help improve beneficiary targeting but would also save public funds.

New technology has also been out to other significant uses. In 2016, the Government of India launched e-NAM (National Agricultural Market) as a pan-Indian electronic trading platform, with the aim to ensure that farmers get remunerative prices for their produce. So far, more than 16.5 million farmers and 1.27 lakh traders across the country have been registered under e-NAM. Till January 2020, 585 mandis in 16 states were connected with e-NAM. As of January 2020, agricultural produce worth Rs 91,000 crores had been traded on this platform.

Agrarian distress

There is no denying the fact that the spate of farmer suicides across India continues to shake the very foundation of the agrarian economy and all political parties, both in their manifestos and in their campaign speeches, bring up the issue of farmers' distress. Even though most state governments deny a direct linkage between agrarian distress and farmer deaths to suicide, the writing on the wall is quite apparent.

According to the National Crimes Record Bureau (NCRB), "Bankruptcy or Indebtedness" and "Farming Related Issues" have been major causes of suicide among farmers/cultivators, accounting for 38.7% (3,097 out of 8,007 suicides) and 19.5% (1,562 out of 8,007 suicides) of suicides, respectively, as of 2015. "Poverty" accounted for 1.1% of total suicides.

Although "farming related issues" is quite a generic term, the main concerns are high input costs, coupled with crop failure or a failure to get a proper market price. It is worth noting that the states of Andhra Pradesh, Karnataka, Madhya Pradesh, Maharashtra and Telangana, which saw more than 200 farmer suicides in 2015, are largely dryland regions. The other states that receive a higher annual rainfall have considerably fewer farmer suicides.

Agrarian distress has become an issue of major concern to policymakers. To address these concerns, the Government of India constituted an inter-ministerial Committee on Doubling Farmers Income (DFIC), which sought inputs from relevant stakeholders, including state governments. Led by Ashok Dalwai, then additional secretary in the Ministry of Agriculture, the DFIC was mandated to examine the immediate, medium- and long-term steps required to transform the agriculture sector, with a major focus on farmers' income – rather than on production and productivity, which was the focus of earlier committees and task forces. This suggests that the Indian government has shifted its strategy to ensure food security from food production to farmers' income. As stated earlier, with the exception of oilseeds, the country has sufficient production capacity and adequate buffer stocks to tide over a drought year. Moreover, thanks to the irrigated areas of the country, and the spread of BGREI in areas marked by abundant rainfall, India has a reasonable food security cover.

The DFIC recognizes agriculture as a "value-led" enterprise and suggests empowering farmers with "improved market linkages" and promoting "self-sustainable models" to ensure continued income growth of farmers. This strategic direction addresses four key concerns: optimal monetization of farmers' produce; sustainability of production; improved resource use efficiency; and the revamping of extension and knowledge-based services.

Towards this end, the focus is on diversification towards high-value crops, improvement of price realization, increasing non-farm occupation, promotion of "smart agriculture" through precision farming, optimalization of nutrient and pest management, increasing cropping intensity by covering fallows and providing water and effective improvement of crop and livestock production.

Conclusion

The ecosystem of India's food security is moving in the right direction. While there are a host of pulls, pressures, unmet expectations and frustrations, the multi-pronged approach is yielding results. Both central and state governments are sensitive to the demands of their political constituencies – both urban and rural, while many farmers still face serious challenges when they try to get fair and right prices for their crops. This includes restrictions on where the produce can be sold, multiple intermediaries and disproportionate bargaining power.

There is obvious scope for improvement in almost every sphere: from enhancing food grain production to ensuring remunerative prices; plugging inefficiencies in the implementation of the Right to Food and Right to Work to ensure near-universal coverage of those entitled to these rights; strengthening the monitoring mechanism and replicating best practices.

In 2020, three new Acts were introduced: The Farmers' Produce Trade and Commerce (Promotion and Facilitation) Act, The Essential Commodities (Amendment) Act and The Farmers (Empowerment and Protection) Agreement on Price Assurance and Farm Services Act. The stated intention of these Acts is to give market and farmers direct access to each other, for better and more efficient transactions. This would also make sure that farmers diversify from growing primarily wheat and paddy and move towards more high-value crops that are more lucrative in and for the market. According to advocates of these measures, this is a necessary step to increase the income of farmers.

The terms of discourse on food security have changed. Prior to the enactment of the "Right to Food", discussions focused on the enlargement of the PDS, with numerous allegations that the "political economy" of the PDS is based on "systemic leakages". The example of Chhattisgarh has shown how technology interventions might eliminate corruption in the PDS and bring about a substantial improvement in terms of outreach. The pointed media attention to farmer suicide also became a major embarrassment, and policymakers up for election have left no stone unturned to avoid farmer distress. The universalization of crop insurance is also a major step forward, while indebtedness is being addressed in a big way through financial inclusion schemes. The ecosystem is hence shifting, from a strong focus on the production of food grains to attention to public procurement to help farmers, and public distribution to ensure access to "food for all".

Acknowledgements

The author acknowledges the contribution of Dr Srishtee Sethi, research fellow at Lal Bahadur Shastri National Academy of Administration, who provided research support and insightful suggestions on the draft paper.

References

Kumar, R., 2016. Putting Wheat in Its Place, Or Why the Green Revolution Wasn't Quite What It's Made Out to Be. *The Wire*, 31 October 2016. Online at: https://thewire.in/agriculture/green-revolution-borlaug-food-security (accessed 29 May 2020).

Sen, A. (1999). *Development as Freedom*. New York: Alfred Knopf.

Sinha, S., 2014. Bihar to Eliminate PDS Leakage in 2 years. *The Hindu Business Line*, 6 July 2014. Online at: https://www.thehindubusinessline.com/news/national/Bihar-to-eliminate-PDS-leakage-in-2-years/article20811970.ece (accessed 19 March 2021).

United News of India, 2018. Khadya Sathi: Food Security for Bengal, 31 August 2018. Online at: http://www.uniindia.com/khadya-sathi-food-security-for-bengal/states/news/1336268.html (accessed 11 May 2021).

Virmani, A., 2001. *India's BOP Crisis and External Reform: Myths and Paradoxes*. New Delhi: Indian Council for Research on International Economic Relation.

Chapter 3

Addressing nutritional challenges for India

T.P. Rajendran

This chapter discusses the role of food security for sustaining nutritional security and seeks to explain the Indian efforts to mitigate nutritional challenges in the Indian population against the backdrop of the legal rights of Indian citizens under the National Food Security Act – NFSA, 2013, which provides a legal right to access food. The premise of this chapter is that nutritional food security can only be achieved through the consumption of a variety of foods that constitute a well-balanced diet. As described in a position paper on "Nutrition Security in India", the Indian National Science Academy (2009) states:

> Nutrition Security implies physical, economic and social access to balanced diet, clean drinking water, safe environment, and health care (preventive and curative) for every individual. Education and awareness are needed to utilise these services. Thus malnutrition has a complex aetiology and its prevention requires awareness, and access to all the above at affordable cost.

It is in this sense that nutrition security is mentioned in the description of targets of the United Nations Sustainable Development Goals.

The World Health Organization (WHO) defines food insecurity as a situation that exists when people lack secure access to sufficient amounts of safe and nutritious food for normal growth and development and an active and healthy life. It may be caused by the unavailability of food, insufficient purchasing power, inappropriate distribution or inadequate use of food at the household level. Food insecurity, poor conditions of health and sanitation and inappropriate care and feeding practices are the major causes of poor nutritional status. Food insecurity may be chronic, seasonal or transitory.

The combination of food insecurity and nutritional challenge in communities becomes a subject of debate on the preponderance of one over the other. It is acknowledged that the economic power of a country does not necessarily solve the nutritional challenges of its population. The permeation of nutritional knowledge among the people, along with the manner in

DOI: 10.4324/9781003272656-3

which nutrition can be secured by one's food habits, provides the trajectory for accessing and enjoying the benefits of nutrition (Joshi et al., 2012).

Food as a source of nutrition

Nutrition through the food that one consumes is the basis for sustaining normal body metabolic activities for growth and procreation. Both energy, in terms of calories, as well as the required nutrient components for the body, are derived from food. The government has fixed the nutritional requirements and recommended dietary allowance for Indians (National Institute of Nutrition, 2020b). In modern times, food commodities are accessed by purchasing from the market or from the government supply in the public distribution system (PDS) in India. Nearly 0.48 million PDS shops or Fair Price Shops (FPSs) support the designed food security system of India, that is managed by states, as supported by the Ministry of Food and Consumer Affairs. Various states have implemented the PDS to make available food grains to the deprived sections of the population. The PDS has stood the test of time for the distribution of cereals (rice/wheat), sugar and kerosene since 1947. The Food Corporation of India (FCI) manages the PDS by procuring food grains to supply through bulk transport to all the states, to ensure timely availability of food grains in the PDS network shops. However, the PDS supplies only cereals, while Targeted PDS (TPDS), commenced in 1997 as a structural adjustment of the ongoing PDS, and provides pulses to communities living below the poverty line (BPL). The doubling of the quantity of grains for the monthly quota to those living BPL through TPDS was done to satisfy nutritional needs.

The food commodities support the calorific and protein requirements of the consumers (National Institute of Nutrition, 2017). The full spectrum of nutrition for an individual such as proteins, vitamins and minerals are available from food components such as eggs, fish, milk, fruits and vegetables. India has over the decades enhanced the production of all these farm commodities to become a globally reckoned producer. However, the majority of its population is deprived of these important nutrient components due to the inequity of access to these commodities. The relatively lower consumption of these nutritional food components by the BPL and other segments of the population is common in every state.

Malnutrition and undernutrition are the maladies afflicting various sections of society. The major concern is with regard to undernutrition that has a direct bearing on their socio-economic, regional and religious influences. Indian women and children have suffered the most in terms of undernutrition, leading to various levels of physical debility and health burden. Economic disparity and the uneven distribution of income have created huge inequalities in the nutritional status of these undernourished sections of the population. While several estimates regarding the impact of undernourishment are available, there is no real-time data relating to the regional dietary nutritional disparity. The complexity in the availability of nutrition to the impoverished is more so because of economic, social and ethnological disparities in society. The deteriorating capacity to access and purchase nutritious food items by disadvantaged persons in the countryside and the hinterland, merits keen attention while addressing the mitigation of undernutrition.

The entire issue of the public effort for reducing malnutrition in the population is a race against time. The national health burden arising out of this situation has been taken into account while developing the National Health Plan. Inter-generational undernutrition cycles compound this situation further. The National Health Plan, 2017 gives a thrust to the promotion of healthy living and disease-prevention strategies. It emphasizes the role of the Accredited Social Health Activist (ASHA) who will be supported by other frontline workers like health workers to undertake primary prevention of non-communicable diseases. These workers would get support from local self-government and the Village Health Sanitation and Nutrition Committee (VHSNC).

Food production impetus

Since the time the country became independent from colonial rule, adequate thrust has been given to enhancing food production to feed the growing population of the country. Through the Five-Year Plans utilizing various special government schemes, the targets for producing adequate quantities to meet the per-capita demand. Focus on per-capita availability, without managing the growth of the human and cattle population in certain states, led to the inadequacy crisis. Food grain production is limited to certain regions of the country, where there is assured availability of water for the uninterrupted production of food grains, for cultivating high yielding crop varieties and high input use under the "green revolution".

Agriculture has been the mainstay of food security that can guarantee nutrition for all. The continuing increase in the national food production (303.34 million metric tonnes as 2020–2021) has strengthened the country's conviction to implement NFSA. Agriculture has supported the fight against undernutrition and malnutrition. The integrated development of all sectors of Indian agriculture has substantially enhanced the production and the productivity of farm commodities over the last few decades. This was ably aided by the timely adoption of various policy support systems such as the: National Agricultural Development Plan [NADP (*Rashtriya Krishi Vikas Yojana*)]; National Food Security Mission; National Horticultural Mission (NHM) with parallel State Horticultural Missions (SHM), now known as National Mission on Horticultural Development (NMHD); Technology Mission on Pulses and Oilseeds (TMOP); Technology Mission on Cotton, and the like. Subsumed with these was the National Mission on Sustainable Agriculture (NMSA), one of the eight missions under the National Action Plan on Climate Change (NAPCC) to facilitate sustainable agriculture in the context of the perceived and the unknown risks associated with climate change. The "climate smart food production system" (Department of Agriculture and Cooperation, 2010) would produce livestock commodities (dairy, meat and dung), cropping systems and food systems (agricultural markets, new generation of agricultural insurance and credit support procedures). The National Agriculture Market (NAM), also known as e-NAM, is a portal that attempts to create a unified Indian market for agricultural commodities, funded by the Agri-Tech Infrastructure Fund (ATIF) since 2015.

It is important to raise food crops in soils that have adequate nutrient reserves. The farm practice of the soil incorporation of compost, farmyard manure and other decomposed plant materials before sowing can provide the required nutrients to crop plants. Appreciating the significant role of balanced crop nutrition in intensive agriculture, the practice of soil testing to assess the soil nutrients and health before the application of supplementary chemical fertilizers to cultivate healthy crops is widely practised in Indian agriculture. The government also launched the Soil Health Card scheme to enable states to implement balanced nutrition for crop production and prevent the injudicious application of fertilizers in farmers' crop fields.

The world's agricultural research community adopted plant breeding and other crop-genetic improvement technologies to enhance nutrition through food for better human health. The world's nutrition- and health-conscious communities should be able to enjoy the benefits of these efforts. Sustainable solutions to the enormous global problem of "hidden hunger" will not come without employing such agricultural approaches. The implications for investments for accelerating the research and evaluation procedures of crop varieties and animal breeds are immense. The success of all these efforts is dependent on the market appreciation of such agricultural commodities and their products.

The government of India through the NMHD has given an added thrust to progressively increasing the production and productivity of vegetables and fruits. Bananas and other seasonal fruits have become highly ubiquitous all over the country. Availability of these in even remote villages due to the over 311.34 m MT of production in 2017–2018 is a silent revolution by itself. Raw materials such as vegetables, spices, condiments and fruits to support the daily nutrition of common people in rural and urban settings has been an extremely significant development in the last five years. India's diverse climate ensures the availability of all varieties of fresh fruits and vegetables. It ranks second in fruits and vegetable production in the world, after China. As per the National Horticulture Database of the National Horticulture Board, India produced 97.35 million metric tonnes of fruits and 184.40 million metric tonnes of vegetables in 2017–2018. The area in the same period under cultivation of fruits stood at 6.50 million hectares while vegetables were cultivated in 10.26 million hectares.

In order to alleviate the rising agro-ecological instability, integrated farming systems that utilize all the biological resources of a village such as livestock, fishery, beekeeping and dairying are being recommended. These system elements enable a better nutrient supply chain in villages and from there up the value chain to all consumers through balanced food baskets. Horticulture crops such as vegetables and fruits have in recent years contributed much to nutrient availability due to the expansion of their area and productivity. The major nutritional security effect is created by the increased production of dairy products. As per estimates, the per-capita availability of milk, fruits and vegetables in the country is 290 grams, 200 grams and 401 grams, respectively, which is comparable to the world average (Singh, 2014).

India advocates an integrated farming system for small-holding farms. Poultry, piggery, milch draught animals and fisheries/aquaculture constitute the basic structure of the available natural resources in these farms. Many small holdings have integrated farming systems for meeting household requirements. Milk and milk products are also freely available in the majority of locations thanks to the white revolution and dairy technology that have promoted micro, small and medium enterprises (MSMEs) in all states and union territories. The weekly village shanties provide ample opportunities for the local populations to access – through barter or purchase – essential farm commodities from neighbouring villages. Access to food for nutritional support for farm labour, landless farming families, national labour force, the population in the unorganized sector and homeless street-dwellers is to a large extent achieved in this manner from such markets. However, the lack of access, equity and inclusiveness (AEI) of the weaker sections of society as well as people who have religious or fads about consuming certain food items has limited the expansion of the nutrition security to all the classes of the Indian population.

Eggs as a protein source are available in rural India. Homestead and farmstead poultry provide eggs for local consumption. The annual egg production in the rural unorganized sector is about 33% of the total eggs produced in the country. These eggs are produced largely by country birds. Backyard poultry and farmstead poultry enterprises have been thriving well. Specific poultry breeds have contributed to the growth of this sector. India produces over 80 billion eggs annually (National Institute of Nutrition, 2017).

Cereals (rice, wheat, maize, millets); tubers such as potato root crops such as tapioca/cassava, yams, aroids (colocasia), taros, etc.; pulses and oil from oil seeds provide calories for human beings. Commonly accessed commodities by people in villages are the preferred cereals, pulses, potatoes, root crops and vegetable oils. Many of these commodities offer minerals, vitamins and proteins too. Hence, staple foods derived from these could substantially supply the much-needed nutritive substances for managing health, besides calories. Cereals, pulses, vegetable oil and dairy products are the major ingredients in the food basket of Indian villagers. These are produced in village farms. The numerous small holdings under the integrated farming system largely produce these commodities which are consumed by the local population.

Changing cropping patterns

Due to the credible changes in weather patterns as well as in the availability of natural resources, especially rainwater, changes have been witnessed in cropping systems in different parts of India. Silviculture became part of the cropping system in northern India in which the wheat/mustard in the *rabi* season was introduced as strip crops in poplar and teak tree plantations. Innovative cropping systems such as these would effectively improve land-use efficiency, to harvest more by using less land and other natural resources, including water. The seasonal rainfall pattern is a major determinant of changes in cropping patterns in addition to the tempting market demand as well as farm profitability, per unit land area. In fact, conventional rice and wheat cropping patterns have destabilized the agroecology due to the increased use of agrochemicals such as fertilizers and pesticides.

The full spectrum of Indian cropping systems with 14 species of pulse crops is given below:

a) For grain/vegetable purposes: cowpea–wheat–green gram (moong)/ chana (Bengal gram), cowpea–potato–black gram (urad bean)/bean, maize/rice–wheat–cowpea, maize–toria–wheat–cowpea, rice–rice–cowpea, rice–cowpea and rice–mustard–cowpea
b) Fodder sorghum + cowpea–berseem–maize + cowpea
c) Maize–berseem/oat–maize + cowpea
d) Sudan grass–berseem/oats–maize + cowpea
e) Cowpea–berseem–maize + cowpea
f) In the plains, *Rajmash* is grown as a Spring season crop after the harvesting of potato and mustard. It is also found to be quite compatible for intercropping with early potato, due to its high nitrogen requirement and wet moisture regime in 2:2 or 2:3 row ratios.
g) Maize–field pea, paddy–field pea–wheat–(being popular in northern India), cotton–field pea, jowar–field pea, bajra–field pea

Crop rotations

1. (i) Maize–pigeon pea (Rabi), (ii) pigeon pea–urad–wheat, (iii) pigeon pea–sugarcane, (iv) moong + pigeon pea–wheat and (v) pigeon pea (early)–potato–black gram (urad bean)

2. Rice–wheat–green gram (summer), rice–rice–green gram (South India), maize + moong–wheat–green gram, green gram–wheat/barley, maize (early)–potato (early)–wheat/green gram
3. (i) Maize + urad–wheat, (ii) maize–potato–black gram, (iii) maize–mustard–black gram, (iv) sorghum + Black gram–chickpea (central and south India), (v) maize–wheat–black gram, (vi) rice–black gram (rice fallow of central and southern India), (vii) paddy–wheat–black gram (summer) north India, (viii) pigeon pea + urad–wheat–black gram (summer) north India and ix) sugarcane + black gram (1:2) (Spring) north India
4. (i) Kharif fallow – gram (chana) (in barani areas), (ii) paddy–gram, (iii) maize–gram, (iv) bajra–gram and (v) jowar–gram
5. (i) Kharif fallow – lentil (rainfed areas), (ii) paddy–lentil, (iii) maize–lentil, (iv) cotton–lentil, (v) bajra–lentil, (vi) jowar–lentil and groundnut–lentil

Intercropping/Mixed cropping

1. Central and southern states: pigeon pea + sorghum (1:2 ratio); upland plateau of Bihar and Jharkhand: pigeon pea + rice (1:2 ratio); Gujarat, Andhra Pradesh and Maharashtra: pigeon pea + groundnut (1:3 ratio); Madhya Pradesh, Andhra Pradesh, Maharashtra and Gujarat: pigeon pea + cotton (1:1 ratio), pigeon pea + soybean (2:2 ratio); Rajasthan and eastern India: pigeon pea + maize/bajra (1:1 ratio)
2. Sugarcane + green gram (summer 1:2), sunflower + green gram (summer 2:2), cotton + green gram (1:3 in central India 60/90 cm paired row), green gram + pigeon pea (red gram/arhar/tur) (2:1)
3. Pearl millet + moth bean (2:1), maize + moth bean (4:4)
4. Horse gram/*kulthi* (*Macrotyloma uniflorum*) crop is grown as a pure crop as well as a mixed crop with sorghum, pearl millet, pigeon pea, sesame or niger
5. (i) Chickpea+mustard (2:1 to 4:1), (ii) chickpea + linseed (2:2), (iii) chickpea + wheat/barley (2:2), (iv) chickpea + safflower (2:2) and (v) chickpea + coriander (2:2)
6. (i) Lentil + sugarcane (autumn) – two rows of lentil at 30 cm row spacing in between two rows of sugarcane, (ii) lentil + linseed (2:2) and (iii) lentil + mustard (2:1)
7. Specific crop sequences/rotations: (i) red gram (arhar/tur) + groundnut, (ii) black gram + cotton, black gram + millets, (iii) green gram + millets, (iv) cowpea + millets (v) horse gram, (vi) Bengal gram + coriander, (vii) red gram + groundnut, (viii) black gram–rice fallows, (ix) green gram–rice fallows (x) cowpea + millets (xi) horse gram, (xii) Bengal gram + coriander

India is the largest producer and consumer of pulses in the world. Pulses are a protein source from crops that yield their grains, and are very critical for vegetarians for whom it becomes a significant source of protein. These include lentils, grams, peas and beans. They contain 22–25% protein. Pulse production is concentrated in the rainy season in central India. During winter, the significant irrigated pulses are also cultivated in central and northern India. Besides, pulse production also takes place in the hills during rainy season. The production of all 14 species of pulse crops shot up to 23.02 MT, in 2018–2019. As India needs about 27.44 MT annually, hence the deficit of 4.42 MT was covered through imports from various pulse-producing countries.

The spurt in pulse consumption in the country, in this millennium, is attributed to higher purchasing power as well as the rising vegetarianism. The youth segment of the population has also contributed to the higher consumption of pulses. The consumption of pulses has shot up from 18 MT to over 22 MT in recent years. However, due to the better pulse production, thanks to the good monsoon rains and suitable government intervention, including creation of huge buffer stocks has reduced the inflationary fluctuation of prices.

Forestry and food for nutrition

Another significant source of food is forestry wherein a number of forestry products and plants offer nutrition to those communities who are settled around forests (Hoskins, 1990). "Food will last so long as forests do" so runs an ancient Kashmiri adage (*Ann poshi tele yeli poshi van* – Sheikh Nur-ud-Din Wali). The large availability of forest land for agriculture permits alternate cropping and natural fallow periods when the tree cover is re-established to boost soil fertility. Trees such as *Faidherbia albida* (formerly *Acacia albida*) in the Sudano-Sahelian zone and *Prosopis* spp. in Mexico serve as fodder for livestock, as in India in Rajasthan and Gujarat. In the food chain of the prevailing agro-ecologies, such forest flora support livestock-based nutrition for humans. Forests do support food and medicinal plant resources in every continent. The food plants support the cyclical famine periods caused by drought to avoid "hungry seasons". The biological resources in forests support the genetic diversity (Johns and Maundu, 2006; Arnold et al., 2011) that stabilizes the forest ecology for human nutrition by providing scope for ancillary food sources such as mushrooms, honey, etc. that form part of the dietary content of food basket in rural ecosystems. These resources are enjoyed by the landless and the rural poor along with tribal communities living on the forest fringes. Management for sustaining forest biodiversity in mangroves has been given high priority in order to sustain the food security of the population of humans and livestock animals. Focused policy support for sustaining the forest activities by dependent communities could address the growing issue of nutrition in the underprivileged populations of most countries. A number of Indian communities depend on the food resources from forests. Cropping food commodities in and around the fringing forests has been the traditional practice by communities that supported their nutritional needs in addition to the supplementation through PDS supply.

Challenges to food security

In spite of the production of 303.34 MT (2020–2021) of food grains, it is noticed that the country tends to lose over 10% of this stock due to poor storage systems in most states. Food commodity loss is treated by the government as a serious economic loss to the country. The other challenge is the issue of AEI. Another major concern is the sustained productivity of food in all states of the country with prudent and judicious agroecological management. Modern agricultural technology offers adequate solutions for improved natural resource use efficiency along with applied input use efficiency in Indian farms in order to reduce their overuse.

Food commodity loss

The advertent loss of food commodities from farmgate to consumers has been a concern in India as much as in many Asian and African countries. Harvest losses have been mitigated to a large extent through the harvesting machines. However, in the post-harvest handling and storage stage commodities get damaged, eaten by pests and contaminated by harmful materials, leaving the commodities unfit for consumption. At a rough estimate, about 7–10% of grains are lost during transport, storage and handling in the country. Minimizing this loss by means of modern storage systems such as silos is being undertaken by the government. Serious loss of grains during natural calamities in the homesteads and farmhouses of farmers is also being taken as food commodity loss. This avoidable loss of food grains and perishable horticultural commodities has been addressed by the government through many schemes to improve grain storage structures, cold chains and modern storage systems that are being adopted to capture the maximum quantity of fruits and vegetables, eggs and meat in order to secure their availability for the consumers.

Farmgate value chain enhancement through connecting with MSMEs could catalyze the mission of providing nutritious processed food to the population (Ministry of Food Processing Industries 2014a, 2014b). Encouragement from the government to the farm sector to cultivate biofortified crops as well as to MSMEs for establishing processing units to utilize them would bring in an adequate environment for assuring optimum food commodity utilization and prevent their avoidable loss.

Issue of access, equity and inclusion (AEI)

In the Indian context, AEI has potential implications for people whose capacity to access food at will is constrained by low incomes and disempowerment. The wages earned from employment would provide them with the means to purchase and consume nutritious food. The Mid-Day Meal scheme and similar social nutrition programmes supply freshly cooked food and do not incorporate finished food products due to various limitations.

In terms of equity and the opportunity to access and enjoy the benefits of nutrients in the available food, the target population has the purchasing power. The government on its own through the Food Safety and Standards Authority of India (FSSAI) notification on the fortification of commonly used food commodities has enhanced the exposure of all sectors of the population to access essential nutrients, vitamins, micronutrients and minerals. The FSSAI has taken suitable steps to give legal status to the fortification of food materials, based on the government circulars relating to the Mid-Day Meal and integrated child development schemes.

One concern of the government is that the health burden of the country is enhanced by the unscientific formulation of food products and the marketing strategies of those who drive consumers to eat unhealthy food and then be plagued by health issues. These food products do not carry any risk assessment-based food-safety recommendations. The risk assessment and risk management (RARMs) of such products by competent agencies is of paramount importance before they are permitted into the market. Often, many imported food preparations and food products find their way into Indian markets without adequate RARMs.

Fresh food has a short shelf-life and thus food is processed for enhanced shelf-life. The food processing industry (FPI) that manufactures and markets many food products needs to make it clear that their products are no substitutes for natural food prepared from cereals, pulses, oil, vegetables, etc. Global food processing and packaging technologies have been widely adopted by the Indian FPI. The load of sugar in dairy products (sugar) is generally considered to be sucrose, but a combination of sucrose with other sugars, consistent with Good Manufacturing Practice, is a major intervention in the food products manufactured by the FPI. The FSSAI regulates the FPI products to bring parity with global food product standards. The provisions specified in the Food Safety and Standards (Health Supplements, Nutraceuticals, Food for Special Dietary Use, Food for Special Medical Purpose, Functional Food and Novel food) Regulations, 2016, regulate the use of probiotics and prebiotics in dairy products. However, a strong oversight system to monitor the label claim of nutritional status of the food product needs to be put in place at the state level by the state food commissioners.

The aggressive food market has thrown up a wide variety of choices for urban consumers. There are maize-based, rice-based, potato-based, minor-millets-based and soybean-based food products in varying flavours and colours. Bakers and confectioners and the fruit-based beverage manufacturing sector attract the urban palate for various reasons. The National Institute of Nutrition has come up with the nutritional requirements for Indians (National Institute of Nutrition, 2020a) and the nutrient requirements and recommended dietary allowances for Indians (National Institute of Nutrition, 2020b).

The Food Safety and Standards Authority of India has laid down standards for all these manufactured products to ensure that the consumers get worthy food products. Many of these, along with instant food preparations, have apparently altered the urban palate. The quick-access nutrients in these, mainly energy-providing sugars and carbohydrates, and in some cases protein supplements, have made consumers fully dependent on them instead of on home-cooked food. The addictive nature of many of these products has affected the health of children, the youth and even adults, due to consistent consumption and the lack of natural foods. Malnutrition has flared up in the urban population leading to systemic ailments such as obesity, thyroid-related ailments, digestive disorders, cardiac problems, hepato-renal disorders, etc. The market-driven changes of the palate lead to changes in food habits in modern human life.

The impact of undernutrition in the Indian population could be due to early marriages, poor medical attention during pregnancy and, of course, the quality of available food. Such sociocultural and economic factors impede the success of even well-crafted programmes. These can be addressed by enhancing the knowledge regarding the adverse effects of such practices in the community. These require more coordinated inter-ministerial and inter-organizational government intervention. Another significant drag on the nutrition of the population is the increased consumption of narcotic products of the target population that affect body metabolism in large measure, impeding digestion and absorption of nutrients from food.

Biofortification as a strategy to correct micronutrient malnutrition

Biofortification is an optimal approach for the inherent deficiency alleviation in populations. Globally this recognized approach has offered the possible correction of pernicious nutritional deficiencies. Tackling the hidden hunger in various countries has become a priority to tackle the inherent ill effects in the population. Global agencies such as Harvest Plus have focused on tackling hidden hunger and empty calories. Biofortification is the best method (Bouise et al., 2011) to tackle nutritional deficiency and consequent ill health. Selection of crops that provide the essential micronutrients and vitamins in addition to proteins become the staple source for biofortification programmes in the world (Bouis and Saltzman, 2017; Saltzman et al., 2017; Welch and Graham, 2004). Asia, Africa and other continents face hidden hunger among vulnerable communities. Several staple crops have been biofortified to provide minerals and vitamins to the vulnerable populations through dietary mixing of these biofortified crop commodities.

Strategies have been drawn up for correcting micronutrient malnutrition through biofortified food commodities and biofortified agricultural commodities such as beans, cereals, pulses, etc. The various research programmes for crop breeding as well as for crop husbandry have the target goal of harvesting biofortified crop commodities. The plans to cultivate naturally biofortified crops by using high yielding varieties are ongoing in various states. It would be befitting if the production plan of such commodities with adequate price support for farmers could incentivize their increased production to fulfil the higher demand in the market. FPIs could chip in by contract farming for processing such commodities in biofortified agriculture commodities in various nutrition programmes of government and non-government institutions.

Food fortification

The FPI can contribute to the food fortification plan of the government under FSSAI as per which wheat flour, salt milk and oil have been chosen for being fortified with vitamins and minerals such as iron, along with iodine, especially for women and children. The vision is to provide double fortified salt; fortified edible oil in the MDMS and in Integrated Child Development Scheme (ICDS); and fortified wheat flour in MDMS and ICDS through the PDS. Food fortification is the best preventive measure for perceived micronutrient malnutrition.

Legal food fortification as in the case of iodization of common salt was the one that was extensively implemented in India during the last five decades. Recent FSSAI mandatory fortification notification of milk and vegetable oil with vitamin A and vitamin D also have a certain outlook for supplementation of the daily requirements. The Ministry of Women and Child Welfare made it mandatory for the oil to be fortified for use in the ICDS programme. However, indicator-based assessment and population survey may be appropriate instead of a mandatory supply of these nutrient supplements may not be substantiated presently with scientific evidence. In India, iodization of salt which has fulfilled all these criteria remains as the only mandatory fortification so far, but with the success of this in reducing goitre, there is now evidence that it contributes to iodine excess, which may be counter-productive. The Food Safety and Standards Regulation considers that mandatory fortification should be notified only after careful evaluation of the "severity and extent of public health need as demonstrated by generally accepted scientific evidence" as per the provisions under the Food Safety and Standards (Fortification of Foods) Regulations, 2018.

Sustainable Development Goal-2: Zero Hunger and malnutrition

Economic, social and ethological taboos relating to nutrition have been impairing the free flow and intake of nutritious food items in various regions of the country. Federal and state government plans to enhance education and sensitivity regarding the need for nutritious food that makes one healthy, through sustained media campaigns, have created good awareness among the young population in the weaker sections of society. Various government programmes such as ICDS have been designed to reduce the ill effects of undernutrition and malnutrition on the health of women, children and the youth along with the aged segments of the population. The indicators of the nutrition levels of the population seen in shorter, weaker, low-weight children or adults do not capture the actual levels of the nutritional challenge. The UN Sustainable Development Goal (SDG)-2 indicates at 2.2 the malnutrition maladies and the adverse health effects of undernutrition.

The inter-ministerial inter-active action plans of states and the federal government may bridge the existing gaps in the implementation of well-intentioned programmes to alleviate malnutrition of target communities in various states. The SDG-2 is linked to most of the other SDG targets (to be attained by 2030) and hence needs a visionary approach for the realization of targets that culminate in the expected impact on health, malnutrition and hunger. Prevailing government schemes could be fortified through the prism of SDG targets to measure the impact of assigned indicators and record the progress achieved. National debate to establish such a matrix plan could be a starting point to align all the ongoing non-government and government efforts in the country to enable efficient and better coordination.

The central and state governments allocate substantial resources to an array of health and nutrition programmes or schemes, such as the Integrated Child Development Services Scheme, mid-day meals, the reproductive and child health programme and the National Rural Health Mission (NRHM). The NFSA, 2013 provides subsidized (at a fixed price not exceeding 50% of the 2010–2011 procurement price for rice, wheat and coarse grains) food grains (4 kg per person per month) to 50% of the urban population, with at least 28% earmarked for priority urban households and the remainder for the general urban households. The NFSA for rural areas proposes to provide subsidized food grains (7 kg per person per month) to 75% of the rural population, with at least 46% designated for the priority rural households and the remainder for the general rural households. Government schemes for augmenting nutrition security with a multi-sectoral programme include maternal and child malnutrition, the Integrated Child Development Service scheme, Mid-Day Meal programme and the Rajiv Gandhi Scheme for Empowerment of Adolescent Girls. Supporting the government programme of MDMP, the following private initiatives are credited for contributing towards providing one nutritious meal a day for school-going children in accordance with WHO Guidelines, 2017.

Many religio-sociological organizations have volunteered to provide free nutritious food under ICDS and MDMP all across the country. Such participation will increase the daily supply of nutritious food for identified groups in socially deprived communities and individuals of defined age/gender.

a) The mid-day meal is a strategic programme of the government of India and is being implemented by ISKCON Food Relief Foundation (IFRF) – under *Annamitra* programme – in select schools across the country. The aim of this project is to liberate children from the vicious cycle of malnourishment and illiteracy. It is a not-for-profit, non-religious, non-sectarian public charitable trust formed on 23 April 2004 and registered under the Bombay Public Trusts Act, 1950. *Annamrita* serves 1.2 million meals every single day, through its 20 kitchens across India. ISKCON has a presence in seven states namely – Andhra Pradesh, Delhi, Haryana, Jharkhand, Maharashtra, Rajasthan and West Bengal and aims to provide nutritious, wholesome, hygienic meals prepared in hi-tech kitchens.
b) The *Akshaya Patra* Foundation started its mid-day meal programme in June 2000 by providing free mid-day meals to 1,500 children in five government schools in Bengaluru, Karnataka. It has been providing free mid-day meals to over 1.76 million schoolchildren in 14702 government and government-aided schools of 12 states. This not-for-profit organization is credited with running the world's largest NGO-run mid-day meal programme. The Bharti Foundation partnered with the *Akshaya Patra* Foundation in 2003 to set up a state-of-the-art kitchen at Vrindavan in Uttar Pradesh to provide mid-day meals to underprivileged children in government schools.

The Corporate Social Responsibility (CSR) obligation has led various food business organizations such as Nestlé, Britannia and Du Pont to contribute towards supplying nutrition to various classes of children in the community.

The Nestlé Healthy Kids Programme was launched in India on 7 April 2010, at a government school in the village of Pattikalyana, Haryana. The Nestlé Healthy Kids Programme provides nutrition education to adolescents. Its objective is to create and raise awareness regarding good nutritional practices and cooking methods to enhance the nutritional content of foods and physical fitness among students in village schools. Education is a powerful tool for ensuring that children understand the value of nutrition and physical activity and continue leading healthy lives as they grow older.

It is run in collaboration with six leading regional universities, viz. College of Home Science, Punjab Agricultural University, College of Home Science, Govind Ballabh Pant University of Agriculture and Technology, Pantnagar, Goa College of Home Science, Goa University, College of Home Science, CSK Himachal Pradesh Agricultural University, Palampur, National Dairy Research Institute, Karnal and the Rajiv Gandhi University of Health Science, Karnataka (Bangalore). The programme is conducted in communities around Nestlé factories, through two-hour sessions spread over six weeks, ensuring sustained nutrition training of 12 hours for each student. Nestlé collaborated with the Drishtee Foundation to set up health camps in villages across the Mathura region. Information regarding micronutrients, such as good locally available sources of food and the symptoms of micronutrient diseases, was imparted to the people attending the camps. Nestlé's Maggi Masala, an affordable taste enhancer fortified with vitamin A, iron and iodine, was also distributed to the participants. Nestlé aims to provide consumers with products that are nutritious, tasty and affordable. Popularly Positioned Products (PPPs) are high-quality food products that provide nutritional value at an affordable cost. With a large proportion of India's population suffering the consequences of deficiencies in key micronutrients such as iron, zinc, iodine and Vitamin A, fortifying these PPPs with micronutrients can help address deficiencies where they are most prevalent, that is, among lower-income consumers.

Britannia Nutrition Foundation is an independent, not-for-profit body that leverages the strengths of Britannia's wide stakeholder network to address malnutrition in underprivileged children using Britannia's fortified products. Multinational companies such as DuPont have addressed protein malnutrition by building up a value chain based on soybean protein. DuPont Danisco Soy Protein is an economical and reliable alternative to meat and dairy proteins, helping food manufacturers control costs and improve the profitability of their products. Soy protein offers nutritional, functional and environmental advantages over animal-based proteins. It is a high-quality, complete protein that contains all of the essential amino acids and is supported by an FDA-approved health claim of its positive effect on heart health.

Addressing the challenges of nutrition

India's commitment under the UN Sustainable Development Goal-2 for ensuring access to nutritious food for the deprived communities was affirmed by the legal food security offered to its population. Food grains including pulses are supplied at subsidized rates under TPDS to the target population in the country. It is significant that the central and state governments have rolled out plans and pragmatic policies and guidelines that are geared towards providing at a subsidized cost the locally available food commodities in villages for the target population. Indeed, sincere and conscientious implementation of such plans could yield great dividends.

Path-breaking policy measures include:

1. Diet diversification in the food basket of the poor in India can bring about change in land use patterns to grow oilseeds and horticultural crops in order to regionally expand the availability of nutritious food components to below- poverty-line citizens.
2. Women's empowerment through education and health is a prerequisite for achieving nutrition security in India, since mother's awareness and education would have a positive impact on the child's well-being.
3. Securing and sustaining forest biodiversity to ensure the continuing flow of resources to the marginalised and underprivileged citizens for their nutrition and that of their animals could reduce the burden on the government, especially in times of famine and natural calamities.
4. Synergy across sectors needs to be achieved. A multi-modal administrative and reporting management approach is required to improve nutrition and health outcomes. Synergy between the processes and programmes of various agencies, departments and ministries directed at: improving drinking water facilities; sanitation and public hygiene; access to elementary education; nutrition; poverty alleviation; and the processes that improve access to public health and medical services is important for ensuring positive nutrition and health outcomes. Providing incentives and encouragement to FPIs in the MSME sector will contribute towards creating value chains that can mitigate the shortfall of cost-effective nutritious processed food for Indians.

Acknowledgements

The chapter is a result of the discussions with Dr Ruchita Beri, Institute for Defence Studies and Analyses (IDSA), New Delhi, on the synthesized issues of food and nutrition security in the Indian context. The deliberations with Dr Sachin Chaturvedi, Director General and other esteemed colleagues at the Research and Information System (RIS) for developing countries on various aspects of nutrition security in India under the prevailing governance, access, equity and inclusion profiles helped in shaping the views in this chapter.

References

Arnold, M., Powell, B., Shanley, P. and Sunderland, T.C.H., 2011. Forests, biodiversity and food security, *International Forestry Review* 13(3): 259–264.

Bouise, H.E., Hotz, C., McClafferty, B., Meenakshi, J. and Pfeiffer, V., 2011. Biofortification: A new tool to reduce micronutrient malnutrition, *Food and Nutrition Bulletin* 32(Supplement 1): 31–40.

Bouis, H.E. and Saltzman, A., 2017. Improving nutrition through biofortification: A review of evidence from HarvestPlus, 2003 through 2016, *Global Food Security* 12: 49–58.

Department of Agriculture and Cooperation, 2010. *National Mission for Sustainable Agriculture for Meeting the Challenges of Climate Change*. New Delhi: Department of Agriculture and Cooperation.

Hoskins, M., 1990. The contribution of forestry to food security, *Unasylva* 41: 160–173.

Johns, T. and Maundu, P., 2006. Forest biodiversity, nutrition and population health in market-oriented food systems, *Unasylva* 224: 57.

Joshi, P.K., Dev, S.M., Kadiyala, M.S. Nanda Kumar, T. and Vyas, V., 2012. A nutrition secure India – Role of agriculture, *Economic & Political Weekly*, 47(8), 21–24.

Ministry of Food Processing Industries, 2014a. *Fruits & Vegetables Availability Map of India*. Ministry of Food Processing Industries, Food and Agribusiness Strategic Advisory & Research (FASAR).

Ministry of Food Processing Industries, 2014b. *Food Availability Overview in India*.

National Institute of Nutrition, 2017. *Indian Food Consumption Tables. Nutrient Requirements and Recommended Dietary Allowances for Indian*. National Institute of Nutrition (ICMR).

National Institute of Nutrition, 2020a. *Nutrient Requirements and Recommended Dietary Allowances for Indians*. National Institute of Nutrition (ICMR).

National Institute of Nutrition, 2020b. *Recommended Dietary Allowances & Estimated Average Requirements for Indians. A Short Report of the Expert Group*. National Institute of Nutrition (ICMR).

National Science Academy, 2009. Nutrition security for India–issues and way forward: A Position Paper, December 2009.

Singh, R.P. 2014. *Status Paper on Pulses*. Department of Agriculture & Cooperation, Ministry of Agriculture and Farmers Welfare, Government of India.

Saltzman, A., Birol, E., Oparinde, A., Andersson, M.S., Asare-Marfo, D., Diressie, M.T. Gonzalez, C., Lividini, K., Moursi, M. and Zeller, M., 2017. Availability, production, and consumption of crops biofortified by plant breeding: Current evidence and future potential. Issue: *Staple Crops Biofortified with Vitamins and Minerals*. Annals of the New York Academy of Sciences 1390: 104–114.

Welch, R.M. and Graham, R.D., 2004. Breeding for micronutrients in staple food crops from a human nutrition perspective, *Journal of Experimental Botany* 55(396): 353–364.

WHO, 2017. Assessing and managing children at primary health-care facilities to prevent overweight and obesity in the context of the double burden of malnutrition. WHO Guidelines.

Chapter 4

Challenges of the Targeted Public Distribution System in Eastern Uttar Pradesh

Anjoo Sharan Upadhyaya

Despite achieving sufficiency in food grain production, India continues to account for a quarter of the global hunger, with nearly 195 million undernourished people. The advances in agricultural sciences beginning with the Green Revolution saw India achieve a five-fold increase in food grain production, from 50 million tonnes in 1950–1951 to about 250 million tonnes in 2014–2015. Clearly, the crux of food security in India is no longer the non-availability of food but the inability of a large percentage of the vulnerable populations to access food to meet their basic needs. India is currently ranked as number 94 out of 107 countries on the Global Hunger Index (2020). It is abundantly clear that has yet to achieve food security in terms of ensuring the constant availability, accessibility and affordability of food for all its citizens. This is despite the various efforts made by past and current governments to ensure that food is accessible for the poor and needy, and to protect them against hunger and unstable food pricing.

The Public Distribution System (PDS), predating India's independence, carries the pivotal responsibility of ensuring food security and has continually advanced its trajectories and coverage to fulfil its mandate. The introduction of the Targeted Public Distribution System (TPDS) and the more recent enactment of the National Food Security Act (NFSA) raised hopes for the preservation of food security. And yet, there still remain a number of challenges, with regard to achieving food security objectives at the grassroots level. Oftentimes, academics and activists have called for a shift towards a system of cash transfers, especially in states where the PDS does not function well (Narayanan, 2015).

Indeed, the implementation of TPDS has been a work in progress and a learning curve for the government in India. While many Indian states have accorded greater priority to implementing NFSA and TPDS and have adopted innovative trajectories to achieve their targets, some other states have lagged behind. The recent improvement in the functioning of the PDS in select states suggests the possibility of adopting and relocating strategies to reinforce the TPDS (Khera, 2011; Sinha et al., 2016). While it is

DOI: 10.4324/9781003272656-4

important to highlight the instructive examples and good practices followed by some of the more successful states, it is equally relevant to examine the impediments and policy constraints that hamper the implementation of the TPDS.

To this end, this chapter analyzes the various trajectories of the TPDS and how they are being pursued in some of the select districts of eastern Uttar Pradesh, which has a critical mass of poor and vulnerable people. Drawing on the inputs from target beneficiaries, PDS officials, local NGOs, local politicians, Fair Price Shop owners and common people, this chapter highlights the several less emphasized factors that impinge on the TPDS in everyday practice and how corrective measures are being applied at the grassroots level. While conceptualizing the problem of food security in India, the discussion suggests how innovative measures implemented in the neighbouring states could prove relevant for nurturing household food security in Uttar Pradesh and other states.

The context

In 1997, the TPDS replaced the earlier PDS, which was a general entitlement scheme for all consumers, with no specific target. Then again in 2013, the NFSA was enacted to provide food and nutritional security by ensuring access to adequate quantities of quality food at affordable prices. The NFSA provides coverage of up to 75% of the rural population and up to 50% of the urban population. The Act expanded the PDS coverage while reducing the subsidized amount from 7 kg to 5 kg per person for all Antyodaya beneficiaries (Bhattacharya et al., 2017).

The Act stimulated the implementation of fresh approaches for streamlining the delivery of subsidized food grains and food items to the underprivileged sections of society. This ranged from identification of the deserving through Unique Identification Cards (UIDAI) or Aadhaar, availability of food items in a Fair Price Shop (FPS), delivery of these goods to the deserving via e-pass machines, etc. The NFSA modified the TPDS programme by shifting from a welfare approach to a rights-based approach. The PDS used to provide food grains as a general entitlement, while the NFSA conferred a legal right to food grain to the poor. The most distinctive feature of the TPDS in relation to the previous policy is the introduction of targeting by dividing the entire population into Below Poverty Line (BPL) and Above Poverty Line (APL) categories, based on the poverty line defined by the Planning Commission (2014). Under the new dispensation, the eligible beneficiaries are legally entitled to receive 5 kg of food grains at highly subsidized prices from the TPDS. The beneficiaries of PDS are divided into two categories: (a) priority households (PHH), entitled to 5 kg of food grains per person per month at subsidized nominal prices and (b) Antyodaya Anna Yojana (AAY) households (the poorest), entitled to 35 kg per household per month. The TPDS is to cover at least 75% of rural households at the national level, going up to 80–90% in the poorest states, and 50% at the urban level. Today the TPDS serves more than 65 million poor families.

Indubitably, the NFSA has energized the TDPS and there seems to be greater awareness among the beneficiaries about their entitlement. The fast-expanding digitization has also brought much-needed transparency into the process. The introduction of Aadhaar has largely addressed the problem of identification and distribution of PDS services. Linking of ration cards with the Aadhaar card, regular update of the beneficiary list and use of point of sale (PoS) machines in the ration shops, are said to have led to the deletion of 2.75 crore bogus ration cards (of the 24.3 crore total ration cards), and reduced grain pilferage (Sinha et al., 2016).

Amidst narratives of food-security achievements, there is also a nagging criticism about the gaps in food delivery and distribution to the targeted beneficiaries. The identification of beneficiaries and the target households remains problematic with inbuilt possibilities of exclusion errors (Jha and Ramaswami, 2012). The charges of "leakages" continue to surface from time to time and the corruption issues remain endemic. Often there are complaints about the beneficiaries being short-changed of their allocated quota or charged higher than the entitlement price. The Aadhaar-based distribution system and real-time online monitoring have posed new challenges for ensuring error-free transparent delivery.

These and allied gaps in TPDS have been redressed in varied ways by the concerned states. It is generally acknowledged that there is a notable decline in leakages over the past decade. While some states such as Andhra Pradesh, Himachal Pradesh, Karnataka, Kerala and Tamil Nadu have consistently reported low leakages, many states such as Bihar, Assam, Chhattisgarh, Jharkhand and Uttarakhand have been able to plug leakages from the PDS (Drèze and Khera, 2015). Personal interviews conducted with various stakeholders suggest that Uttar Pradesh has a long way to go before it can join the band of the states that have successfully plugged leakages. There are multiple dimensions to the problem.

Challenges in Uttar Pradesh

While some of the states have tried to plug the gaps and deficiencies in PDS, some others have been less forthright in doing so. Ensuring food security in the most populous Indian state of Uttar Pradesh, with its high percentage of poor and needy people, has always been a challenge. In fact, it became the last state to implement the NFSA on 1 March 2016 with the projected target of benefitting more than 15.21 crore people. The level of food security in the province is far from satisfactory to the extent that many hunger deaths have been reported. The cases of hunger deaths are either hushed up, or so managed as not be counted as hunger deaths. Most starvation deaths took place among disadvantaged groups like Dalits, Adivasis and Muslims due to the non-accessibility of "rations" from PDS shops to the poor (Mehta, 2018).

Despite continual reforms including the digitization of the PDS, Uttar Pradesh has not been as successful as some other states in plugging the gaps and inefficiencies in the TDPS. Against this background, the chapter examines the recent efforts to improve the accessibility, utilization and efficiency of TDPS in three districts of eastern Uttar Pradesh, to highlight some of the common, yet less emphasized constraints that routinely impair the implementation of TPDS at the grassroots level. While conceptualizing major shifts in the problematic issue of food security, the discussion suggests how innovative measures adopted by neighbouring states are relevant for ensuring food security in Uttar Pradesh.

This chapter draws on secondary sources as well as experiential insights related to the TPDS practices gained in three districts of eastern Uttar Pradesh, namely Varanasi, Sonebhadra and Mirzapur. The fieldwork was conducted in several phases between September 2018 and March 2019. The inputs came majorly from the target beneficiaries, PDS officials, local NGOs, local politicians, Fair Price Shop owners and common people. Data was collected with the help of student volunteers through open-ended qualitative interviews.

Identifying beneficiaries

In Uttar Pradesh, like elsewhere, the TPDS is run jointly by the central government and the state. While the central government is responsible for the procurement, allocation and transportation of food grains up to the selected depots of the Food Corporation of India (FCI), the state government is responsible for allocating and distributing food grains to the target population. The identification of eligible beneficiaries/households, issuing of ration cards and monitoring of the working of the FPSs rests with the Uttar Pradesh government.

Our study reveals that despite greater public awareness and government attention, the identification of BPL beneficiaries remains problematic. The beneficiaries are identified by the local rural/urban council, which often misuses this privilege to benefit their clientele. Our fieldworkers came across several narratives from interior villages, which revealed how the genuine claims of the deserving population were denied by the village headmen and officials. There are also omissions that are attributed to a misspelling of a name, or a minor discrepancy in other details, that often becomes a reason for the beneficiary being denied ration. Many respondents believed that somewhere around 10–12% of the deserving population remains unrepresented in the list of beneficiaries. The fieldwork uncovered several genuine rations claimants, such as Kalawati (aged 60) of Atesua village, and Budhni (aged 65) of Chittupur village, who didn't receive rations for a long time due to delays and inertia in obtaining an Aadhaar card. The repeated promises of the village chief in this regard were of no avail. Also, a sizeable number of PHH cardholders complained that, due to the non-inclusion of their entire family members, they didn't receive their due entitlement.

Similarly, the members of nomadic tribes such as the *Musahars*, *Buntangias*, *Tharus*, *Baigas* and *Koles* are less aware of their TDPS entitlements and often not included in the list of TDPS beneficiaries. For instance, many members of these nomadic tribes were not issued Aadhaar cards in the district of Sonebhadra. However, lately, the concerned district authorities have taken the initiative to proactively identify such tribes. A local-level campaign, the *Sone Antyajan Kaya Kalpa Abhiyan* (campaign to transform the poorest people), was launched to identify the *Musahars* and the *Buntangias*, get them to make their Aadhaar cards and include them in all the schemes meant for the least developed category people.

There are also gaps with regard to the eligibility of people as beneficiaries. For instance, the clause that disqualifies the owner of an automobile often disqualifies the needy claimant. The sizeable presence of migrant labour constitutes another stumbling block. Families migrate in search of work and are thus deprived of their legitimate claims. So, for instance, if an entire family migrates to live on a brick kiln site, their names would be omitted from the list and so will their entitlement.

However, there seems to be a greater urgency to exclude bogus beneficiaries from TDPS compared to the relatively fewer efforts to include authentic beneficiaries, who are left out for one or the other reason. In Chhattisgarh, where the NFSC is a relative success, the attitude is just the opposite, that is, not to lose out on a single genuine beneficiary even though it means that ten bogus beneficiaries are included (Krishnamurthy et al., 2014). The touts and corrupt officials still mediate for procuring or amending the AAY/PHH cards. Twelve percent of our respondents reported instances of bribes demand by the village headman (*Pradhan*) or his touts, for the issuance of ration cards. Of late, people's awareness has been enhanced, but only marginally.

Procurement and delivery

The state's performance with regard to PDS through FPS leaves much to be desired. A recent study based on data from the 68th Round of the National Sample Survey Office (NSSO), Consumer Expenditure Survey (CES) and primary data collected from six villages of western Uttar Pradesh, finds that "with high levels of corruption and lower income margins, ration dealers syphon off a part of the PDS quota for sale in the open market or charge higher prices to cover their losses" (Gupta and Mishra, 2018).

The extensive chain of over 80,000 FPS shops in Uttar Pradesh is responsible for distributing food grains to the target households. The FPS owners, known as *Kotedars*, directly cater to the beneficiaries and as such the effective distribution of food supplies to the needy, hinges on them. These private individuals appointed by the elected local councils are generally influential people, who have clout within the local community.

The FPS owners have often publicly expressed their resentment regarding the mismanagement of food supplies to them. The grains made available to them are never weighed and only counted per bag. Many FPS owner respondents complained that the bags are underweight from three to seven kg per bag. The carriage cost of the food grain is also borne by FPS owners. Similarly, the cost of maintaining the shop too is met privately by the *Kotedars*. The burden becomes enormous in urban settings. In short, there seems to be an unstated "understanding" that the *Kotedars* will offset these costs by adopting unfair practices.

The All-India FPS Owners Association (AIFSDF) has staged several protests in the recent past, demanding reasonable monetary compensation for their work. The AIFSDF in its recent meeting in Varanasi in October 2018, launched a protest against the government for undoing the NFSA by discriminating against the FPS owners. They demanded that each dealer be paid a salary of Rs 20,000 per month and a commission of Rs 250 per quintal of ration. The *Kotedars* also demanded that the government should compensate for the rent and electricity bills of the PDS shops.[1]

On the other side, the beneficiaries too made several complaints about FPS: under-weighing, overcharging, the multiple trips required for procuring each commodity, irregular opening of shops and the highhandedness of the FPS salesmen. In addition, the FPS was blamed for the lack of transparency, accountability and community participation. The study also found that there were sporadic complaints about "leakages" at various points: from procurement from warehouses, to delivery to the end beneficiary.

Large numbers of people, especially among vulnerable groups such as widows and the elderly, are often excluded from the PDS, for not being able to follow up on the tedious procedures. Elderly persons with rough fingerprints are routinely deprived of their rations. Those who were still able to buy their rations, faced considerable inconvenience due to connectivity and biometric failures. It was found that sporadic power failures, internet faults or simply the malfunctioning of the e-pass machines, imply delays of hours and at times days, before the beneficiaries can receive food grains. Digitization and the end-to-end computerization of the TPDS is still a work in progress. Meanwhile, the addition of Aadhaar-based biometric authentication threatens to disrupt recent progress with PDS reforms. It also deprives millions of people of essential food entitlements (Drèze, 2016).

This is because for one, it is not easy to operate the PoS machines at PDS shops which require numerous tenuous technologies to work in tandem to ascertain the identity of cardholders by matching their fingerprints against the Aadhaar database over the internet. In Sonebhadra district, for instance, if the machine is moved even marginally to get better internet connectivity, it starts showing errors to the extent as if, it has been shifted to the neighbouring state of Chhattisgarh.

At times, malfunctioning machines and ill-trained personnel deprive the genuine beneficiaries of their due claims. The incorrect entry of the beneficiary's name or Aadhaar number in the PDS database frequently hampers the verification process. The private company (OASIS) responsible for uploading data often ignores the dates of ration distribution, causing the machines to hang, thus making it difficult for the beneficiaries to claim their next instalments.

Our study also noted that the proper maintenance and timely repair of the computerized system have been a common problem. Some of the respondents showed us records of the flawed system which delayed their food supplies. In villages with dismal internet connectivity, it guarantees inefficiency.[2] In the remote villages of Varanasi, food distribution was stalled several times due to the malfunctioning of either the PoS machine or the failure of the internet. At times, the computer server was down for days, compelling beneficiaries to make more than three rounds of the shop, to get their ration. The beneficiaries being mostly daily wagers have to forego their earnings to receive their rations. Often children are sent by working parents to collect the rations and they lose a school day in the process.

Though the court has allowed the use of Aadhaar in PDS, it has been categorical in stating that it should not be made compulsory. It can be safely stated that imposing new technologies on populations, without having a structure in place, can be more harmful than constructive for the overall performance of a system.

Like other states, Uttar Pradesh too has put in place a grievance redressal machinery to deal with the complaints regarding the food supply. However, this has hardly been invoked in the past years. The state grievance redressal board remains mostly inoperative with more than two vacancies, at any given point of time. The same inertia pervades the vigilance committee at the village or the urban ward level. These vigilance committees were expected to monitor the activities of the FPS on a regular basis and consisted of members of the gram panchayat or city council. In all the three Uttar Pradesh districts, that our team visited, we found virtually no felt presence of the vigilance committee. Either the vigilance committees had not been constituted or they remained non-functional. The public are either not aware or they are not empowered enough to benefit from the systems of grievance redressal. For instance, 45% of the respondents under the PHH category had a lower number of units mentioned on their cards. This can be easily rectified by cross-checking the same, from the census data or through the community resources. However, there was not a single case in which this omission was found to be rectified.

Besides these technological challenges, the civil supplies department in Uttar Pradesh continues to countenance the menace of diversion and corruption. In August 2018, the Uttar Pradesh government admitted that food grains meant for the poor under the PDS, were in many cases being diverted to the open market by ration shop owners with the connivance of the officials. The Aadhaar numbers of genuine beneficiaries were replaced by those of imposters, according to many respondents.

The corruption and diversion practices in PDS seem to be unstoppable in Uttar Pradesh. In August 2018, a major scandal was reported, wherein the owners of ration shops in many districts used fake Aadhaar cards to withdraw tonnes of rations. As per the official claims, the agency responsible for linking the Aadhaar cards to the FPS system was one of the main culprits (Shukla, 2018). The fact is, that much of the corruption in the PDS occurs because of the nexus between the PDS officials, the *Kotedars* and the politicians. Routinely, one comes across cases wherein the non-deserving has been included in the list of beneficiaries to siphon off the ration. One such undeserving beneficiary has even opened a ration shop of his own in one of the blocks of Vidyapeeth (Varanasi) to sell the ration he fraudulently obtains from the FPS. There are known cases of undeserving people, related to influential politicians who were given the AAY by the officers, to save themselves from the wrath of the politicians.[3]

The village scenario in Uttar Pradesh is still extremely patronage driven. It is a common sight to see the *Pradhan* sitting in the FPS and getting the rations distributed as per his whims, giving the impression, that it is some kind of mercy mission or charity. Such feudal practices defy the "rights-based" approach to food security, which is about people being entitled to demand ration as their right.

Lessons from Chhattisgarh

Many other states like Chhattisgarh, Odisha and Bihar in recent years have undertaken PDS reforms in recent years (Aggarwal, 2011). There are several lessons to be learned from successful states like Chhattisgarh, that have inspired PDS practices in other states. In Chhattisgarh, a transformative reform programme, known as the Centralized Online Real-time Electronic PDS (CORE PDS) has been undertaken in the structural, financial and legal spheres (Sheel, 2013). Most significantly, the government has done away with privately owned ration shops which have been handed over to public bodies like women's self-help groups (SHGs), or the village panchayat, cooperatives or forest protection committees. Strong efforts have been made to make the shops viable by increasing the commission received by shop operators, earmarking (where possible) public buildings for PDS shops, training in accounting and providing soft loans for infrastructure and working capital. Similarly, the innovative system of doorstep delivery directly to all FPS, eliminated the malpractice of brokers and the middlemen. The Chhattisgarh model also improved the viability of FPS by extending an interest-free working capital loan of Rs 75,000 payable in 20 years in EMIs, one-month stock on credit, commission on food grains and increased quota of kerosene (Puri, 2012).

Another innovative measure introduced in Chhattisgarh is the "portability" of entitlement, through the use of smart ration cards (SRCs), in combination with real-time monitoring (RTM) of uptake. Through this portability, the beneficiary has the choice of picking up his ration from the shop of his choice. This innovative approach introduced fair competition among FPS for customers. The new dispensation also made a provision for issuing a printed receipt for cash paid by the beneficiary.

Other states, like Odisha and Bihar, also adopted the good practices of the well-publicized Chhattisgarh model. Odisha replicated such several innovative trajectories in some of its food insecure districts like Kalahandi, Bolangir and Koraput to begin with, and later extended them to other districts as well (Aggarwal, 2011). Accordingly, the BPL entitlements were also extended with the doorstep delivery of the food grains to improve the regularity of distribution and quality of food grains. Also instructive is Bihar's recent experience which curtailed the leakages and embezzlements, by the introduction of a system for tracking coupons (Choithaniand and Pritchard, 2015). Yet, even in Chhattisgarh, all is not well with its CORE PDS. Studies suggest that the CORE reforms took the earlier reforms to their logical conclusion and further reduced corruption by capturing transactions at the shop level, but the gains were limited. CORE PDS reforms could not address the issues of the power imbalance between shop owners and cardholders which continue to shape interactions between them. Neither did the reforms put in place robust and effective grievance redressal systems that could enable cardholders to report poor performance without fear of reprisal (Sinha et al., 2016).

Another significant finding is that technological fixes for social protection programmes are only feasible, insofar as they work within the political logic of the context in question. The CORE PDS reforms could not address the issues of power imbalances between shop owners and cardholders which continue to shape interactions between them. Introducing transparency, accountability and quasi-market reforms in this context thus offered limited possibilities in what they could achieve (Gupta and Mishra, 2018). The UP government showed a keen interest in the Chhattisgarh model of PDS soon after the Yogi government took office. In March 2017, the new chief minister publicly declared that UP will transform its PDS based on the Chhattisgarh model. Soon thereafter on 27 March 2018, a high-level delegation of food supply officers, led by the minister for food supplies, went to Chhattisgarh to study their experience. While the delegation submitted a report of their learnings and a perspective sketch of PDS reforms in UP, not much was heard of this proposal thereafter. It is suggested that the UP government does not wish to use its own resources to augment the PDS, as was the case with Chhattisgarh.[4]

Challenges ahead

Clearly, the past decades have witnessed enhanced awareness, both at the government and the public level, about the pivotal importance of good food governance. The transformation in information and communication technology (ICT) has provided innovative approaches for upgrading the delivery mechanism of public services and also for tackling the chronic problems of corruption and inefficiency. However, despite the NFSA and a meaningful change in PDS, there are still gaping holes in the system for ensuring food security for the poor. While some states that took the NFSA earnestly have done better to handle the problems of leakage and diversion, many others have been less forthcoming in implementing the much-needed PDS reforms. Several new models, including the Chhattisgarh model, have emerged for rendering transformative changes. However, there seems to be a lack of political will to go the whole hog in this direction.

The study highlights some of the less prominent issues which the "reviving" states like Uttar Pradesh need to consider for meaningful PDS reforms. To begin with, the weighing of the food grains at the time of handing over to the FPS should be the first priority. Now that the quality of the grain procured is supposedly better than was the case earlier (verified by all the beneficiary respondents), the major point on which the end beneficiary gets short-changed is the quantity. Then comes the issue of the FPSs being privately owned. Chhattisgarh has moved the FPS from private hands to SHGs, cooperatives and women's groups. This arrangement is working much better. In Uttar Pradesh, the continuing nexus between the *Kotedars*, food supply officers and political elites needs to be addressed urgently. At the least, they can make the FPS over to the SHGs here too, on a trial basis. Reducing inclusion and exclusion errors, or in short, correct identification of beneficiaries is one of the most critical issues for improving food grain deliveries to the poor. Another point is the portability of FPS. Sizeable sections of the poor population from eastern Uttar Pradesh are migrant workers. In this situation, either they have to forego their monthly entitlements or skip work/school to secure the food grain – that too, only if their workplace is close to their allocated ration shop. Another dividend from this will be the growth of healthy competition between the FPSs which will enhance the quality of their services. Studies on the Chhattisgarh food supplies reveal that the portability of FPS has encouraged fair competition there.

Most of all, a robust grievance mechanism has to be put in place to ensure hassle-free delivery. Our fieldwork leads us to conclude that although much ground has been covered to ensure food security, yet a total coverage of beneficiaries and deliveries has a long way to go. The real challenge is to create, multiply and expand grassroots level civil society processes, movements and social action under the agenda of the right to food and nutrition for socially excluded and marginalized groups with a particular focus on women, the elderly and children. Some relief has been provided by conducting interface camps, social audits, *Jan Sunwai* (public hearing), etc. in the "un-served" locations. One instructive example is that the Uttar Pradesh government has accepted that starvation deaths are taking place. The state and district administration have further taken note of the vulnerability of certain communities and taken immediate steps for addressing food security issues (Sinha, 2016).

Crucial for the success of a COREPDS is a dependable internet. Adoption of any new technology has to be preceded by the extensive training of all stakeholders (especially government agencies and FPS managers). There is an urgent need to carry out widespread awareness campaigns to ensure that all beneficiaries are informed of their entitlements, so as to be able to access and use new technologies. Good quality PoS machines and smart cards are equally critical. It should also be mentioned that the department of food and civil supplies in Chhattisgarh provided the option for offline transactions in case there were technical difficulties. Though Uttar Pradesh also has a similar provision, it is rarely invoked, as per our fieldwork responses.

Uttar Pradesh is still trying to complete the process of digitization. According to our respondents' estimates, only 40% of the cards have been digitized. The e-pass is still not successful. Though it is working in urban areas, it is still a work in progress in rural areas. There are diverse reasons for the same: software compatibility, availability of network, lack of trained *Kotedars*, etc. There have been efforts to train them, but these are hampered, by the absence of motivated trainers and the capacity of the *Kotedars* to be trained. "The company that has been outsourced for training these *Kotedars* is working for profit, not for education"[5] has been the general impression. In some of the villages, the FPS owners have delivered the grains, pending verification, but this is more of an exception. Most of the FPS owners have gone by the book and delayed distribution till such time that the system became fully operative. The portability of ration cards is yet another issue.

There is no doubt that significant reforms are underway for improving PDS, which for long remained a symbol of systemic inertia, inefficiency and corruption. The enhanced public awareness and end-to-end use of ICT have proved crucial in this transformation. However, it is clear that the ICT reforms alone cannot resolve all issues of diversion and corruption at the grassroots. These technologies could be effective if they are accompanied by the desired transformation in the sociopolitical power dynamic. For instance, the inefficiencies and leakages at the FPSs level are largely due to the power differentials between the shop owners (and their collusion with local elites), and most PDS consumers (Sinha et al., 2016). These issues can only be tackled through duly empowered and independent mechanisms of vigilance and grievance redressal. Uttar Pradesh being a "reviving" state has many lessons to learn from its own failings as well as from the good practices elsewhere. A constant vigil over the systemic fault lines in PDS, along with the imperative of a dynamic social audit, is the call of the day.

Notes

1 Based on fieldwork conducted in October 2018.
2 Ibid.
3 Personal interview with a serving District Supply Officer.
4 Ibid.
5 Personal interview with Kotedars in March 2019.

References

Aggarwal, Ankita, 2011. "The PDS in Odisha: Against the Grain?," *Economic & Political Weekly*, 46(36), September 3, 2011: 21–23.

Bhattacharya, Shrayana, Vanita Leah Falcao and Raghav Puri, 2017. "The Public Distribution System in India," in Alderman et al. (eds.), *The 1.5 Billion People Question: Food, Vouchers or Cash Transfers?* Washington, DC: The World Bank. Online at: http://pubdocs.worldbank.org/en/901801506434971394/Chapter-2.pdf (accessed 25 May 2021).

Choithaniand, C. and B. Pritchard, 2015. "Assessing Bihar's Coupon-based PDS," *Economic & Political Weekly*, 50(3), January 17, 2015: 61–68.

Drèze, Jean, 2016. "Dark Clouds Over PDS," *The Hindu*, New Delhi, September 10, 2016, p. 9.

Drèze, Jean and Reetika Khera, 2015. "Understanding Leakages in the Public Distribution System", *Economic and Political Weekly*, 46(21), 39–42. Online at: http://www.epw.in/journal/2015/7/insight/understanding-leakages-public-distribution-system.html (accessed 12 October 2020).

Global Hunger Index, 2020. "India". Online at: https://www.globalhungerindex.org/india.html (accessed 23 May 2021).

Gupta, A. and D.K. Mishra, 2018. "Public Distribution System in UP: Access, Utilization and Impact," *Indian Journal of Human Development*, 12(1), 2018: 20–36.

Jha, Sikha and Bharat Ramaswami, 2012. "The Percolation of Public Expenditure: Food Subsidies and the Poor in India and the Philippines," in Shekhar Shah, Barry Bosworth and Arvind Panagariya (eds.), Conference: India Policy Forum 2011–2012, Volume 8. New Delhi: Sage Publications.

Khera, Reetika, 2011. "Revival of the Public Distribution System: Evidence and Explanations," *Economic & Political Weekly*, 46(44–45), November 5, 2011: 36–50.

Krishnamurthy, Prasad, Sharad Tandon and Vikram Pathania, 2014. "Public Distribution System Reforms and Consumption in Chhattisgarh," *Economic and Political Weekly*, 49(8), February 22, 2014: 74–81.

Mehta, Avantika, 2018. "In a UP District Death From Hunger, As Governance, Social Security Collapse," *IndiaSpend*, 23 October 2018. Online at: https://www.indiaspend.com/in-a-up-district-death-from-hunger-as-governance-social-security-collapse/23/ (accessed 20 March 2021).

Narayanan, Sudha, 2015. "Food Security in India: The Imperative and Its Challenges," *Asia & the Pacific Policy Studies*, 2(1), January 12, 2015: 197–209.

Puri, Raghav, 2012. "Reforming the Public Distribution System: Lessons from Chhattisgarh," *Economic and Political Weekly*, 47(5), May 2012. Online at: http://www.epw.in/journal/2012/05/commentary/reforming-public-distribution-system-lessons-chhattisgarh.html (accessed 25 October 2018).

Sheel, V., 2013. "Executing Food Security: Experiences from the Grassroots," *The Discussant*, 1(4), October 2013: 54–62.

Shukla, Nelanshu, 2018. "Corruption in PDS Distribution of Ration in UP, Probe Ordered," *India Today*, New Delhi, 27 August 2018. Online at: www.indiatoday.in/india/story/corruption-in-pds-distribution-of-ration-in-up-probe-ordered-1323579-2018-08-27 (accessed 28 March 2019).

Sinha, A.K., 2016. "Experiences from the Grassroots," paper presented at the International Seminar on Food Security Debates in India: Varanasi, 2016, Organised by the UNESCO Chair for Peace and Intercultural Understanding in collaboration with the Peace Research Institute Oslo (PRIO) and the Institute of Defence Studies and Analyses (IDSA).

Sinha, Dipa, Anuradha Joshi and Biraj Patnaik, 2016. "Credibility and Portability: Lessons from CORE PDS Reforms in Chhattisgarh," *Economic & Political Weekly*, 51(47), September 10, 2016: 51–59.

Chapter 5

Entitlements for the deprived

An empirical study of household food security in Karnataka and Bihar

Arne Dulsrud and Unni Kjærnes

The social condition of not having enough food to eat may be characterized as "food insecurity", along with its effects including caloric undernutrition, malnutrition due to the lack of certain nutrients and malnutrition due to caloric imbalances (usually too much sugar and/or fat). In 1996, the World Food Summit emphasized the need to address food security at the household level, referring to "a condition where all people, at all times, have physical and economic access to sufficient, safe and nutritious food that meets their dietary preferences for an active and healthy life" (Food and Agriculture Organization, 2006). In the extensive academic literature on food security, three distinct solutions seem to dominate: (a) economic growth, (b) food production and (c) public institution building. All of these are not only on the Indian academic, but also on the public agenda, where food and food security have featured since independence. There are huge numbers of publications on food security in India, including reports, books and journal articles. This chapter will not attempt to give any overview of this literature but will instead mention specific references wherever relevant.

In recent years, economic growth has been high and food production has been intensified. There is, overall, sufficient money and sufficient food. Moreover, multiple policies and systems of governance have been developed to address problems of food insecurity (see, e.g., Mishra, and Agrawal, 2013; Jain, 2014; Dubey and Srivastav, 2011). At least to some extent, India has even managed to maintain some protection against the effects of neoliberal globalization. Yet, although famines have been avoided in the last decades, under- and malnutrition are still endemic – in rural as well as urban settings (Mishra, 2013). Neither economic growth nor major efforts to increase overall food production have been sufficient to solve the serious problem of food insecurity in India. Millions of people lack realistic access to an adequate and healthy diet.

Despite its obvious importance, challenges to food supply in terms of the quantities of food available are rarely enough to explain food insecurity at the household level. Poorly developed logistical systems are sometimes

DOI: 10.4324/9781003272656-5

restraining local supplies: limiting food availability of people living far away from shops or being dependent on inadequate food services. However, limited household access, strongly framed by socio-economic structures, is repeatedly found to be the dominant explanation for food insecurity (Drèze and Sen, 1989). This seems to be the case in poor as well as in rich societies, in normal times, as well as in times of crises. Yet, food supplies and poverty cannot be seen as isolated factors that influence household food security but need to be studied as a concrete and institutionalized dynamic (Ingram, 2011). While production quantities have increased globally, poor people lose out on the production, as well as on the consumption side, and food insecurity among poor people has persisted (Agarwal et al., 2009). Ingram (2011) argues for a food systems approach that integrates an analysis of the full set of food system activities with the food security outcomes for poor households, including stability of food access, utilization and availability, while taking into consideration even the impacts of environmental change.

Food security at the local and household level is influenced by the shifting interrelationships between production systems, food distribution systems and state involvement. Regardless of its rapid economic development and democratic institutions, India has been less successful than China and even Bangladesh, in improving the levels of satisfaction of basic needs among the poor (Sen, 2011). Sen in his classical study of the Bengal famine of 1943 demonstrated that the severity of this famine did not emerge from a lack of food supplies per se, but rather from inequalities built into the mechanisms for distributing food (Sen, 1982). The tendency of poor people losing out even in terms of basic food access is still evident. Today, the poor Indians' food insecurity is aggravated by environmental degradation and climate change, as well as social and economic development. A case study in the Himalayas illustrates this point, by showing that food security in the region depends on interactions between local agricultural productivity, family income, availability of employment outside the region, food purchasing power and infrastructural facilities for the transportation, storage and distribution of food (Tiwari and Joshi, 2012). They find that food insecurity in the region has increased due to the combined effects of deforestation and erosion, reduced job security, as well as shifts in the social relations in the villages.

We lack critical research on how local food security systems are affected by changes in climate, as well as labour markets, food trade and public policies (Vyas, 2000; O'Brien and Leichenko, 2004). Several studies have been conducted on the impact of climatic change on the food production, national and international food trade and policy initiatives taken to mitigate food insecurity (Butler, 2009; Dorosh, 2009; Jha and Bhattacharyya, 2011). However, few have been aimed at understanding how these macro-level changes together impact food security at the household level in India. This calls for the development of a meso-level approach, that can capture how social and climatic changes together affect food security for vulnerable population groups.

In this chapter, we conduct a small case study on how the various aspects of food security operate together and impact the situation at the household level, in different settings. We contrast poor villages with the urban slums in the two states of Karnataka and Bihar, states with very different outcomes when it comes to nutritional status.

Entitlements to food

In order to capture the significance of the above factors on household food security, it is crucial to study the interplay between relevant institutions and household practices (Tiwari and Joshi, 2012). Amartya Sen has stated that the law stands between the food and the eater. In our view, this opens up to an institutional approach that links basic social, economic and political structures with household practices. Sen's concept of "entitlement" is often understood as social rights. Building on the original study in West Bengal, we think the concept may capture various societal conditions for household food security. This broader understanding of the concept was used by, for example, Charles Tilly in his historical study of social change and food riots in France (Tilly, 1975).

Entitlements are defined as, "the set of alternative commodity bundles that a person can command in a society using the totality of rights and opportunities that he or she faces" (Sen, 1984). With its formal and societal references, the concept of entitlement points to a relational and institutional approach to food insecurity, which may be seen as the lack of entitlements that can be exchanged for food. A household may be in command of means of production or capital, exchange work for money and/or food, or have social rights. We operationalize this as three distinct types of legal entitlements for providing stable access to food:

1. a household's own production, which presupposes access to agricultural land or other sources of food (like fishing, hunting and gathering)
2. market distribution of food, which presupposes purchasing power (relative to the price of nutritious food)
3. public schemes (income replacement, price regulation, distribution in kind), which presuppose social rights and functioning social security programmes

A household may rely on one or more of these types of entitlements. When entitlements obtained through a person's own labour or own production fail, access to adequate alternatives, such as social security or food relief, becomes crucial. A situation of household food insecurity depends not only on the bundle of legal entitlements that each person and household hold at a given point, but even on how these entitlements function, how they are realized. Thus, we need to consider the influence of market institutions, the labour market, structures of ownership – especially ownership of land, as well as public policies regulating markets and social security. Although part of social distribution systems, charity is not an entitlement, nor are norms of reciprocity within families and neighbourhoods. None of these provides legal entitlements.

Access to land may be of fundamental importance to the availability of food. In India, the dispersion of poverty in rural areas is highly correlated with access to land, making the landless population particularly vulnerable to food insecurity. Most vulnerable households depend on wage labour, many within agriculture (Pritchard and Rammohan, 2014). Traditionally, these households have accounted for a third of all rural households but make up almost half of those living under the poverty line in India. At the same time, those who own land have exercised disproportionate power over rural institutions, including labour and credit institutions (Thimmaiah and Aziz, 1983). Added to that, older forms of land use, such as share-cropping, continue to prevail. In both Bihar and Karnataka, land reform legislation became an important measure of socio-economic change in the rural agrarian structure after India's independence, followed by several legal reassessments at state level. Whether the initiated land reforms have been successful in providing land for the poor in India, has been contested by several studies, as is the case in Bihar and Karnataka (ibid.). In Bihar, in particular, repeated land reform efforts have proved very difficult to implement.

A dominant argument, strongly promoted by Gulati and others (Gulati et al., 2018), is that economic development is the most crucial way of improving living conditions, assuming that an increased GDP will trickle down, eventually, to benefit the poor. Open and competitive labour and commodity markets are seen as the most efficient way of distributing limited resources (Fan et al., 2008). Goods such as food will be distributed where demand is allocated, and demand stimulates production. Regulatory interventions, such as fixed prices, public subsidies and protectionism, slow down the effectiveness of markets. In the long turn, such capitalist processes will, it is argued, promote the welfare of all (Bhagwati and Panagariya, 2013). Within this perspective, employment is the key factor, increasing buying power, household budgets and thereby accessibility to food. However, according to the Planning Commission of India, more than 94% of the workforce belongs to the informal or the unorganized or informal labour market (Planning Commission of India, 2007). The informal sector in India refers to all unlicensed, self-employed or unregistered economic activity such as owner-manned general stores, handicrafts and handloom workers, rural traders, farmers, etc. In most cases, informal work implies (very) low and unstable income.

For a long time, however, direct worries relating to undernutrition have been linked to the need for functioning social security systems (Mishra and Agrawal, 2013). The National Food Security Act (NFSA) of 2013 converted former rules of access to such systems into a legal entitlement to governmental food security programmes. It includes subsidized food from the food distribution system (PDS), nutritious meals for children (Mid-Day Meal Scheme), Integrated Child Development Services (ICDS) and maternity entitlements, accessed through Anganwadis. The Mid-Day Meal Scheme and Integrated Child Development Service are universal services, while the PDS reaches about 75% of the population in rural areas and 50% in urban areas. The PDS is based on ration cards, which are used to establish identity, eligibility and entitlement. There are three categories of ration cards: Antyodaya, Below Poverty Line and Above Poverty Line. BPL or Antyodaya cards give the cardholder access to subsidized staples, primarily wheat and rice, through the PDS. According to the NFSA, the PDS entitlement for BPL cardholders is 5 kg of food grains per person per month at nominal prices (Rs 3, 2 and 1 per kg for rice, wheat and millet, respectively) for all households in the "Priority" household category. The Act continued the Antyodaya programme aimed at the poorest, wherein households are entitled to 35 kg of food grains per month at the same price. The identification of eligible households is a major challenge in implementing the NFSA scheme (Drèze et al., 2015).

We argue here for the need to address the whole bundle of entitlements for poor households; access to land, waged employment and social rights. What are the dominant patterns in the two states? What characterizes those with the fewest overall entitlements? Third, to what degree do social rights to food in effect compensate for the lack of other types of entitlements emerging from socio-economic inequalities? On this basis, we discuss the extent to which compensatory mechanisms are influenced by the institutional setup in the two states.

Methods of data collection

Empirical studies were undertaken as part of the project "Food Security in India: The Interactions of Climate Change, Economics, Politics and Trade" supported by the Research Council of Norway. One of its aims was to find a way to study the implications of poverty and the lack of entitlements for household food security among vulnerable groups. The study focusses on two Indian states, Bihar and Karnataka. Both states have significant agricultural production, but they also face challenges in food production and rural development due to climate change, as Bihar is a flood-prone state and Karnataka is drought-struck. However, the two states differ in many other respects. According to the Human Development Index, Karnataka is ranked 12th and Bihar 25th among Indian states (Mukherjee and Chakraborty,

2014). Karnataka is among the better-functioning southern states when it comes to public programmes, compared to Bihar which is an example of the more problematic, populous North Indian states. While the situation in Bihar has been closely monitored, Karnataka has received comparatively less attention.

Household surveys were carried out in rural districts (Raichur in north-eastern Karnataka and Sheohar in north Bihar) and in the urban slums of Bangalore and Patna in 2016. The rural districts were selected in accordance with specific criteria based on indicators of poverty, complemented by indicators of the effects of climate change on food production. The five most vulnerable districts were shortlisted based on the indicators of exposure, sensitivity and adaptive capacity, with reference to the Central Research Institute for Dry-land Agriculture (an institute of ICAR) under the National Initiative of Climate Resilient Agriculture (NICRA). The indicators to assess vulnerability at the household level were: slum population above 5% of the total population of the district, the incidence of poverty above 35%, SC/ST population above 25%, agricultural labour to total worker above 35% and marginal worker to total worker above 18%, as recorded by 2011.[1] Considering the two criteria together, the rural districts of Raichur in north Karnataka and Sheohar in north Bihar were selected, in addition to the urban areas of Patna and Bangalore defined as slums. Two blocks within each district were selected, within these three Panchayats: one female-headed Panchayat, one SC/ST community-headed Panchayat, one general category-headed Panchayat and finally nine villages spread out within the three Panchayats. Within each village, the selection of households was random, choosing every second household until the desired number of units were accomplished. The selection of blocks, Panchayats and villages considered a fair representation of religion, the inclusion of agricultural labourers/landless, etc. About 25 households were selected within each village (9*25 = 225). Two slums were selected in each capital, with 75 households in each slum. The overall final sample was 776 households. Trained personnel speaking the local language conducted personal interviews with female representatives of the households. The questionnaire was piloted within each setting.

A largely pre-coded questionnaire included questions on eating (a recall of meals of the day before plus food frequency), food procurement practices, and a detailed account of socio-economic background, including their connections with food production in the rural areas. In addition, a series of questions addressed the use of, and experiences with public services providing food (or cash).

Due to the intended concentration on poor areas, the final samples are more disadvantaged than the averages for the two states. While half the population of Bihar is illiterate, according to recent statistics, 79% of the rural sample and 77% in the urban sample, were illiterate. In Karnataka, the figure is 34% for the whole state, while it is 44% and 20% in our rural and urban samples, respectively. The concentration of disadvantaged in our samples is even larger in terms of caste. While the average proportion of scheduled castes and scheduled tribes in Bihar is 17%, it was 31% in the rural sample and 71% in the urban sample. In Karnataka, the average is 24% and 21% in the rural, and 74% in the urban sample, respectively.

In this chapter, we will report some simple findings on meal patterns, food procurement and the respondents' reports on their food security situation. We will then link this to accounts of their various entitlements to food.

Household food security

Meals on the day before

Our focus during the household interview was on meals served in the household during the day before. Asking about yesterday's eating is a reliable way of identifying everyday eating practices in terms of number of meals and the food items included, as well as the social context and circumstances (Kjærnes and Holm, 2009). We will here present some observations on key dietary elements (for more details, see Dulsrud et al., 2015). Table 5.1 shows the number of meals during the day before that included one or more staples (rice, grains) and pulses or dhal, respectively. All households in all four settings had served at least one meal including staple food, that is rice, wheat and/or other staples. This category includes even potatoes in Bihar and ragi in Karnataka. Potatoes are nutritious, but much less calorie dense than ragi. Most likely, this indicates the number of substantial meals on the day before. While a clear majority had eaten staples three times, quite a few had had only two such meals, more so in Bihar than in Karnataka. This was especially the case in the Patna slum, where nearly half the sample had eaten only twice.

Table 5.1 The number of times staple food (rice, wheat, other) and dhal were served yesterday

	Bihar Rural		Bihar Slum		Karnataka Rural		Karnataka Slum	
No. of Meals	*Staple*	*Dhal*	*Staple*	*Dhal*	*Staple*	*Dhal*	*Staple*	*Dhal*
0	0	33	1	31	0	1	0	2
1	5	43	1	45	5	13	1	14
2	22	21	45	23	9	33	17	36
3	71	3	54	1	87	53	80	47
4	2	0	0	0	0	0	2	2
Total	100	100	101	100	101	100	100	101

Per cent of households. N = 776.

Very few had eaten once, no one had no rice or wheat at all on the day before. The variation is larger with regard to dhal. In Karnataka, most meals included dhal. Here, less than one in five households had eaten dhal less than twice on the day before and hardly anyone had not had dhal at all. The difference between the urban and the rural samples is small. In Bihar, however, one meal with dhal on the day before was most common, with one-third having had no dhal at all. Even here, the urban/rural difference is insignificant.

Thus, apart from urban Bihar, a three-meal pattern dominates. This is not sufficient information to conclude whether they overall have enough calories, apart from the limited meals suggesting that people in the Patna slums have too little to eat. The presence of dhal is an indication of nutritional quality, especially when it comes to protein. Here the division line is between the two states, with small differences between urban and rural settings.

The foodstuffs available through the PDS system appear to have a major influence on the composition of meals in both states, with heavy reliance on rice and wheat and few additional meal ingredients. The most common addition was dhal (or sambhar in Karnataka). Very few included animal protein in terms of dairy and meat, in their meals. A vegetable sauce was usually added, but there was very little food of animal origin, nor had the households served much sugar, biscuits, etc. apart from some sweetened milky tea (data not shown). There is a divide between the two states. The rural households were generally somewhat better off for certain food items such as dairy and dhal, but the picture was not consistent. For some items, consumption seems to be higher in urban areas, especially when it comes to processed food, such as biscuits.

Food procurement

The food distribution channels that people use indicate the types of entitlements that are functioning when it comes to food acquisition. Table 5.2 presents forms of procurement for wheat, rice, pulses, vegetables, cooking oil and milk within the four different settings, referring to the food served on the day before. The table shows that the major food items were primarily bought from government (PDS) shops or through the ordinary market. Only in rural Bihar is own production of any significance as a direct source of food. Pulses are nearly always bought from the market. In both Bihar and Karnataka, people from the urban slums get a lower proportion of their staple food from government shops. We also have data for other staple foods, such as ragi, as well as for vegetables, oil and animal products. Nearly all of these are procured through ordinary markets, with some home production of ragi in rural Karnataka. People in rural villages do get some milk from their own production, their family and neighbours. Apart from that, sharing with other households is insignificant.

Table 5.2 How main food items consumed in the household yesterday were procured (from own production, a PDS shop, other shop or being a gift or sharing with neighbours/relatives)

		Wheat	*Rice*	*Ragi*	*Pulses*	*Veg*	*Ghee/Oil*	*Milk*
Bihar rural N = 220	own production	79	75	18	38	13	12	34
	PDS shop	146	144	0	2	1	1	1
	other shop	139	141	144	206	228	222	117
	gift/sharing	0	0	1	2	1	1	72
	not rel/DK	0	0	67	1	0	0	12
Bihar slum N = 150	own production	0	0	0	0	1	0	0
	PDS shop	58	52	1	8	1	6	2
	other shop	124	124	31	141	143	147	94
	gift/sharing	1	0	2	1	0	0	12
	not rel/DK	1	0	81	0	5	1	41
Karnataka rural N = 234	own production	13	38	35	2	2	3	3
	PDS shop	205	190	6	9	5	27	4
	other shop	125	131	180	201	210	185	181
	gift/sharing	2	1	2	2	2	24	32
	not rel/DK	0	0	0	0	0	0	0
Karnataka slum N = 171	own production	4	5	22	9	0	0	0
	PDS shop	80	91	62	14	0	75	0
	other shop	98	146	125	161	171	163	161
	gift/sharing	0	0	4	2	0	1	0
	not rel/DK	9	0	11	0	0	0	9

Total number of households: 775

In order to capture the households' own judgement of their food security situation, people were asked whether they always have enough food to eat or not (Figure 5.1). About two in five households in rural Bihar agreed to this, three in five households in rural Karnataka. There were significantly fewer positive answers in the slums where only about one in ten always had enough. If this was not the case, they were asked about the primary reasons for not always having enough food. From Figure 5.1, again we see the contrast between rural Karnataka and urban Bihar. However, everywhere, two factors stand out as reasons: unemployment and low income. A few rural respondents mention climatic factors influencing their own production, but not many. Obviously, when asked in this way, the lack of income – i.e. exchange entitlements – represent the main problem. Many respondents in the Bihar slum, whenever they could during the interview, added that not having a BPL card was a major obstacle for them. These problems of accessing food are consistent with how food is most often procured; through markets, where purchasing power is the major requirement, and government shops, requiring social rights, in practice, first of all, a ration card. A few among the rural respondents also accessed food through their own production and here we find some referring to problems caused by bad weather. In the following, we will discuss in more detail how the various types of access depend on specific kinds of entitlements.

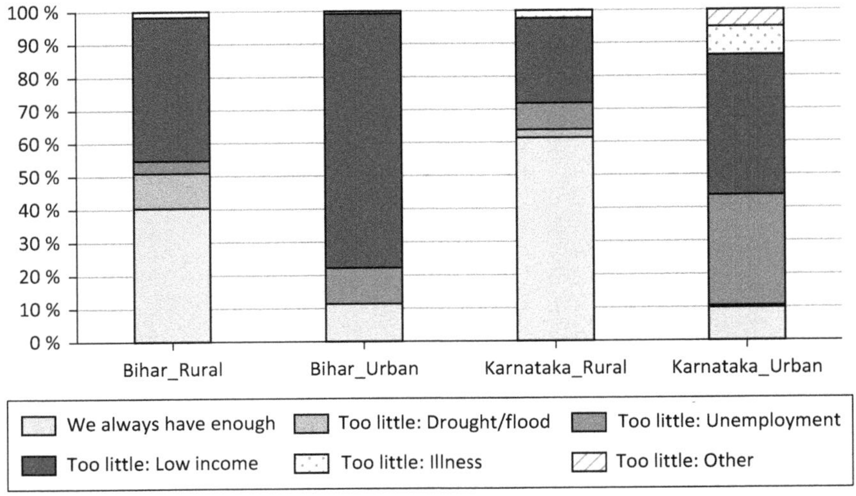

Figure 5.1 Do you always have enough food to eat? If not, what are the primary reasons? Per cent

Food production and access to land

The majority of poor people live in the countryside, which might direct attention towards production. Not surprisingly, around 60% of the rural households in both states were involved in farming activities and food production in one way or another. However, as we saw above, little food was procured directly through own production. There may be two reasons; food from own production is sold to markets to gain purchasing power or they are not in direct command of the food they produce. Our rural samples varied significantly with regard to land access; nearly half of the households in Karnataka owned land, while none in the Bihar sample, did. Most lacked even a back garden to grow vegetables. Instead, 26% of the Bihar households had access to land through sharecropping. Sharecroppers do not own land, the landowner supplies the inputs, and the supplier of labour – the sharecropper – receives a share of the output, usually one-third. In some areas, parts of input costs and output are equally shared between landlords and tenants (Sharma, 2005). In Bihar, 31% of those sampled were agricultural labourers, compared to 1% in Karnataka. It is questionable whether agricultural employment increases access to food; it will depend on the form and size of payment. In addition, the food procured through the use of common land or other shared resources, such as fishing or hunting was, as we also saw in Figure 1, insignificant. Thus, the low proportions of using own food sources are in Bihar mainly due to a lack of command over food production, while the situation in rural Karnataka is rather that the produced food is being sold to generate income (Table 5.3).

Table 5.3 Access to land among rural households (in per cent). Multiple answers

Access to Land	*Rural Bihar N = 220*	*Rural Karnataka N = 231*
Involved in farming activities	60	59
Have own back garden	2	3
Owning land	13	46
Access to rented land	2	6
Sharecropping	26	1
Work as agricultural labourer	31	1
Total		

Table 5.4 Employment and access to the labour market

	Rural Bihar	*Bihar Slum*	*Rural Karnataka*	*Karnataka Slum*
Kinds of work agreements				
Self-employed (farming, trade, etc.)	31	8	43	8
Permanent employment	3	5	4	16
Casual labour	60	78	43	69
Contract work	4	1	11	5
Other	0	3	0	1
Not relevant/no answer	0	0	0	1
Migrant worker in household	59	3	26	5
Occupations among adult household members				
Service/trade	6	12	12	1
Government employee	6	3	1	4
Rickshaw puller	2	21	1	1
Auto driver	0	6	4	3
Industry work	1	0	9	9
Work in house	1	1	10	1
Domestic help	0	15	0	4
Farmer	6	0	40	0
Agricultural labourer	40	1	31	0
Other	36	42	15	0
Sick	9	0	4	3
Unemployed	8	1	1	7
MGNREGA	0	0	44	0

Number of households. Multiple households. Total N = 776

Exchange entitlements

We asked the respondents about the households' main source of income, work agreement and occupation. The majority of rural and urban respondents rely on some kind of employment as their source of income, dominated by informal agreements (Table 5.4). Very few had permanent employment. A few even had contract work, especially in rural Karnataka (i.e. with dependencies involved in the relationship). Self-employment is more common among rural households, mostly as farmers. Urban self-employment might be to for example owning a rickshaw or a market stall. We also see that in the rural settings, many households had one or more members staying away because of work. This was particularly significant in the Bihar villages, where a clear majority of the respondents had a migrant worker in the household.

When it comes to occupation, agricultural labourers are most common in the rural samples. But there were significant differences. While 40% were farmers in Karnataka, only 6% gave that answer in Bihar. It is noticeable that this was reflected not only in the higher proportion employed as agricultural labourers, but also in more households relying on other casual work and small trade. There were some variations across the urban settings in terms of occupations, perhaps also indicating different income levels. While many in the Bihar slum were rickshaw pullers and domestic workers, we find several auto drivers and industrial workers in the (more well-off) Karnataka slum. Also, in Bihar, we found many listed as having "other" occupations, which might refer to even more informal and unstable sources of income. Overall, incomes through employment appear to be unstable for most of the respondents. This was reflected even in the high proportion of households earning less than Rs 5,000 per month, especially in Bihar (84 and 80%, respectively, in rural and urban Bihar, compared to 30 and 21% in rural and urban Karnataka, respectively).

Social rights

In the survey, we asked detailed questions about access to various types of public services. Here, we will briefly report some results that will allow us to discuss the role of social rights, in our various samples.

The employment programme, the Mahatma Gandhi National Rural Employment Act (MGNREGA) aims to enhance buying power among poor households in rural areas by providing a minimum of paid employment for women during a financial year. MGNREGA typically offers work on roads and other development of public infrastructure and construction. Table 5.4 showed that MGNREGA appears as a significant source of income. Forty-four percent of the households in the rural region of Karnataka, also here selected for its relative backwardness (Raichur), report getting work through the MGNREGA scheme. In contrast, none of the households in rural Bihar was part of this, despite the selected region (Sheohar) being one of the most economically backward in India. The poor implementation of MGNREGA in Bihar has been flagged as a cause for concern over the years, by the Controller and Auditor General of India (CAG), implying that only a limited number of rural Bihar households have been able to benefit from the employment scheme. The 2014 report of the government's auditor points out that only 13% of job cards holders could actually get work under this employment generation scheme.

The main public programmes offering food directly include the Public Distribution System (PDS), free mid-day meals in public schools (MDM) and the Anganwadi or Integrated Child Development Services (ICDS) provided for mothers and preschool children.

The answers to the procurement question (Table 5.2) revealed that most people relied heavily on government provisions, clearly the most significant source being the PDS. A ration card is a prerequisite for accessing PDS shops. The ration card depends on the income level according to census data; above the defined poverty line (APL), below the poverty line (BPL), and with very low income (Antyodaya). In Table 5.5, we see that around nine out of ten households in the rural areas in both states, hold either a BPL card or an Antyodaya card. In the urban slums, the proportion of cardholders is much lower, particularly among slum dwellers in Patna. Here, only 43% had a BPL or Antyodaya card. This proportion is far below the expected coverage, considering the incomes reported in this study. The share of BPL cardholders thus serves as a poor indicator of poverty. The urban slum dwellers belong to the lowest income strata, the situation being much more serious in Patna, compared to Bangalore. These patterns were also reflected in the respondents' satisfaction with the functioning of PDS, which was the highest in rural Karnataka and lowest in urban Bihar, a common complaint being missing a ration card (results not shown). The poor functioning of the PDS governance in Bihar is discussed in a recent paper published by Drèze et al. (2018). There are staff problems at all levels, from top to the bottom. The government tend to rely on PDS dealers, where there are tendencies of corruption, in order to carry out tasks and to collect ration-card applications.

A third important category of public services is services providing food for children. The Mid-Day Meal Scheme supplies free lunches on school days for children in the primary and upper primary classes in government-aided schools. We asked our respondents whether mid-day meals were provided regularly in school. We find that school lunches were served regularly in the rural areas, with a regularity of 74% in Bihar and 94% in Karnataka. Irregularity was most widespread in the urban slum of Bihar, where the

Table 5.5 Holders of Below Poverty Line (BPL) and Antyodaya (AAY) ration cards (in per cent)

	Bihar Rural	*Bihar Slum*	*Karnataka Rural*	*Karnataka Slum*
BPL card	68	39	47	49
Antyodaya AAY	18	3	45	5
No card	14	58	8	46
Total	100	100	100	100

schoolchildren from only 39% of the households were served lunch on a regular basis. Here, only 10% of the households' children had eaten in school on the day before. In other settings, this figure ranged from 38% in urban Karnataka to 60% in rural Bihar.

Infants, small children, and pregnant women receive some food and food supplements through Anganwadi centres that are established under the ICDS programme. In our study, this proved to be less significant as a source of daily food access, compared to the other programmes, most commonly operating in urban Karnataka, where 18% of the households reported having an Anganwadi meal on the day before, while the percentage was lowest in urban Bihar (5%).

Concluding remarks

There is a large and growing literature on the food security situation in India. However, most studies focus on only one type of issue, such as agricultural development, market logistics, the functioning of public services – or household consumption. The concept of "entitlement"[5] has allowed a middle-range institutional approach of linking consumption patterns to provisioning sources and social structure. Importantly, the question has been how various entitlements combine into "bundles" that decide the overall food security situation and its dynamic, including not only income through employment, but even own production and social rights.

Our survey has addressed the poorest sections of society in rural and urban Bihar and Karnataka, respectively, thus offering few surprises in terms of their generally poor living conditions. Meal patterns are mostly simple, dominated by starchy staples. Even from our simple observations, we see that this may be inadequate for small children who need higher caloric and nutrient density, thus giving support to national statistics. Dhal is included in most meals in Karnataka, but in much fewer meals in Bihar – signifying a considerably more monotonous and less nutritious diet in Bihar (information on other dietary components such as vegetables, fruits and cooking oils supports this conclusion). This state difference is in accordance with national household surveys.[2] It is therefore not surprising that a considerably higher number of Bihari respondents complain of too little food. The situation is particularly dire in the Patna slums. In Karnataka, we find less variation between the urban and the rural settings.

Most poor people live in the countryside and it is often claimed that better farming methods are crucial for improving household food security. In this study, own production complements rather than forming the basis of food provisioning. Importantly, among the poorest in rural villages, very few have access to any land at all, not even a plot to grow vegetables. Furthermore, in Bihar sharecropping is more common than ownership, thus drastically reducing the possibility of feeding the family from the land. On the whole, it is only in Raichur (rural Karnataka) that ownership is significant. Since own production here is rarely used directly for consumption, we must assume that commercial agriculture dominates.

So, our informants have to, more or less, buy all the food they need – they depend on "exchange entitlements". The price–income ratio for basic foodstuffs is therefore fundamental for vulnerable households. Incomes are generally very low and unstable. Like the rest of India, casual work (plus some contract work) dominates. Nearly everyone in our Bihar samples has very low (and unstable) incomes, giving them extremely limited purchasing power. Family members migrating for work may improve the situation somewhat but will also put pressure on the functioning of the household. The higher proportion of farmers in Raichur is reflected in the lower dependence on casual work in this region.

The reliance on government shops as a source of procurement, the significance of ration cards, and the informants' focus when describing their situation revealed that a functioning PDS system is crucial for food security. Bihar PDS shops offer only rice and wheat, as reflected in the informants' diet. In Karnataka, where other food items may be offered as well, such as lentils and cooking oil, this is mirrored in our dietary observations. Other than this, people rely on buying from the ordinary market. Where purchasing power is most limited, that is, in most of Bihar, the diet is also most monotonous and not likely to suffice as nutrition for children. School meals are therefore a significant addition to the households in this study, reflecting an improvement (especially in rural Bihar, much less so in the slums) that has been observed in several studies (Drèze and Khera, 2014).

However, overall, we see that social rights, especially ration cards and a functioning PDS system, form the basis of food security, but a security with clear limitations in terms of sufficiency. And there are still gaps. A review of their bundles of entitlements reveals few signs that households missing one type of entitlement, can then rely on other types. On the contrary, the effects seem additive. In Karnataka, more rural households own land and considerably fewer households in the rural as well as the urban samples have very low incomes. Migrating from the countryside to a slum in Bangalore may mean improving the situation, as signified by relatively well-paid employment in, for example, construction or as auto drivers. Considering the rapid development of this capital, this is hardly surprising. Despite these comparatively better socio-economic conditions, more people in this state also benefit from public services, especially in the rural district, where also the MGNREGA employment programme is well established. In the urban slum, there are still problems of accessibility, with quite a few missing a ration card.

Bihar is a rural state with fertile land and a large agricultural sector. Yet, land reforms have not worked and hardly anyone among the poorest own land. With very low levels of urbanization and industrialization, there are few alternatives to (casual) farm work or migrating to other states of India. With the poorly paid work, dependence on public provisions is high, which is clearly reflected in the diet of the rural Biharis. This is in accordance with reports that public provisioning has improved significantly in recent years (Khera, 2011, 2015). Responses to direct questions about the functioning of the system were generally positive. In that regard, we can conclude that social rights do, at least to a certain extent, compensate for the lack of other entitlements in rural Bihar. It must be emphasized, however, that this is a very, very basic compensation, hardly sufficient for providing a nutritious diet. Direct starvation is prevented, but not undernutrition at a young age (or during pregnancy and lactation). In the Patna slum, social rights are not functioning. These are the poorest in every respect and the lack of entitlement to public provisioning clearly adds to their severe misery.

Our findings support the entitlement and livelihood approach, premised on the understanding that hunger and malnutrition are primarily caused by the lack of purchasing power among the poor to meet their food requirements. If the poor could gain access to income and the means to earn a livelihood, they would purchase a variety of food, available in the local markets. The functioning of labour markets, at the state and local level, is crucial for their food security. Lack of income limits access to food and poverty may increase, depending on how vulnerable households are to food price spikes.

In our samples, even the rural ones, access to food through own production is highly inadequate. The key foundation for food security, considering their very limited potential for income through work, is therefore the functioning of public services. Here, the PDS system is most important. The key limitation is access to ration cards, a prominent problem in the urban slums, especially in Patna. Considering its dominant influence on the diet, the limited range of items that are offered also has serious implications for dietary sufficiency. Patel (2008), Deaton (2013) and Drèze and Sen (2013) all suggest that subsidized distribution of wheat and rice, supplied by the Green Revolution regions, has undermined the nutritional and cultural diversity of the people in the food recipient regions. This has contributed to malnutrition and a decline in dietary diversity among the poor in India. In our study, this is particularly salient in the poor state of Bihar. Still, the public distribution might be seen as a fall-back when other sources fail. With the dominant reliance on public distribution for ordinary food procurement, there is no scope for further flexibility or compensation in cases of unemployment, failing harvests, illness, etc. As observed by Khera (2011), the proportion of those who are vulnerable to hunger remains large in India, because casual employment in the informal sector is high. Access to food will be severely affected if the breadwinner in a family is out for work due to unemployment or sudden illness even for a shorter period of time. Considering India's severe experience of the Covid pandemic, we may expect that this becomes even much, much more urgent and direct starvation may reappear, especially in the most vulnerable states with poorer functioning of public institutions.

After studying these four settings, we conclude that entitlements are additive rather than complementary, creating distinctly different conditions for satisfying the need for food. This seems to be linked to the dynamic between socio-economic factors and the functioning of social rights, that are (relatively) beneficial in rural Karnataka and much more difficult in rural Bihar. Moreover, while migrating to urban slums may provide better opportunities for landless and low-caste people in Karnataka, this is hardly the case in Bihar.

Notes

1 See Directorate of Census Operations – Karnataka: 2011 Census, online at: http://censuskarnataka.gov.in/kpca2011.htm

2 Household Consumer Expenditure: National Sample Survey 66th Round, online at: https://data.gov.in/resources/household-consumer-expenditure-66th-round; see also Dulsrud et al. (2015).

References

Agarwal, S., Sethi, V., and Gupta, P., et al., 2009. "Experiential household food insecurity in an urban underserved slum of North India," *Food Security* 1, 2009: 239–250.

Bhagwati, J. and Panagariya, A., 2013. *Why Growth Matters: How Economic Growth in India Reduced Poverty and the Lessons for other Developing Countries*. New York: Public Affairs.

Butler, C.D., 2009. "Food security in the Asia-Pacific: Climate change, Phosphorus, Ozone and other environmental challenges," *Asia Pacific Journal of Clinical Nutrition* 18(4), 2009: 590–597.

Deaton, A., 2013. "What's going on in India," *The Lancet* 382(9897), 2013: 1015–1016.

Dorosh, P.A., 2009. "Prize stabilization, international trade and national cereal stocks: World price shocks and policy response in South Asia," *Food Security* 1(2), 2009: 137–149.

Drèze, J., Gupta, P., Khera, R., and Pimenta, I., 2018. "Casting the Net: India's public distribution system after the Food Security Act," *SSRN*. Posted 24 May 2018. Online at: https://papers.ssrn.com/sol3/papers.cfm?abstract_id=3177691 (accessed 11 March 2020).

Drèze, J. and Khera, R., 2014. "Understanding leakages in the public distribution system," *Economic and Political Weekly*, 14 February 2014: 39–42.

Drèze, J., Khera R., and Pudussery J., 2015. "Food security. Bihar on the move," *Economic and Political Weekly* (34), 2015: 44–52.

Drèze, J. and Sen, A., 1989. *Hunger and Public Action*. Oxford: Oxford University Press.

Drèze, J. and Sen, A., 2013. *An Uncertain Glory. India and Its Contradictions*. Princeton & Oxford: Princeton University Press.

Dubey, A., and Srivastav, N., 2011. *Poverty, Public Distribution System and Food Security in India: A Household Level Analysis Shillong, India*, North Eastern Hill University.

Dulsrud, A., Kjærnes, U., and Austgulen, M.H., 2015. *Institutional Conditions for Food Security in India. Exploring a Model of Household Food Security through the Study of Literature, Key Concepts and Statistics*. SIFO Project Note 3. Oslo.

Fan, F., Gulati, A. and Thorat, S., 2008. "Investment, subsidies, and pro-poor growth in rural India," *Agricultural Economics* 39(2), September 2008: 163–170.

Food and Agriculture Organization, 2006. *State of World Food Insecurity 2006*. Online at: ftp://ftp.fao.org/docrep/fao/009/a0750e/a0750e00.pdf (accessed 20 May 2021).

Gulati, A., Sharma, P., Samantara, A. and Terway, P., 2018. *Agriculture Extension System in India Review of Current Status, Trends and the Way Forward*. Indian Council For Research on International Economic Relations (ICRIER).

Household Consumer Expenditure: National Sample Survey 66th Round. online at: https://data.gov.in/resources/household-consumer-expenditure-66th-round

Ingram, J., 2011. "A food systems approach to researching food security and its interactions with global environmental change." *Food Security* 3, 2011: 417–431.

Jain, N., 2014. *National Food Security Act of India, 2013. A Compendium*. CUTS International.

Jha, M., and Bhattacharyya, S., 2011. "Social safety nets and nutrient deprivation: An analysis of the national rural employment guarantee programme and the public distribution system in India," *Journal of Asian Economics* 22, 2011: 189–201.

Khera, R., 2011. "Revival of the public distribution system: Evidence and explanations," *Economic and Political Weekly*, 46(44–45), 5 November 2011: 36–50.

Khera, R., 2015. "Implications of India's National Food Security Act," in: Kathuria, R. and Nagpal, N., eds, *Global Economic Cooperation*. New Delhi: Springer, pp. 75–80.

Kjærnes, U., and Holm, L., 2009. "The Study of Nordic meals: Lessons learnt," in: Meiselman, H.L., ed., *Meals in Science and Practice: Interdisciplinary Research and Business Applications*. London: Woodhead Publishing, pp. 69–91.

Mishra, A., 2013. "Food consumption and health," in: Mishra, S.K. and Agrawal, B., eds, *Food Security in India. Policies and Challenges*. New Delhi, New Century Publications, pp. 1–13.

Mishra, S.K., and Agrawal, B. eds, 2013. *Food Security in India. Policies and Challenges*. New Dehli: New Century Publications.

Mukherjee, S., and Chakraborty, D., 2014. "Three decades of human development across Indian states: Inclusive growth or perpetual disparity?" Working Paper No. 2014-139, June 2014, National Institute of Public Finance and Policy, New Delhi.

O'Brien, K.R., and Leichenko, U., 2004. "Mapping vulnerability to multiple stressors: Climate change and globalization in India," *Global Environmental Change* 14, 2004: 303–313.

Patel, R., 2008. *Stuffed and Starved Markets, Power and the Hidden Battle for the World's Food System*. New York: Melville House.

Planning Commission of India, 2007. *Technical Note on Employment for the Eleventh Five Year Plan (2007–2012)*. Planning Commission Order No.P-12099/6/08/LEM/ERS dated May 27, 2008, Labour, Employment & Manpower Division, 2008.
Pritchard, B., and Rammohan, A., 2014. *Feeding India: Livelihoods, Entitlements and Capabilities*. Croydon: Earthscan from Routledge.
Sen, A., 1982. *Poverty and Famines: An Essay on Entitlement and Deprivation*. Oxford: Clarendon Press.
Sen, A., 1984. *Resources, Values and Development*. Cambridge, Mass.: Harvard University Press.
Sen, A., 2011. "Quality of life: India vs. China," *New York Review of Books*, 12 May 2011.
Sharma, A.N., 2005. Agrarian relations and socio-economic change in Bihar. Working paper No. 30. New Delhi: Institute for Human Development.
Thimmaiah, G., and Aziz, A., 1983. "The political economy of land reforms in Karnataka, A South Indian state," *Asian Survey*, 23(7), 1983: 810–829.
Tilly, C., 1975. "Food supply and public order in modern Europe," in: Tilly, C., ed., *The Formation of National States in Western Europe*. Princeton: Princeton University Press, 1975, pp. 380–455.
Tiwari, P.C., and Joshi, B., 2012. "Natural and socio-economic factors affecting food security in the Himalayas," *Food Security* 4, 2012: 195–207.
Vyas, V.S., 2000. "Ensuring food security: The state, market and civil society," *Economic and Political Weekly* 35(50): 4402–4407.

Chapter 6

Food entitlements

Political will versus preparedness of the state in Odisha

Nita Mishra and Edward Lahiff

Incidences of hunger-related deaths brought all food entitlement schemes into the realm of public debate in the late 1990s. The Constitution of India stipulated direct and indirect food entitlements for vulnerable groups under different food security schemes, such as the Integrated Child Development Services (ICDS), Targeted Public Distribution Scheme (TPDS), Antyodaya Anna Yojana (AAY), Mid-Day Meal Scheme (MDMS), and the Emergency Feeding Programme (EFP). On 10 September 2013, the Indian Parliament legislated the National Food Security Act (NFSA) which made the Right to Food a fundamental right for citizens of India. Since then, the above-mentioned welfare programmes relating to food entitlements, have fallen under the purview of the NFSA. The Ministry of Law and Justice (2013) defines the NFSA as follows:

> an Act to provide for food and nutritional security in human life cycle approach, by ensuring access to adequate quantity of quality food at affordable prices to people to live a life with dignity and for matters connected therewith or incidental thereto.

Drawing upon evidence from primary data (2013–2015), this chapter shows that the realization of food provisions by the poor, however, depends not only on the adoption of rights-based policies by the state, but also on its preparedness for operationalizing such policies. This chapter first argues that the NFSA is a rights-based Act, followed by a discussion on the response of the Odisha government to the Supreme Court directives on hunger-related measures in the state which reflects government political will and commitment to tackle hunger. It then uses interviews with 12 duty-bearers, both government officials (four) and non-state development practitioners (three), including Right to Food campaigners (four) and union activists (one), to analyze Odisha's preparedness for operationalizing its policies.

The National Food Security Act 2013: a rights-based approach to food entitlements

In the absence of a constitutional guarantee, rights are nothing more than aspirations to be fulfilled at some indefinite future date (Drèze, 2004). By

DOI: 10.4324/9781003272656-6

making the Right to Food a fundamental right, the Indian state, however, moved beyond the merely aspirational political will and commitment, to making the rights justiciable in practice. The second aspect of a rights-based approach can be gleaned through its focus on a "lifecycle approach" to food security (Ministry of Law and Justice, 2013) which means that the human right to food must be realized at every stage of human life, through policies and entitlements for vulnerable groups. The use of the phrase "live a life with dignity" lends the Act the idea of well-being, dignity and respect, that scholars have argued for, in different ways, in the rights' discourse (Sen, 2005; see also Nussbaum, 2003). Thirdly, the Act identifies "priority households" as those of vulnerable groups such as the disabled, older people, poor single women and children, and further specifies that there is a "right to receive food security allowance in certain cases" (Ministry of Law and Justice, 2013: 2–4). For example, the Act has special provisions for preventing malnutrition amongst young children and providing nutritional support for pregnant women and lactating mothers. Provisions for ensuring food security for vulnerable groups in hilly and tribal areas have been separately included in the NFSA. These special provisions for priority households indicate that the political will and commitment of policymakers were directed towards tackling hunger by raising the capabilities of the poor and vulnerable groups.

Fourthly, the NFSA has initiated a new pathway that challenges traditional gender norms in Indian society by declaring that women, above 18 years of age, will be deemed "head of the household for the purpose of issue of ration cards" (Ministry of Law and Justice, 2013: 5). Furthermore, in cases where women are not yet 18 years of age, there can be a male head of the household, until such time that the woman is 18 years of age. This is an important step towards women's empowerment, and a landmark decision in the Indian context where previous policies have unquestioningly taken men as head of households, based on prevailing cultural norms. Fifth, is the use of a rights-based language in the Act which imposes the primary duty-bearing obligation on the government, at all levels, not just as a provider, but to ensure food and nutritional security (Ministry of Law and Justice, 2013: 8–10).

The sixth rights-based aspect of the NFSA is the setting up of grievance redressal mechanisms, such as helplines for people, in addition to the appointment of nodal officers at panchayat levels to link people with their specific duty-bearers. In addition to the appointment of the District Grievance Redressal Officer (DGRO), the NFSA has provisions for periodic social-audit procedures to be conducted by independent agencies. As a step towards ensuring accountability and transparency at the district level, the Act delineates punitive measures for duty-bearers, such as a fine of Rs 5,000 if a public servant or authority on any complaint is found guilty of failing to provide suitable relief, as recommended by the DGRO (Ministry of Law and Justice, 2013: 11). The NFSA (2013) also recommends, in Section 32 of Chapter XIII (ibid.) that "the state Government may" introduce additional entitlement schemes, if and where necessary, to alleviate hunger and poverty.

The NFSA, as discussed above, can thus be argued to be rights-based. However, for the NFSA to be impactful, state preparedness for operationalizing the various food provisions must be taken into account to get a complete overview of its effectiveness.

Political will and commitment: Supreme Court directives

A writ petition (Civil No.42/97) filed by the Indian Council of Legal Aid and Advice (ICLAA) and others on 23 December 1996, before the Supreme Court of India under Article 32 of the Constitution alleged that deaths by starvation continue to occur in some districts of Odisha. This was followed by periodic Supreme Court directives based on a dialogue with the National Human Rights Commission (NHRC), and others, on the type of measures governments must adopt to tackle hunger. In its regular monitoring activities, since then, the NHRC, with the assistance of a Special Rapporteur, regularly monitors the progress of the implementation of SC directions, with the underlying assumption that misgovernance leads to starvation deaths. Since freedom from hunger is a fundamental right of the people of the country, therefore, governance issues were of direct concern to the Commission under the provisions of the Protection of Human Rights Act, 1993. The Commission further felt the need to formulate a programme of action for making Right to Food a reality in the country. With this in view, following a meeting with leading experts on the subject, in January 2004, the NHRC approved the constitution of a Core Group on the Right to Food to act as an advisory group and suggest appropriate programmes which can be undertaken by the Commission.

Here, a focus on the Supreme Court Order of 29 April 2004, which directed governments to involve local women's groups in food procurement would be pertinent to the chapter. The Odisha women and child development (WCD) department responded to the directive by initiating the formation of women's self-help groups (SHGs) at the village level. The school and mass education (SME) department employed SHGs to prepare hot-cooked meals in schools under the Mid-Day Meal Scheme. Different departments took an in-principle decision to implement the decentralized procurement of food items with effect from April 2011 under the Supplementary Nutrition Programme and the Emergency Feeding Programme in response to the Supreme Court orders to streamline and strengthen ICDS. According to the WCD secretary, the SHGs are trained to prepare nutritious Take Home Rations (THR) for pregnant women beneficiaries.

> We provide training to the SHG women with clear guidelines about the nutrition component and recipe, and this process builds capabilities of, and empowers, the women not only with advice on nutrition, but also as responsible duty-bearers at grassroots level.[1]

The importance of local procurement was deemed as promoting culturally appropriate, nutritious locally grown food, that engages local communities, especially poor women, in the production and marketing process. According to the State Institute for Rural Development (SIRD) director, it also encourages decentralization, increases accountability of local duty-bearers and reduces leakages of food stocks during the long distances travelled by trucks across state borders. In a letter (Saxena and Mander, 2012) to the WCD secretary dated 7 February 2011, the Commissioners of the Supreme Court noted that Odisha was only one of the three Indian states that have given procurement contracts to SHGs to produce THRs at the panchayat, cluster and Block levels, unlike other states that have given the contract to private contractors or procure food through state food and agro-corporations. The Commissioners suggested that the Odisha model should be one of the models for the production of THRs studied independently by the National Institute for Nutrition, to help create the best model for decentralized procurement of THRs, for children between six months to three years of age.

State government officials such as Child Development Project Officers (CDPO) of Cuttack and Banapur, in separate interviews, discussed the 2013 Public Evaluation of Entitlement Programmes (PEEP) Survey which ranks Indian states (as leaders, learners and laggards) on the basis of their overall performance with regard to the delivery of five food-related entitlement programmes. According to the PEEP survey, Odisha, along with Maharashtra and Rajasthan, is grouped under "learner" states which means that its overall performance, marks a positive step forward in the direction of delivery of entitlements to rights-holders. The secretary of the Panchayati Raj (PR) department, for instance, said that the finding that Odisha is a "learner state" is evident in the state's political will and commitment to push for a rights-based agenda for development activities.

Thus, while interviews with the higher-level officials of the government of Odisha (GOO) show that they were happy with the direction food-related policies were taking in the state, issues raised by people highlight that there was a mismatch between rights-based food policies and the level of state preparedness for operationalizing such policies. The problems faced by people in accessing the Right to Food provisions have been discussed below.

In practice: preparedness of the state

An analysis of the primary data, collected by means of interviews with duty-bearers, at different levels of administration and with non-government development practitioners, highlights the various difficulties that emerge while making food entitlements accessible to poor people. Problems range from inadequate entitlement amounts, exclusions, absence of real decentralized governance and grievance redressal mechanisms and corruption.

In spite of the many initiatives undertaken in the last few years, the state of Odisha was unprepared in terms of its resources (finances, infrastructural and human resources) and the actions required to take forward the provisions of the NFSA 2013. For example, the NFSA (Ministry of Law and Justice, 2013: 4–5) has specific instructions for state governments to, within 365 days, undertake the preparation of guidelines to identify priority households and to update and make public the list of households eligible for the food security allowance. Informal interviews in November 2015, however, revealed that the GOO has not been able to complete the process of listing all new (and old) beneficiaries ("priority households") under the NFSA 2013 guidelines.

Discussing the newly enacted NFSA, Right to Food campaigners argued that several aspects of the old system of policy making such as the targeting, identification and selection of beneficiaries, are continuing in the NFSA 2013, and therefore, the most marginalized will still be left out. For instance, in the NFSA, marginalized groups such as bonded labourers, migrants and others with no identity cards will remain outside the purview of the basic food security system. The problems of starvation and the destitution of child-headed households of migrant families has also not been addressed by the Act. Thus, just because there is an Act, does not mean hunger and starvation will disappear. Distance, fear, the cost factor and local power relations determine poor people's responses to problems.

Continuous civil society engagement and public action is required to make officials accountable and responsive to people's complaints. For instance, the previous government brought the debate on hunger to the national level with the support of the media, by continuously reporting on the poor people's right to food to avoid starvation deaths. However, the implementation of entitlements under the various Acts, in keeping with the spirit of the Constitution, was not very encouraging because of the lack of participation of civil society including donors and NGOs. Enshrined rights can empower poor people when translated through trainings to enhance people's existing skills, by providing opportunities for skill-building, and exposure training trips to enable learning from others. The provision of cash benefits is a temporary measure and only satisfies an immediate need for many families and is unsustainable. Translating rights into practice is, therefore, a challenging task.

> NGOs, earlier, were not interested in implementation activities but spent all their efforts in making funding applications and following funding instructions. The gap in implementation is observed at the

> lower administrative levels as well. For example, the judicial space provided in the lower courts such as the District Courts, has not been used by local communities to demand employment opportunities, or petition officially. People have not used the services of the state Legal Aid Cell in the last seven years of MGNREG Act.[2]

The Bharatiya Mazdoor Sangh (BMS) union leader, Sahoo, directed attention to, what he described as, serious short-sightedness on the part of the government. Sahoo argued that political will is motivated by individual interests at the higher levels, which sometimes can be detrimental for duty-bearers at the lower end of the administration who were duty-bound to follow orders from above, without being able to voice their concerns within the administrative set-up. In the absence of mechanisms whereby grassroots duty-bearers can voice the problems they face while implementing entitlement related provisions, the operationalization of rights-based approaches to development becomes problematic.

> Has the Secretary of WCD realised that it will take at least a year for SHGs in remote areas such as Malkangiri district to set up an egg production unit, unlike chatua mix, and only when once such a unit has been established, then only can eggs be supplied to the local Anganwadi centres. Until then, should the Secretary not send directives to the District Social Welfare Office (DSWO), the Child Development Project Office (CDPO), and the Collectorate to cover the extra cost as per local prices (which differ) so that Anganwadi centres can function without the workers investing in eggs from own pockets? Schemes come out of some officer's head, and the worker bears the brunt of it.[3]

Elsewhere, while discussing schemes for the disabled, an official of the SIRD highlighted the lack of infrastructural facilities for the differently-abled, especially for access to public spaces such as markets, or even for boarding local buses which makes the entitlements non-usable.

> Footpaths, transport vehicles, as well as public buildings including state offices, currently, are not wheelchair friendly. It is interesting to note the gap between intention and implementation on the part of the government. For example, on the one hand, while the state is distributing free bus passes, on the other hand, these passes cannot be used because the bus is not wheelchair friendly.[4]

An important indication of people's lack of awareness regarding their entitlements, and the claiming processes if their rights were violated, was the non-use of available redressal mechanisms. According to Mishra, one of the chief reasons for this unawareness is that the district- and state-level government initiatives for information dissemination on the same, in Odisha, have not been as adequate as in other states such as Andhra Pradesh and Tamil Nadu. A second reason is that for the poor, the judicial process is the last resort, because it is laced with a fear of the process, the costs involved and the distance to courts in towns and cities. Additionally, the complaint made by the poor may be influenced by existing social and economic power relations locally which may result in her being affected negatively.

Theoretically, rights are justiciable but at the grassroots level, in real life situation, it is far from being a reality. There needs to be more public action, and more active involvement of non-state actors in addressing the root cause of all inequalities to be able to ensure that rights are justiciable and implemented in the spirit of the Constitution.

> One of the ways to do so is to activate the legal Aid Cell before the NFSA 2013 is rolled out in the state, and this would mean that local issues are reflected in policy choices.[5]

Elsewhere in Balianta Block, interviews with the block development officer (BDO), revealed that designated officials were quick to respond to grievances within given time-frames.

> Mondays were designated as grievance hearing days, and these were well attended by villagers from different parts of the district.[6]

Responses of officials, according to development practitioner Mohanty, depended on the individual's sense of responsibility and the accountability of duty-bearers to poor citizens. This, to a large extent, determined whether the citizens would receive their entitlements or not. In many cases, the officials had a superior attitude towards the poor. Citing the case of Indira Awaas Yojana, Mohanty said that people had to go from one desk officer to another before they finally received their entitlements.

> Government attitude and approach is still on the welfare mode. If welfare schemes were rights-based and the mindset of duty bearers was rights based, 60-70% of villages would have been empowered. For instance, if a woman files a First Information Report (FIR) at the police station, the attitude of the police is: let her wait, we will attend to her when we are free. There is no immediate relief, no emotional support or help, and she gets victimized yet again. This is a mindset which is against inclusiveness of all people, and we need to change this.[7]

According to Pangi, a community-based NGO worker, high levels of illiteracy and inadequate living conditions render poor people's social position as "under-developed", and more often than not, local duty-bearers have "a disrespectful and brazen attitude" towards them. On the other hand, the rights-holders develop a deferential attitude towards the duty-bearers, as the latter have the authority to grant them access to various entitlements, possess all knowledge of the state, and therefore are referred to as *mai-baap* (mother-father). This perceived unequal social status impacts the general well-being and the dignity of the poor, especially ethnic minorities and genuine policymaking. Development practitioners argue that the challenge to overcome this unequal social status if any rights-based change at the grassroots level is to be achieved through policies alone. In cases where the duty-bearer's attitude towards poor people is disrespectful, it further reinforces inequalities and creates a culture of silence. A legal expert points out that it was unthinkable for the poor, struggling for two meals a day, to find the courage or the means to register complaints against duty-bearers.

> The State usurps the language of rights such as the slogan of Your Right is Our Duty without any real change in the attitudes of its officials responsible for operationalising its entitlement schemes.[8]

Nalini, a development practitioner, was sceptical of the ability of the Food Security Act to address vulnerable people's hunger needs without a corresponding change in the attitude of the duty-bearers, from being masters to service-deliverers or facilitators. If the people are not comfortable about demanding their rights from unhelpful duty-bearers, it would be challenging to implement any rights-based entitlement scheme.

> Policy is great. Intention of the duty bearer is also okay. The NFSA modifies all other older Acts ... However, the people are the same.[9]

Arguing that the personality of the duty-bearer at high levels of decision-making and policy initiatives is crucial to the success of any rights-based policy, the chief Right to Food campaigner in Odisha gives the example of the WCD secretary as a path-breaking duty-bearer, who took a personal interest and introduced innovative changes in the Anganwadi system. According to Mishra, the secretary implemented the Supreme Court directives on decentralized procurement in April 2011 by forming and training, women's SHGs. The secretary clearly demarcated the role of each duty-bearer at the grassroots level. So, for example, the duties of an Anganwadi worker were printed and announced in panchayat offices to keep villagers informed. Initiatives such as the creation of Mother's Committees and Jaanch Committees at the village level engaged the community in its development process. The secretary introduced quality checks in the supplementary nutrition programme (SNP), and ensured a regular supply of nutritious food items to the Anganwadi centres. Additionally, unlike in other states, the secretary laid down the protocols for THR and made public the rules and regulations relating to the ICDS at the district level.

> Secretary Ahuja had been able to dismantle centralised cartel of dealers of food items in 2011 when the corrupt minister was exposed by the media and had to resign. She acted upon SC directives and made food procurement decentralised by giving it to the SHGs. Another pathbreaking action was a simple step, namely listing duties of the AWW and AWH in panchayat offices and AWCs, and this action had a major impact in the villagers in terms of their awareness of the ICDS provisions. What Ahuja madam did was to implement provisions which have been in the policies at the central level, and this reflects her political will and commitment.[10]

In many cases, middle-level officials shared instances where the expectations and demands of duty-bearers at higher posts, as well as the ever-changing demands of the various local stakeholders such as ministers and businessmen, had impacted adversely on the operation of rights-based policies at the village level. The Balianta BDO said that he was transferred every few months, because of his attempt to "honestly" discharge his responsibilities. The BDO further clarified that individual officials still had the option of deciding how to discharge their obligations, and that active citizen participation in the development process would make it easier for the official to work.

> The implementation of the Right to Public Services 2013, depends on the officer in charge, his reaction to people and to his own duty, and to the environment. Does he react actively, or does he freeze? Our honest duty is to activate and implement any law, but people should be conscious of what should be "our right, our duty" to be able to exploit existing laws and claims.[11]

Problems relating to rights-based policies vary with the context, said the Right to Food campaigner, Jena. For instance, the amount of cash given under the different entitlement schemes was considered as being inadequate for a decent life unless the beneficiaries had an additional source of income.

> A comparison with prices for 2012 shows that Rs.300 per month for the age group of 60-80 years, for instance, is very meagre. In 2012 December, potatoes were Rs.60 a kg, rice was Rs.35 per Kg (under PDS), sugar was Rs20 per kg, and kerosene was Rs.20 per litre. To be meaningful, well-intentioned policy initiatives must have adequate budget provisions.[12]

The process of claiming entitlements for the extreme poor, in the case of the death of a beneficiary, is a complex process. For instance, when the primary wage earner of a BPL family dies, the benefits are either withdrawn from the family, or given to the father of the deceased, and if the father already has a BPL card then no card is given because only one BPL card per family is allowed. This impacts adversely on the widow and in many cases, she becomes either destitute or dependent on her in-laws because she is not entitled to her deceased husband's ration card and the benefits therefrom. For example, interviews with a few Anganwadi helpers (AWH) in Banapur Block revealed that upon the death of their husbands, these women were ousted from their husbands' family homes, and ended up in makeshift living arrangements, before they were selected by the WCD to work as AWHs. In Chinmayi's (an AWH) case, she and her five-year-old daughter took shelter at the local orphanage before she fought for her share of her deceased husband's home. For unemployed poor widows, the situation can be worse, according to the Extension Officer (EO) of Banapur Block.

> The norm of one BPL card per family then becomes an issue of power within the family, where the wife always loses out to her in-laws.[13]

Thus, inadequate entitlement amounts which did not cover all household members reinforced existing sociocultural inequalities, based on gender or age. This posed difficulties in the execution of well-intentioned rights-based policies, as social realities were not taken into account.

Discussing the shortcomings in the government entitlement schemes, Right to Food activist Sinha directed attention towards the policy of provision of cash transfers to poor women only for the first two pregnancies. Additionally, while maternity-leave schemes for government employees were available, poor women in other formal and informal employment sectors did not enjoy this privilege.

> If we are all equal under the Indian constitution then why should only government employees have maternity leaves? Why this discrimination? And why are conditional cash transfers provided to poor women only for the first two pregnancies? What happens to the same poor woman for her other pregnancies? Why is food security linked to family planning issues?[14]

The absence of special provisions for migrants created a cycle of continuous hunger for seasonal migrant families. Interviews with migrants revealed that they were typically landless with no sustainable means of livelihood and the food scarcity between the months of October and June led many to neighbouring districts in search of daily wage labour at brick kilns and construction sites. In some cases, their names were not on the BPL list due to: (i) their absence during the enlisting period, (ii) frequent migration from the native village with no forward address and (iii) corruption on the part of the duty-bearers. This, in turn, impacted upon their entitlement to different food programmes, including the government scheme of 100 days of employment.

Problems were compounded, according to NGO workers, and took unusually longer to be dealt with because local governance bodies were not authorized to execute decisions related to issues, such as those discussed above. According to Sricharan, while the Constitution, under the Panchayati Raj Extension Services Act (PESA) of 1996, confers responsibilities on the Gram Sabha (Village Council) for all village development activities and for self-governing its natural resources, it does not provide it with either the decision-making authority nor does it give financial authority to the panchayat at the village level. Giving an example, the EO in Galua panchayat pointed out that the sarpanch as the executive head of the panchayat initiated the work of pond restoration, by cleaning out the collected debris, to allow fishing. However, the head of all development activities undertaken at the Block level is the BDO, who is appointed by the state administration, and not by the local panchayat. The BDO has the charge of finances and budgeting, which means that the panchayat can only request for funds for any activity but has no authority to disburse any finances related to development activities in the villages. Critiquing the decentralization process, an official at SIRD argued that the devolution of powers was ineffective because it did not translate into political or administrative authority at the panchayat level.

> By not giving financial powers to the Gram Sabha, the PESA has no teeth, and reflects the absence of genuine political will and commitment. In many cases decisions regarding panchayat plans have often been changed at the Block office level without informing the panchayat itself, which reflects on where real power lies. When the village panchayat has not been invested with real powers, the creation of other panchayat level grievance or accountability committees such as Jaanch Committees (JC), or Mothers' Committee (MC), in schools is merely an act of goodwill. ... this contradiction between intention and actual functioning of the Act, shows that government intention on RBA can be seen as meaningless.[15]

Furthermore, the creation of different bodies at the local level by the state led to multiple administrative bodies at the village level. Giving responsibilities to the AWCs along with the panchayat ward member, the health worker and to other local bodies answerable to different government departments, challenged the authority of the panchayat as the centre of decision-making authority at the village level. In other words, the creation of parallel centres of authority at the local level is creating disharmony and distrust amongst community members.

> If the panchayat is the primary unit of administration for all development activity at village level, then where does the *Anganwadi* worker fit in? Why are AWCs becoming the focal point of development activities?[16]

NGO workers such as People's Cultural Centre (PECUC) director, also argued that if decentralization had to be meaningful, the monitoring of the AWC, the School Management Committees (SMC) and the JC should be vested with the panchayats, and not with different government departments, as is the practice currently.

> Why cannot there be a system in place wherein the beneficiary doesn't have to waste time, and grievances be addressed immediately, and why cannot the state activate the decentralized system under the PESA which we already have in the Constitution? For example, although the state has established a SMC, it doesn't have the required qualifications or the autonomy to take decisions. The School and Mass Education Department of the state has kept all responsibility on decision making on any incident as its prerogative. The selection of members on the SMC suggested that it is not participatory, nor transparent, and most were not actively engaged with schools where PECUC works. Some SMCs raise funds and have used it for building boundary walls to demarcate school grounds. A need for leadership in the community is felt because although there are committees and constitutional requirements to facilitate a right to development, there is a gap which communities have not been able to seize it. This gap can be filled, and has to be filled by the community, and its panchayat for which collective public action is needed.[17]

Development practitioners stress that all is not bad. For example, the WCD actively seeks out the support of civil society organizations with a grassroots base for providing third party observations and conducting social audits, of state entitlement schemes. According to Jena, the Right to Food social audit (2012) found that the *jaanch committee* members were unaware of their responsibilities as duty-bearers at the panchayat level, and the report recommended the need to train them on the same. A relationship of mutual trust between duty-bearers of the state and civil society was essential for such collaborations between the government and NGOs.

> The WCD department, spent Rs. 48 lakhs on training and capacity building of the *Jaanch* committee members which included a two-page training manual prepared by us. We collect complaints from rights-holders at village level, try and understand why an AWC is not functioning and what could possibly hinder the AWW's active role, and then draft letters on behalf of the department which is sent to the department

> for a final edit and approval. We have been able to establish a relationship of mutual trust, credibility and faith because we check our facts three to four times at least.[18]

On another issue, i.e., the protocol for THRs, Mishra said that decentralized procurement of food produce was a step in the right direction because it gave control to communities and checked corruption. However, if the state wished to create an ideal situation, it would have to ensure that there is one SHG per Anganwadi centre and the train women in accounting procedures and marketing techniques.

> Earlier decentralised procurement was a Rs 800 crore business for a few people. If 30gms of dal is used per child in each AWC, in Koraput, for example, it means at least 12 kgs will be consumed in one panchayat and one quintal of dal will be required per month. If the panchayat produces 12 quintals, processes and feeds its own children, will it not be sustainable? Same arguments can be made for eggs and other food items.[19]

Preparedness of the state for operationalizing rights-based policies, according to NGO worker, Nayak, was not a primary concern for many development practitioners. Describing government welfare schemes, such as the ICDS, as necessary, but not necessarily rights-based, Nayak directed attention to various scenarios. Suppose the state decides it does not want to provide for all these entitlements, as is observed in the withdrawal of many welfare programmes such as the cuts in the Mahatma Gandhi National Rural Employment Guarantee Act (MGNREGA), or the NFSA in 2015, following the change in the political dispensation, then people are at a loss. Even the TPDS which ensured that basic food items were sold to poor people at highly subsidized rates, and as such, gave no control to people over their food security, but to retailers. The direct cash transfers, as seen above, into bank accounts also pose a challenge for communities which live in geographically remote areas and are illiterate. The "help" provided by literate sections to poor people to access the cash transfers into their bank accounts is given for a small consideration in percentage terms.

> But access to the scheme does not necessarily empower poor people. It ensures that poor people live at survival levels and be dependent on the state. The delivery of any of the state welfare schemes and services is not in the hands of the poor people, nor is the production of the service including food. At all levels people are the "receivers", and not owners and decision makers. Is it not time to critique this model of entitlements where pensions are not equal to the cost of living, for instance?[20]

Furthermore, according to Nayak, these entitlements run parallel with populist approaches to secure electoral votes. If the state wishes to be rights-based, then the strengthening of the village economy would be the first step. On the one hand, the state provides for entitlements through ICDS, PDS and cash transfers and ensures that the communities depend on outside factors for their survival, which in turn hurts the economy. On the other hand, the state takes away land rights by leasing land to mining corporations, and other industrial bodies. Seed sovereignty is taken away. Monocultures of coffee and cashew plantations make communities food insecure, and dependent on the state for survival. The amendments of rules and procedures are just that, so long as, larger corporate interests are not at stake, and industrialization policies are not changed, the state does not mind making nominal changes in policies. This is again observed in the mining industries continuing their activities, with state support in Odisha, in spite of people's protests and their loss of land and livelihood systems.

There is a lack of institutional coordination between the various government departments dealing with the same subject matter, as observed in the case of bonded labour. Giving the instance of bonded labour, Nayak argues that there are multiple departments, and it becomes difficult for the poor labourer to identify any of these, and therefore be in a position to demand his safety or food security entitlements. The subject of bonded labour is not with the labour department of the government, but with the panchayat raj department. To further complicate make matters, the job of identifying bonded labour rests with the social welfare department; their rescue is the responsibility of the police department, and their rehabilitation is the responsibility of the PR department. A second instance is that of the PDS where the consumer and civil supplies department is responsible for the provision of food items in the retail shops. However, complaints relating to this process and cases of corruption are registered with the PR department. This is very confusing for ordinary people, and more so for the tribals as they live on the margins of mainstream society. For a right to be claimed, a single identifiable duty-bearer would make it easier for ordinary people to claim their entitlements. As described by Nalini, an NGO worker:

> The GOO has the administrative capacity to make food entitlements a reality, but does it utilise this capacity to its fullest? Perhaps not yet, and this could also be due to behavioural reasons, personality, work ethics, and attitudes of duty bearers at many levels. And that is why political leadership is crucial. Political will is the thread that can connect all the disparate ends of policy making and its effective implementation. The rest of us are like puppets in this process, while the final impact is felt at the village level.

Concluding remarks

This chapter presents findings from a study into political will and commitment of the state government in Odisha, by examining the state government's preparedness for making operational rights-based food entitlements. The findings show that there is, often, a mismatch between political will, and the actual delivery of rights-based services. Although the constitutional framework and policies are rights-based, the lack of attention to the practice and experience of middle and local duty-bearers in policymaking has led to difficulties in operationalizing well-intentioned rights-based policies in practice. Unless the government addresses the concerns of NGO workers, campaigners, union activists and other development practitioners at all levels, state preparedness for reducing hunger will remain a distant dream.

Notes

1 Author's interview with Secretary, Women and Child Development Department, Government of Odisha.
2 Author's interview with R.K. Mishra, Right to Food campaigner, Odisha.
3 Author's interview with Sahoo, Bharatiya Mazdoor Sangh (BMS) union leader.
4 Author's interview with official of State Institute of Rural Development (SIRD), Odisha.
5 Author's interview with R.K. Mishra, Right to Food campaigner, Odisha.
6 Author's interview with Block Development Officer, Balianta Block, Khorda District, Odisha.
7 Author's interview with A. Mohanty, Director of NGO People's Cultural Centre (PECUC).
8 Author's interview with L.K. Ram, legal expert, Banapur village, Khorda district.
9 Author's interview with Nalini, NGO worker.
10 Author's interview with R.K. Mishra, Right to Food campaigner, Odisha.
11 Author's interview with Extension Officer, Banapur, BDO office.
12 Author's interview with N. Jena, Right to Food campaigner, Odisha.
13 Author's interview with Extension Officer, Banapur, BDO office.
14 Author's interview with D. Sinha, Right to Food campaigner, New Delhi.
15 Author's interview with official of State Institute of Rural Development (SIRD), Odisha.
16 Author's interview with Balianta Panchayat Ward member.
17 Author's interview with A. Mohanty, Director of NGO People's Cultural Centre (PECUC).
18 Author's interview with N. Jena, Right to Food campaigner, Odisha.
19 Author's interview with R.K. Mishra, Right to Food campaigner, Odisha.
20 Author's interview with S. Nayak, NGO worker.

References

Drèze, Jean, 2004. 'Democracy and Right to Food', *Economic and Political Weekly*, 39 (17), 24 April: 1723–1731.

Ministry of Law and Justice, 2013. 'The National Food Security Act', *Gazette of India*, 10 September 2013.

Nussbaum, Martha, 2003. 'Capabilities as Fundamental Entitlements: Sen and Social Justice', *Feminist Economics*, 9(2–3), 2003: 33–59.
Saxena, N.C. and Harsh Mander, 2012. Commissioner and Special Commissioner of the Supreme Court in the Case: PUCL v. UOI & Ors Writ Petition (Civil) No.196 of 2001. Online at: http://www.righttofoodindia.org/data/icds/March_2012_letter_to_secretary_women_and_child_development_sc_commissioners_7_february_2012.pdf (accessed 12 June 2018).
Sen, Amartya, 2005. 'Human Rights and Capabilities', *Journal of Human Development*, 6(2), July 2005: 151–166.

Chapter 7

Global governance and India's food governance and security

Shalini Kala

> *The true source of world hunger is not scarcity but policy, not inevitability but politics. The real culprits are economies that fail to offer everyone opportunities and societies that place economic efficiency over compassion.*
>
> – Dr Peter Rosset, Food First

Over the past several decades, the fight to reduce world hunger has progressed well. In the past 20 years in particular, many countries across the world have reduced undernourishment significantly (FAO, 2003). Yet, Southern Asia, home to the largest number of food-insecure people, has struggled excruciatingly to feed people caught in poverty and conflict. Chronic hunger reduces people's ability to lead a healthy and productive life, thus perpetuating the vicious hunger–poverty–hunger linkage. Banishing food insecurity from India will mean moving about 200 million people out of this hunger trap. While the numbers may be daunting, does its economic stature, policy assuredness and rising contributions to involved and complicate discussions on related global issues place India in a position to race to the goal quickly and convincingly?

This chapter starts by briefly tracing the history of food challenges in India, their changing nature and the domestic policy response in the period starting after independence in 1947 to now. This is followed by a look at the Indian role and contributions to international negotiations on food and agriculture policies relevant to food security. The final section discusses the possible Indian efforts to eliminate food insecurity at home and strengthen global governance.

The Food and Agricultural Organization (FAO) of the United Nations defines food security as a situation where all people have, at all times, physical and economic access to sufficient, safe and nutritious food that meets the dietary needs and food preferences for a healthy and active life (FAO, 2003).

DOI: 10.4324/9781003272656-7

History of food governance in India

At the time of its independence in 1947, over 80% of the Indian population was left poor and vulnerable as a result of 200 years of colonial depredation and squeeze. Additionally, the recent history of famines claiming millions of its people was still vivid in public memory. Understandably, food self-sufficiency was a top priority for political leaders in rebuilding the nation. Later, in the era of Cold War politics, policymakers were also keen to reduce dependence on imports and food aid, at the earliest to avoid any kind of political compromise arising from it. Wheat transfers from the US under its Public Law 480 were widely seen as a tool used to influence Indian foreign policy.

This meant not only having adequate food stocks of its own but also a food distribution system in place to reach citizens in all corners of the country. First, to quickly expand agriculture production, especially of staple grains, investments were made in agriculture technology in the mid-1960s. This involved use of high yielding varieties (HYVs) of seeds starting with wheat, intensive use of inputs such as fertilizers and water associated with HYVs, and building an irrigation network. Initially, a relatively small area was targeted for what came to be known as the "Green Revolution" – mainly, Punjab, Haryana and Western Uttar Pradesh – where this strategy led to a rapid increase in wheat production. Second, the Public Distribution System (PDS), first introduced by the British during World War II as a tool to ration food supplies, was repurposed and expanded to provide essentials like wheat, rice, sugar and kerosene at subsidized prices. This basket of goods expanded over time as the availability of other items deemed essential improved.

Along with this, the Food Corporation of India (FCI) and Agriculture Prices Commission (APC, renamed in 1985 to Commission for Agricultural Costs and Prices) were set up in 1965. The latter was aimed at guiding crop price fixation for staples to encourage farmers to expand their production. The Minimum Support Price (MSP) is aimed at assuring farmers of a remunerative and stable price in case the market price is not attractive or is volatile. Announced at the beginning of the sowing season, the MSP is offered as a guaranteed price for several crops to protect farmers from excessive fall in market prices. The FCI supports PDS operations by buying selected crops, mainly grains, from farmers at the stated MSP, storing these and moving them through the PDS from surplus to deficit areas of the country.

By the late 1970s, even with a rapidly expanding population, Malthusian doomsday predictions for India had withered under reality and wheat and rice production had increased beyond consumption needs. Buffer stocks started building up with the FCI. Both yields and area under HYVs had expanded considerably along with the irrigation infrastructure. Concurrently, the PDS network grew allowing access to an increasing number of people to food grains at subsidized rates.

In addition, Integrated Child Development Services (ICDS) were launched experimentally in 33 blocks in the mid-1970s, focusing on nutrition security for children, and pregnant and lactating mothers. It offered subsidized food, nutritional supplements, primary healthcare, immunization and health check-ups.

Over the years, the paraphernalia of schemes supporting food needs of the poor, vulnerable consumers (some of these are described in Table 7.1) and those aimed at increasing food crop production kept growing. However, the surplus food and a widening food distribution system failed to ensure food security for all at all times. PDS leakages became notorious with claims of subsidized food bypassing those that needed it the most. Starvation deaths and hunger were reported alongside rotting grain stocks and rat infestation at the bulging FCI warehouses.

Table 7.1 Government of India food security initiatives

Government Scheme	*Target Beneficiaries*	*Year Established*
PDS	Poor citizens especially those Below Poverty Line (BPL)	1947
Food Corporation of India	To procure, store and move essential food crops	1965
Essential Commodities Act	General public	1955
Integrated Child Development Scheme	Children and pregnant women	1975
Mid-Day Meal (MDM) Scheme	Primary school students in government schools and those run by local bodies	1995
Village Grain Banks Scheme	BPL families from food deficit areas in 11 states	2004
National Food for Work Programme (NFFWP)	Rural poor in need of employment and desire to do manual and unskilled work residing in the most 150 backward districts	2000
Antyodaya Anna Yojana	5% of the population (about 1 crore of families) in the country who go without two square meals a day	2000
Sampoorna Grameen Rozgar Yojana (SGRY)	Women, scheduled castes, scheduled tribes and parents of children withdrawn from hazardous occupations of all the states and Union Territories (UTs)	2001
National Rural Employment Guarantee Act (NREGA)	Semi-skilled or unskilled workers of rural Households below poverty line.	2005
National Food Security Mission	Increased food grain production.	2007
Rashtriya Krishi Vikas Yojana	Farmers of all states and UTs.	2007
Right to Food Security Act	About 810 million Indian citizens	2013

Source: Lathi and Narkhede (2010)

Critics of the Green Revolution technology blamed it for increasing rural inequality and exposing small farmers to high risks, thus, making them vulnerable and food-insecure (Dhanagare, 1987). Though there were great hopes from ICDS, in its early years of operation, there was little progress on maternal and child nutrition. In all this, the country was weighed down by low economic advancement, which stagnated at the "Hindu Rate of Growth" averaging 3.5% per annum till at least the early 1980s (Central Statistical Organization). Per capita income grew by a very slow 1.3% per annum during this period. Without the ability to purchase food, it wasn't possible for the food-insecure to access it. Thus, producing sufficient food for consumption needs wasn't enough.

Even after the deep and substantive economic policy reforms starting in the mid-eighties that shook the country out of its economic lethargy, progress on food security indices remained slow. Under the New Economic Policy, reforms aimed at improving productivity and promoting private enterprise were launched in 1985. As the Indian balance of payments neared a crisis, this new thinking gathered steam culminating in another and stronger wave of economic reforms in the early 1990s. In the following years, the economy grew, consistently breaching the 3.5% growth rate. While the pace of poverty reduction also accelerated in the 1990s (Mehta and Kala, 2002), the hope and prosperity created did not reflect in improved food and nutrition security (Lancet, 2019).

It was feared that the economic progress was bypassing the poorest – what Sheila Bhalla called "economic development disaster" – and India's growing integration into the world economy was increasing vulnerability resulting in hunger and starvation (Bhalla, 2000). In a sense, this frustrated all the effort behind rising food production and buffer stocks. In fact, the latter had started contributing heavily to the ballooning food subsidy bill which grew at a compound annual growth rate of over 17% between 1991–1992 and 2011–2012. For this period as a whole rice procured was more than double the mandated requirement and wheat was over one and a half times (Sharma and Alagh, 2013).

The puzzling persistence of food insecurity even as the economy grew and grain stocks overflowed, led to several attempts at policy improvements to tackle hunger and malnutrition better. In 1997, to sharpen the reach of PDS it was restructured to target the most needy. Aimed at school-going children, the Mid-Day Meal (MDM) scheme was launched in 1995 to get them to school and feed them nutritious food. A restructured ICDS was launched in 2012 for faster progress on maternal and child nutrition. Several other initiatives were started such as the narrowly targeted schemes like Antyodaya Anna Yojana for the poorest of the poor, Emergency Feeding Programme for the Kalahandi–Bolangir–Koraput region in the state of Odisha considered the most backward and most food-insecure in the country, Annapurna Yojana for those above 65 years of age with no pension, along with several directed at the increasing output of various crops.

Meanwhile, during the last decade, with the push from civil society institutions, media and other sections of society, the government set up a committee under the leadership of the Supreme Court that recommended legislating for the right to food security. The National Food Security Act (NFSA) was passed in 2013 amid controversy regarding its almost universal nature, as more than 800 million Indians are expected to receive food support – and the costs involved. Both at home and abroad, it has been hailed as a great success for those fighting for people's right to access sufficient and nutritious food.

Despite all these efforts, hunger and malnutrition still continue to lurk threateningly. Over half of all Indian women between the ages of 15 and 49 continue to be anaemic. Even with steady progress made in the last two decades, almost 35% of children under five are stunted. Wasting that rapidly reduces weight has been persisted without much change. It affects more than 17% of Indian children under five years of age, which is among the highest in the world (Global Nutrition Report, 2020). Tied to a fixed location, food entitlements are hard to access for migrating families as they move from place to place in search of livelihood; some of the victims of conflict or recurring natural disasters. In selected pockets of the country, the situation is similar to or worse than sub-Saharan Africa (Himanshu, 2021).

Global food governance and the role of India

There are many institutions and mechanisms that contribute to global food governance. Since the formation of the FAO in 1945, there has been a proliferation of international institutions (Table 7.2) committed to reducing world hunger.

In addition to regional and multilateral organizations, private institutions add to the effort. Even as they jostle for legitimacy, space and authority, together they shape and impact global food governance. Following are some of the key platforms where, currently, these institutions connect and deliberate with national governments on the subject.

Prime among these is the intergovernmental agency World Trade Organization (WTO) and its earlier avatar the General Agreement on Tariffs and Trade (GATT). GATT was formed in 1947 on a proposal by the United States to reduce global trade barriers. G8, the Global Partnership on Agriculture, Food Security and Nutrition, is a subgroup of the WTO. Currently, several subgroups of the WTO – G10, G8/G20 and G33 – are discussing issues related to agriculture that directly or indirectly impact food security. India participates in all these groups.

There is also the United Nation's World Committee on Food Security (CFS) that was formed in 1975, as an intergovernmental unit, in response to

Table 7.2 Selected international institutions relevant to food security

Year of Establishment	*Institution*	*Mandate Related to Food Security*
1945	UN Food and Agriculture Organization (FAO)	Eradicate world hunger and improve nutrition.
1963	UN World Food Programme (WFP)	Eradicate hunger and malnutrition; Coordinate international food aid.
1967	Food Aid Committee (FAC) of the International Grains Council	Contribute to world food security by ensuring a minimal level of international food aid
1974	UN Committee on Food Security (CFS)	Coordinate global approach to food security.
1974	UN World Food Council	Coordinate among national ministries of agriculture to help reduce malnutrition and hunger.
1975	Consultative Group on International Agriculture Research (CGIAR)	To reduce poverty and hunger, improve human health and nutrition through security.
1977	UN International Fund for Agriculture Development (IFAD)	Provide loans directed at eradicating rural poverty and hunger.
1996	World Food Summit	Affirmed the human right to food and established international targets to reduce world hunger.
2008	UN High-Level Task Force on the Global Food Security Crisis	To promote a comprehensive and unified response to the challenge of achieving global food security.
2008	G8 Global Partnership on Agriculture, Food Security and Nutrition	To increase the efficiency of the fight against hunger at both local and global levels.

Source: Margulis (2012)

the food crisis of the early 1970s and on the recommendation of the 1974 World Food Conference. The triad of UN's food-based agencies FAO, WFP and IFAD supports it. CFS is a broader multilateral space that includes other agencies such as the UN High-Level Task Force on Global Food Security (HLTF); representatives from transnational peasant movements, such as the Via Campesina; INGOs, such as Oxfam; and philanthropic organizations, such as the Bill and Melinda Gates Foundation. While CFS is increasingly recognized as a key platform, its leadership role in global food governance is not unambiguous. There have been other attempts at influencing international food security governance. For instance, the G8's New Alliance for Food Security and Nutrition, formed in 2012, is focused on eliminating food insecurity in Africa.

The Comprehensive Framework for Action (CFA), "is a multilateral consensus policy document … (and) is best understood as an aggregation of the policy priorities and preferences of multilateral institutions … that are members of the HLTF" (Margulis, 2012). It is led by the UN and has 22 members. These include UN's related specialized agencies, and others such as the World Bank, WTO and OECD.

For several decades after independence, not only did India focus on self-sufficiency in food production, it also followed inward-looking trade and manufacturing policies. On the global platforms mentioned above where the developed nations have consistently argued for reducing policy protection and liberalizing trade, India has been vociferous in upholding farm and food subsidies as critical to protect its food-insecure populations.

From the very beginning, it participated actively in global discussions under GATT, often taking a leadership role in bringing developing country concerns to the table. Agriculture, a sector of great interest to developing nations was largely outside of GATT until the 1986 Uruguay Round. Earlier in 1982 India and Brazil had led a group of developing nations strongly complaining that "the industrialized nations had not lived up to their obligations with regard to trade in ... agricultural products" (IIE, 2003).

By the time the WTO replaced GATT in 1995, some of the key developing nations including India and Brazil had done a domestic policy rethink and opened up their policy regimes allowing for greater participation in the world economy. Yet, domestic protection of agriculture in the form of subsidies and trade tariffs remained a contentious issue and continues to create serious obstacles to progress in the current round of WTO talks. With the United States of America at the forefront, developed nations have continued to favour an open trade regime putting their force behind the reduction in policy barriers to free trade globally. Policies protecting domestic production through subsidies or high import tariffs have been severely criticized. But this has been mainly with regard to industrial and services sectors.

In the case of agriculture, the developed world has fought hard to protect the interests of its own farmers through production subsidies, trade-related tariffs and non-tariff barriers. This double standard has long irritated the developing nations especially since it has been well established that unlike in the developed nations, agriculture in India and many other developing countries was net taxed historically (Cervantes-Godoy and Dewbre, 2010; Gulati and Narayanan, 2003), until related policies were reformed. India along with other developing nations have also regularly called out the developed countries for blocking exports of its agriculture products into their markets.

This became particularly relevant from the early 1980s. Having achieved grain self-sufficiency by the end of the 1970s and a rapid increase in fruits, vegetables and other crops, particularly after the policy liberalization of the 1990s, there was rising interest in India at tapping the export market beyond traditional items such as tea and sugar. Post-harvest wastage was significant, India's share in the world agriculture exports was minuscule and the international markets, though volatile, glittered with the promise of lucrative returns in both fresh and processed agriculture products. APEDA was set up in 1985 under the Ministry of Commerce to promote Indian agricultural exports. Agriculture being the mainstay of the rural economy, growth in the sector was seen as necessary for a reduction in rural poverty and in food insecurity.

In attempting to open up international markets for their agriculture exports, India and other developing countries have made progress in securing a reduction in tariff and non-tariff barriers through long and controversial rounds of discussion. However, while the international markets have opened opportunities and Indian exports of high-value agriculture items such as fruits, vegetables, meat and fisheries have increased, India's share in the world market remains insignificant – it is less than 2% in global processed food exports (IL & FS, 2015). Liberal trade policies also led to rising imports of agricultural products. In the years immediately after domestic policy reforms and the Agreement on Agriculture (AoA), under WTO there was only a "modest increase in per capita income of farm and labour households ... There is also significant reduction in poverty. However, household food security and nutrition have worsened" (Chand, 2004). Thus, the global agreements on agriculture did not result in the reduction in food insecurity.

Potentially then, more than looking to international markets, it is the changing basket of domestic consumption due to rising incomes and urbanization that may have a greater impact on demand for agriculture products. From cereals and other staples, there has been a growing shift towards high-value crops such as fruits and vegetables, milk, oil and meat products and is expected to continue in the same direction as indicated by the Planning Commission in its report on the 12th Five Year Plan. To what extent this impacts farmer incomes, and thus their food security will depend on what percentage of the market price they can realize and if they are able to increase crop productivity. In general, productivity has been persistently low across a large number of crops grown in India. Farmer realization in retail price varies across crops and has been reported to be as low as 28% as per a study conducted by the Reserve Bank of India (Bhoi et al. 2019).

For developing nations, food security remains a sensitive issue whether they are net importers of food or, like India, they produce enough to be able to potentially tide over episodes of low production. Domestic support targeted at rural and farming populations is seen as necessary to protect the poor from hunger and malnutrition as a large majority of them reside in and depend upon the agriculture sector of developing nations. Understandably then, in international discussions, this is seen mostly as non-negotiable by the developing world.

In the case of India, its very high and rising food subsidy bill has attracted a lot of attention internationally and at home. India has been unable to cap this expense in the past many decades mainly due to its continuing commitments on pricing support for farmers and subsidized food for poor consumers, many of whom are the farmers themselves. At present, the MSP is announced for 23 crops, including paddy, wheat, maize, sorghum, pearl millet, barley and ragi, five pulses (gram, tur, moong, urad, lentil), seven oilseeds (groundnut, rapeseed/mustard, soybean, sesamum, sunflower, safflower, niger seed) and four commercial crops (copra, sugarcane, cotton and raw jute).

Selected staple food items are sold to consumers through the PDS at subsidized rates. Commodities namely wheat, rice, sugar and kerosene are being allocated by the central government to the states and Union Territories for distribution. The latter also distribute additional items of mass consumption through the PDS outlets such as pulses, edible oils, iodized salt, spices, etc.

Almost 86% of the agriculture plots in India are less than 2 hectares. Farmers operating these small and marginal farms commonly face livelihood vulnerability. These farmers also form a large section of the poor consumers, as they are net buyers of food.

The nation's ability to support farmer livelihoods along with making affordable food available for the poor became particularly important with the passing of the NFSA that currently purports to cover over 800 million citizens. India actively lobbied for requisite flexibility in the WTO rules under the AoA to allow subsidized procurement and public stocking of grain for food security in the 2013 Bali round.

Added to these are new and complex challenges to global food security that have emerged in recent times. What has come into sharp focus is the changing climate and its impact on food production systems. As farmers struggle to adapt, agriculture is seen as one of the main contributing factors to climate change, specifically to greenhouse gases and the environmental degradation that is leading to it.

Meanwhile, globalization of agricultural markets has increased access to a variety of food for many, but it has also exposed farmers and consumers to its risky volatility. Powerful private corporate interests have come to dominate the international food value chains. They facilitate the movement of food products across the globe to satisfy shifting consumer demands even as food production is under pressure due to the uncertainty induced by climate change.

Episodes of sudden and sharp food price spikes, controversial land acquisitions for agriculture by international parties, and suspicion that global food corporates follow unfair trade practices have led to increasing civil society and activist voices speaking for the rights of the hungry. Consumers have begun to demand evidence of ethical and sustainable practices from global food corporates. International governance for food security and nutrition has probably never been as difficult and complicated as it is now. India will need to rise to the challenge of steering global discussions on these issues which is fair to the developing countries and adds to strengthening food security across the world.

What needs to change at home to improve food security governance?

Apart from focusing on growth in agriculture and the rural economy, the other key to tackling hunger lies in improving the delivery of related programmes along with sharper targeting of the poorest and most vulnerable sections. This two-pronged approach might bring quicker and more long-lasting returns to ensure food security than depending on international markets in any significant manner.

Special programmes for particularly poor and vulnerable groups that are prone to miss the economic growth paths, including those affected by recurring disasters, pregnant women and children, migrants and the old and infirm, ensure that these groups do not fall through the cracks. Many such programmes already exist; regular monitoring to sharpen their targeting and improving implementation will help enhance their performance as has been demonstrated by the experience of states referred to earlier.

In general, greater emphasis on improving policy implementation is imperative to make faster progress on food security. India has consciously tried to address its food security challenges since its independence in 1947. Even with a rapidly growing economy in the last three decades, its struggle with poor progress in this regard has resulted in a web of a large number of schemes and initiatives. There has been no dearth of formulation of new and attempts at refining existing policies. Poor implementation performance has been the bane of most of them especially the large and national-level initiatives including PDS, ICDS and the MDM scheme (see for instance, George and McKay, 2019; Saxena and Srivastava, 2009; Khera, 2006; Katiyar, 2019).

Implementing any national effort is a challenge for a large country like India and decentralization is necessary to ensure effectiveness at the last mile. This makes the participation and effectiveness of the states and their implementation machinery critical. Politically, it has been easier to announce new and larger schemes than focus on the more complex and difficult task of improving implementation that requires heavy lifting on reaching agreements with political adversaries on key priorities for the country. Success on the latter can enable reform of the implementing machinery and improving its ability to achieve stated goals without being chained to changing political rulers. The considerable political disagreement on the Right to Food Act passed in 2013 is a case in point that the current government which was in the opposition at that time did not support and is now mandated to implement (Banik, 2016). Its lack of enthusiasm in doing so is thus not surprising.

Political vision and leadership are critical for attention to implementation performance that helped improve PDS, ICDS, MDM scheme in some of the Indian states even when in general their performance across the country remains wanting even after changes in the programme design. States such as Chhattisgarh, Bihar (Himanshu, 2013) and Odisha (Kumar and Bhatla, 2017) have seen significant improvement in the outreach of PDS as they strengthened monitoring systems and transparency using information technology tools to plug leakage and expand coverage. Kerala, Tamil Nadu and Gujarat have been efficient and effective in the execution of the MDM scheme going beyond its stated mandate to expand coverage and offer more nutrition. After the launch of a restructured ICDS in 2012, even though among the poorest states in India, Chhattisgarh, and Odisha significantly improved (Saxena and Shrivastava, 2009) implementation with close supervision to ensure timely supplies and services.

Proper identification of PDS beneficiaries and end-to-end computerization of its operations are some of the reforms that are expected to improve PDS performance. Hopefully, improving the reach and efficiency of the PDS across the country would also improve the pace of reducing hunger. This is not to say that new or rationalized policies are not needed. However, it seems that for faster and better outcomes, the emphasis on strengthening implementation, especially at the state level, could be considerably more than it has been in the past. Launched in 2018, the National Nutrition Mission represents an effort to holistically and more intensively improve nutrition outcomes for children, pregnant women and lactating mothers, and is focused on improving intersectoral service delivery, building on the ICDS.

At the same time, there is a case to bring coherence to a large number of policies, schemes and initiatives of the government related to food. Policies such as the Essential Foods Act were passed in response to the needs of a previous and now long-gone era. Many of the historical initiatives like PDS, ICDS and Agriculture Produce Market Committees (APMC) Act have had to be reinvented for their relevance to current times. Improving nutrition necessarily requires access to clean water and sanitation along with adequate and balanced diets. Going beyond reforming individual initiatives to create a holistic ecosystem by linking them to sharpen emphasis on food security will likely multiply returns. Additionally, government policies and schemes need to bring in and connect with initiatives of other interested agencies in the non-government and private arena to bolster the fight against hunger and malnutrition. To overcome this formidable challenge, all efforts need to be targeted and well aligned.

Beyond these measures, enabling agriculture growth for rural prosperity will be critical for wide-reaching and long-term gains to address hunger and malnutrition. Improving the pace of growth of the largely smallholder agriculture in India is a necessary step towards lifting the majority of its poor out of their food insecurity status. Being decentralized and disaggregated agricultural growth is known to improve farmer incomes, make food cheaper for both rural and urban poor, energize the non-farm rural economy, and stimulate and sustain economic transition away from agriculture to manufacturing and services (DFID, 2004). There is a rich body of literature establishing that agriculture growth is more poverty-reducing and impacts the poorer sections of society more than growth in other sectors (Cervantes-Godoy and Dewbre, 2010). This is reflected in the case of India where almost half of its workforce is dependent on agriculture even though its share in national output has fallen to less than 15%. Growth in the sector will impact "the largest proportion of the low-income population in India" (NITI Aayog, 2015).

While agriculture prosperity is necessary to reduce rural poverty and food insecurity, it is arguable whether international trade can serve as an engine of growth in the case of a large country like India. Its main drivers of growth lie within and the need to be strengthened for its rural economy to prosper. Though it faces a formidable challenge in eliminating hunger for a large number of rural poor, there are also opportunities in agriculture to improve incomes and strengthen food security. Typically, productivity in most crops is lower than the world averages and nowhere close to that of top-performing countries; post-harvest wastage in perishables is high; and processing of fresh produce is less than 2%. Moreover, rapid urbanization is expanding domestic markets for high-value agriculture and food products. Tapping this potential presents a clear opportunity to create value and raise incomes. As per the apex think tank of the Indian government – NITI Aayog – fresh thinking and investments in technology and institutions along with market and policy reform are expected to double farmer incomes by 2022 (Chand, 2017).

For growth in agriculture crop productivity needs a push, market mechanisms need to reform, farmers need to be able to negotiate fair and remunerative prices probably through collective bargaining, and wastage needs to reduce through enhanced processing and robust marketing infrastructure. NITI Aayog (Chand, 2004) recommends targeted policy and institutional support for this purpose.

For instance, rationalization of agriculture subsidies will not only disincentivize sub-optimal use of resources but could also raise additional investment for farm growth. In the past 20 years subsidy to agriculture (excluding food subsidy) has increased as a percentage of GDP while public investment has been reducing (12th Five Year Plan, 2013). Subsidies have led to poor agriculture outcomes due to overuse of subsidized inputs and, "high use of chemical fertilizers and power is causing excessive mining of other soil nutrients and of groundwater, ... this is also leading to loss of quality of both soil and water". Being the largest importer of fertilizers in the world, efficiency in fertilizer use is a good practice that anyway needs to be promoted in the country. This makes for a case to shift expenditure on subsidies to infuse fresh investment in agriculture growth.

Similarly, rethinking the MSP and links between domestic production and imports could help the better allocation of scarce resources. On the one hand, expanding cereal production, mainly of wheat and rice, has led to excessive stocks year after year, in turn increasing storage costs. On the other, imports of edible oils and pulses are rising in response to growing consumption demand beyond the limited domestic production. Continuous assessment of MSP and trade policy to better align domestic production with consumption needs could improve efficiency by helping reduce storage and import costs. Again, the resources thus freed-up could be invested more judiciously to promote agricultural growth.

In this context, the three new farm bills hurriedly promulgated by the central government in September 2020 are aimed at encouraging private investment in the agri-food supply chain to improve the overall efficiency that would result in improved returns for the farmer (Narayanan, 2020). Apart from the discomfort displayed by several Indian states at the manner in which these were pushed through, the benefits expected to accrue to farmers have been contested widely. In fact, there is suspicion among farmers that the bills will facilitate a corporate takeover of their lands and livelihoods. Some have hence proclaimed them anti-farmer. Punjab, Chhattisgarh, Rajasthan, Delhi and Kerala have reformed state policies to bypass the latest farm bills. While no one doubts the necessity to improve returns to farmers, there is little consensus – whether among political parties as well as between the central government and the protesting farmers – on what these bills will achieve.

What might be India's role in international food governance?

By working towards eliminating hunger and malnutrition for the significant proportion of the world's food-insecure that live in the country, India could make the single most important impact on global food insecurity and malnutrition. Strengthening domestic policy and policy implementation ecosystem would be a critical step in this direction. Domestic policies need to be implemented well and assessed regularly to clearly identify the best options for the country's food-insecure. Can domestic food subsidies be rationalized for better food security outcomes? Is domestic politics driving the continuation of sub-optimal and wasteful subsidies? How can states be encouraged to take the lead on wide and deep changes to reduce malnutrition at a fast pace? Agile resolution of such and related issues need to become a top national priority.

Additionally, in international negotiations, India would do well to continue being a key contributor to discussions on food and nutrition insecurity to protect the interests of poor consumers and small and marginal farmers across the developing world. In representing the developing nations, India's ability at forging alliances to bring attention to common interests can continue to benefit the quality of discussions and outcomes at and within international forums. As much as it can benefit from the experiences of others, its own experience of difficulties and successes in facing food security challenges adds substantially to the world's experience. It has been supporting other more disadvantaged nations by sharing its excess grain stocks and by assisting their agriculture growth. As an economic powerhouse, its skills in high-level negotiations and the ability to fend off severe opposition adds necessary weight to the developing countries block especially in dealing with the developed world's diverging interests in agriculture. And thus, helps a more equal standing for developing nations on international forums with a better chance at negotiating for fair terms of engagement especially on trade in agriculture and food products.

A large number of international actors, both public and private, have emerged to play their part in global food security. Over time, they have evolved and each of them aims to serve important roles. However, there is still some work needed to ensure they can function collectively as an effective and coherent global food governance system. With an increasingly complex food security challenge and the need to find appropriate policy solutions to address it, coherence and convergence in efforts are necessary to make it easier and quicker to successfully address the challenge of hunger and malnutrition globally. India needs to continue to play its role in this process.

Conclusion

The challenge of global food insecurity is formidable and is receiving unprecedented attention. Food security and nutrition have come to be considered by some commentators as "global public goods" just like clean air that benefits everyone and increased consumption by one does not reduce it for others. Alongside, agencies supporting the cause have been redefining themselves to tackle this challenge contributing to and influencing the global governance system.

Food insecurity in India has not been addressed as fast as the country's economic progress in the last three decades would indicate. Prime Minister Manmohan Singh has repeatedly referred to it as a matter of national shame during his tenure in office. In addressing this, a large part of the work is cut out at the domestic front, whether it is in improving access to adequate and nutritious food, reaching the most vulnerable to reduce malnutrition or improving income from agriculture that supports the largest chunk of the poor and food-insecure. Reforming and reinforcing its domestic governance is the first and the most crucial step towards solving this puzzle. This will involve improving the implementation efficiency of domestic policies, promoting agricultural growth to energize the rural economy on which, most of the food-insecure depend and ensuring that the most vulnerable groups are not left out.

In playing its part further in improving international governance, India will need to continue to negotiate hard and smart for the "best" solutions for itself to avoid any domestic policy compromises, to take leadership in bringing together common interests of nations facing food insecurity and helping to strengthen the global governance architecture.

References

Banik, Dan, 2016. The Hungry Nation: Food Policy and Food Politics in India. *Food Ethics*, 1: 29–45.

Bhalla, Sheila, 2000. *Behind Poverty: The Qualitative Deterioration of Employment Prospects for Rural Indians*, Working Paper No. 7, Institute for Human Development.

Bhoi, Binod B., Sujata Kundu, Vimal Kishore and D. Suganthi, 2019. Supply Chain Dynamics and Food Inflation in India. *RBI Bulletin*, October 2019. Online at: https://rbidocs.rbi.org.in/rdocs/Bulletin/PDFs/1SUPPLYCHAINDYNAMICSE29D2F2AC0BF4F1DB05731C6E9B64885.PDF (accessed 5 May 2021).

Chand, Ramesh, 2004. *Impact of Trade Liberalization and related Reforms on India's Agricultural Sector, Rural Food Security, Income and Poverty.*

Chand, Ramesh, 2017. *Doubling Farmers' Incomes*, NITI Aayog, National Institute for Transforming India, Government of India.

Cervantes-Godoy, D. and J. Dewbre, 2010. *Economic Importance of Agriculture for Poverty Reduction*, Food, Agriculture and Fisheries Working Papers, No. 23, OECD Publishing.

Dhanagare, D.N., 1987. Green Revolution and Social Inequalities in Rural India. *Economic and Political Weekly*, 22(19–21), May 1987: 137–144.

DFID, 2004. *Agriculture Growth and Poverty Reduction.* http://www.dfid.gov.uk/Documents/publications/agri-poverty-reduction.pdf

FAO, 2003. *Trade Reforms and Food Security: Conceptualizing the Linkages.*

FAO, IFAD, UNICEF, WFP and WHO. 2017. *The State of Food Security and Nutrition in the World.*

George N.A., and McKay, F.H., 2019. The Public Distribution System and Food Security in India. *International Journal of Environmental Research & Public Health*, 16(17): 3221, 2019 doi:10.3390/ijerph16173221.

Global Nutrition Report, 2020. Online at: https://globalnutritionreport.org/

Gulati, Ashok and Sudha Narayanan, 2003. *The Subsidy Syndrome in Indian Agriculture*. Delhi: Oxford University Press.

Himanshu, 2013. PDS: A Story of Changing States. *The Mint*, 7 August 2013. Online at: https://www.livemint.com/Opinion/TTLqU0Cg2iF4hYtJSHtMRI/PDS-a-story-of-changing-states.html (accessed 20 May 2021).

Himanshu, 2021. Solving the Child Malnutrition Puzzle. *The Indian Express*, 20 January, 2021. Online at: https://indianexpress.com/article/opinion/solving-the-child-malnutrition-puzzle-7154617/

IL & FS, 2015. *A Strategy Paper for Augmenting Exports of Value Added Products from India*, APEDA. Online at: http://apeda.gov.in/apedawebsite

/Announcements/Strategy_Paper_Value_Added_Products_IL&FS_Clusters_14915.pdf

Institute for International Economics, 2003. *India in the GATT and WTO*.

Katiyar, Prerna, 2019. What's Ailing India's Mid-day Meal Scheme? *Economic Times*, 22 December 2019. Online at: https://economictimes.indiatimes.com/news/politics-and-nation/whats-ailing-indias-midday-meal-scheme/articleshow/72918265.cms?from=mdr (accessed 28 October 2020).

Khera, Reetika, 2006. Mid-Day Meals in Primary Schools: Achievements and Challenges, *Economic and Political Weekly*, 41:4742–4750. doi:10.2307/4418915, 2006. Online at: https://www.researchgate.net/publication/262126858_Mid-Day_Meals_in_Primary_Schools_Achievements_and_Challenges (accessed 25 November 2018).

Kumar, Anjani and Seema Bhatla, 2017. How PDS Can Be Made Effective Through Better Governance. *Financial Express*, 28 December 2017. Online at: https://www.financialexpress.com/opinion/how-pds-can-be-made-effective-through-better-governance/992421/ (accessed 25 November 2018).

Lancet, 2019. The Burden of Child and Maternal Malnutrition and Trends in Its Indicators in the States of India: The Global Burden of Disease Study 1990–2017. *Lancet Child & Adolescent Health* 2019, 3: 855–70. doi:10.1016/ S2352-4642(19)30273-1 (accessed 5 May 2021).

Lathi, B. J. and Parag Narkhede, 2010. Food Security in India: Concept, Realities & Innovations, 2010. Online at: https://www.researchgate.net/publication/228096218_Food_Security_in_India_Concept_Realities_innovations (Accessed 25 November 2018).

Margulis, Mathias E., 2012. *Global Food Security Governance: Committee for World Food Security, Comprehensive Framework for Action and the G8/G20*, 2012. Online at: https://pdfs.semanticscholar.org/66c1/499a7d1a492518eaab0a46266ed5207a3660.pdf (Accessed 25 November 2018).

Mehta, Aasha Kapur and Shalini Kala, 2002. *Hunger and Starvation*, Alternative Economic Survey 2001–2002: Economic 'Reforms': Development Denied, Alternative Survey Group, Indian Institute of Public Administration, Delhi.

Narayanan, Sudha, 2020. The Three Farm Bills. *The India Forum*, 2 October 2020. Online at: https://www.theindiaforum.in/sites/default/files/pdf/2020/10/02/the-three-farm-bills.pdf (accessed 5 May 2021).

NITI Aayog, 2015. Raising Agricultural Productivity and Making Farming Remunerative for Farmers, Occasional Paper, 2015.

Planning Commission of India, 2013. *12th Five Year Plan (2012–12017)*, Volume 2. Online at: https://mofpi.nic.in/sites/default/files/vol_2.pdf.pdf (accessed 25 November 2018).

Saxena, N.C. and N. Srivastava, 2009. ICDS in India: Policy, Design and Delivery Issues. *IDS Bulletin*, 40(4): 45–52, 2009. Online at: https://opendocs.ids.ac.uk/opendocs/handle/20.500.12413/8095 (accessed 25 November 2018).

Sharma, Vijay and Munish Alagh, 2013. Food Subsidy in India: Its Components, Trends, Causes and Reforms for Public Policy. *Indian Journal of Agricultural Economics*, 68(2), April-June 2013: 195–221.

Chapter 8

The role of Israel in India's food security

Manjari Singh and P.R. Kumaraswamy

When Narendra Modi visited Israel in July 2017, not only did he become the first Indian prime minister to visit that country, but this visit transformed the mainstream discourse of the bilateral relations (Kumaraswamy, 2018). Until then, Indo-Israeli relations were dominated by security-strategic issues such as arms trade, counterterrorism, intelligence cooperation and a convergence of interests for confronting emerging challenges, such as cyber security. Regional and international tensions, religion-centric extremism, political violence and the resultant instability are the key issues which would continue to dominate India's engagement with the outside world, including Israel. However, the Indo-Israeli relations encompass more than military cooperation, weapons imports and technology transfers. Less attractive, but more valuable soft issues are gradually gaining prominence and it was not accidental that the joint statement issued by Prime Ministers Benjamin Netanyahu and Modi focused more on soft issues such as cooperation in agriculture and water management than hard-core security issues.

Discussions on food security revolve around four core areas, namely, *availability*, *accessibility*, *utilization* and *stability* (FAO, 1996; Kumaraswamy and Singh, 2017). How successfully a country addresses these issues would determine the level of its food security. While the latter three rest entirely with India, Israel comes into the picture in terms of *availability*. This implies the existence of a sufficient quantity of good quality food that is available for the entire population of the country and is achieved through increased domestic production, imports or foreign aid. If food aid is a sign of the economic collapse of a country, importing large quantities of food items undermines the socio-economic stability of an agrarian nation like India. Hence, the increased production of basic food items and their possible export on a regular basis would form the core component of the *availability* part of the food security. Can Israel help India to increase its quantity of food and in the process contribute to its food security?

While India will not be able to confront its food security challenges only with Israel's help, the latter could enable India to mitigate its problems and provide avenues for adopting innovative approaches for feeding

DOI: 10.4324/9781003272656-8

its population, which would enable it to consider agricultural items as a major export commodity. For understanding this, the chapter delves into four major issues: the status of the food security situation in both countries; areas of Israeli expertise; Indo-Israeli cooperation in agriculture and allied industries; and the challenges facing both countries.

With a robust economic growth rate of 4.5%, India is considered as world's seventh-largest economy with a nominal gross domestic product (GDP) of US$2.72 trillion and the third-largest with a purchasing power parity of US$10.51 trillion (PHDCCI, 2019). Moreover, the changing global power dynamics, from uni-polar to multi-polar, has placed India as one of the rising powers. Strengthened by its rapid economic growth, the huge population which yields in demographic dividend and quest for growing energy security has placed India as a regional and global actor. However, the country ranks among the lowest in terms of hunger and poverty indices and is ranked at number 102 of 117 countries in the Global Hunger Index in 2019 (ibid.). This calls for methods and innovations in terms of securing food for its population through unconventional means and in this regard Israel's role as a facilitator in enhancing the production of crops will be crucial in times to come.

Relative equations

In terms of demography, geography, natural resources and other attributes of power and influence, India and Israel are vastly different and, in some cases, incomparable. Their historical trajectory and post-independence journeys have been different and often at cross purposes. The asymmetry in political ties was reflected in the four decades of recognition-without-relations policy, adopted by India since its recognition of the Jewish state in September 1950 (Kumaraswamy, 2010). Given its limited politico-diplomatic options and natural resources, Israel has been pursuing its foreign policy objectives primarily through the military-security diplomacy of arms trade and other forms of security cooperation.

At the same time, in terms of a number of other socio-economic indicators, Israel fares far better than India and often outperforms some of the advanced Organization of Economic Cooperation and Development (OECD) countries of Western Europe. To mention a few, Israel's poverty rate stood at 2.70% (2016 estimates) which was a drop from 5.20% in 1979; life expectancy at birth is 82.60 years (2017); human development index (HDI) is 0.906 and ranks 22nd in the world among 189 countries (2018) and thus is put under very high human development category (World Bank, n.d.; UNDP, n.d.; Macrotrends.net, n.d.). A significant proportion of the Israeli population (1.8 million) has been identified as "poor" and is living below the poverty level (Newmann, 2017); however, malnutrition and food shortage do not exist. Israel, for example, does not figure in *The State of Food Insecurity in the World* report published by the FAO in 2015 (FAO-IFAD-WFP, 2015). The same report identifies that though India's situation has been improving, especially since the early 1990s, a significant portion of its population has been undernourished; it stood at 23.7% in 1990–1992, marginally improved to 20.5% in 2005–2007 and stood at 15.2% during 2014–2016. In real terms, it means that about 194.6 million– or 25 times the Israeli population– Indians were undernourished. According to another FAO report on the *State of Food Security and Nutrition in the World*, about 14.5% of Indians are severely undernourished (FAO-IFAD-UNICEF-WFP-WHO, 2017). Likewise, India ranked 74 on the Global Food Security Index for 2017, while Israel was placed 19th.

When it comes to the food security index, in terms of natural resources and resilience performance calculated in 2019, India ranks 98 with a score of 46.7 while Israel ranks 101 with a score of 44.8 (Global Food Security Index, 2019). While in the same index the ranking of both the countries in demographic stresses stands at 53 and 67, respectively for India and Israel. In terms of adaptive capacity, the ranking is 68 and 55 for India and Israel in that order. These figures are suggestive that in India, there is no dearth of natural resources and the population stress is also lower than in the case of Israel. Despite these, India's inability to eradicate poverty has been daunting and according to *Global Hunger Report* published by the UN in September 2017, an additional 33 million undernourished people joined those from the previous year. Out of the 815 million undernourished people worldwide, India has 190.4 million or 14.5%. In the Global Hunger Index 2019, India's position further dropped to 102nd rank of 117 countries. The point being that since Asia has the largest population concentration, India has more than a third of the undernourished people in the continent (UNDP, 2016). These largely consist of women and children, the most vulnerable segment of the population; if 38.4% of the children have stunted growth, more than half of the women are anaemic. As many critics have argued, India's progress in meeting sustainable development goals one and two– No Poverty and Zero Hunger – has been abysmal and well below that of its South Asian neighbours and the poorer countries of the Middle East (UN in India, 2016; Bahri, 2017; Singh, 2020).

This asymmetry between the two countries is accompanied by another major difference and is hence a potential component of Indo-Israel bilateral relations, namely, productivity. When the state was established in May 1948, Israel had limited natural resources, including water. As a Mediterranean country, its annual rainfall ranges between 100 mm in the south and 1,100 mm in the north, per annum and because of the dry, long and hot summer the natural evaporation levels are very high (Weatheronline, n.d.). Rainfall is unevenly distributed and decreases sharply as one moves southwards. Owing to the nature of its climate, most of the rain occurs between November and March while June to August are dry. The Sea of Galilee that is shared with Syria is the only natural lake and the Jordan River that it shares with Syria, Palestine and Jordan are its main freshwater sources. Israel resorted to military offensives and unilateral action to acquire the water supplies to meet the needs of its growing population, which increased ten times, from 807,000 in 1948 to over 8.1 million in 2017. Israel's political journey was accompanied by political isolation and an economic boycott, spearheaded by the Arab League.

Thus, for achieving self-sufficiency, Israel adopted innovative methods to increase its food and agricultural production to meet the growing demands and needs of its population. Some were social and socialist measures such as the setting up of *kibbutzim* and the adoption of *moshav* farming which acquired national importance after 1948. Driven by political compulsions as well as economics, self-sufficiency became the cornerstone of Israel's agriculture and allied sectors. The results were not inconsiderable and through a host of measures such as innovative farming, hybrid development, water management, scientific intervention in seeding, cultivation and harvesting, Israel made a quantum jump in food yields, higher productivity and large-scale production. Over time, fresh products have become its major exports and it has been recognized as the world leader in agricultural technologies.

Only a fifth of its land is arable but agriculture accounts for more than 2% of its GDP and as of 2015, agricultural exports were to the tune of US$1.1 billion, while its total exports stood at US$63.9 billion (Israeli Ministry of Economy, 2016; Indexmundi, 2018). A host of vegetables, citrus fruits, cotton and flowers, not native to the Mediterranean climate, are grown in the country and make up the bulk of its agricultural production (ibid.). Vineyards that produce high-quality wines are found in different parts of the country as are a host of fruits. It also grows a variety of flowers which mainly cater to the export markets in Europe. Through hothouses which have controlled temperatures, Israel has been able to enlarge not only the quantity of its produce but also increase the frequency of cultivation. The same holds true for animal husbandry and the dairy industry.

Some of its accomplishments in agriculture and allied industry are the envy of many. For example, only 100,000 hectares of land are available for wheat production yet the wheat harvest in Israel stands at 145,000 metric tonnes (Shaked, 2016), as against the 95 million tonnes in India despite, the nearly 29.25 million hectares of land under wheat cultivation (Directorate of Economics and Statistics, 2011). The comparison in the dairy sector is even more profound; the average yield of milk per day in India is 927.1 litres per year ideally, however, the lactation period is very short (Community data .gov.in, 2016) as against the 1,200 litres of milk per cow per lactation over 305–310 days in Israel which amounts to around 40 litres per cow per day, as against 2.54 litres per cow per day, in India (ISHITECH, 2012). All this has been made possible through systematic and scientific intervention and periodic upgrading.

Above all, Israel has emerged as the leader in water technology, including, harvesting, water management, distribution and efficiency. It has mastered and modernized the ancient drip irrigation technology – often associated with a Chinese ruler a century before Christ – and transformed it into its major plank for agricultural self-sufficiency and agricultural diplomacy. Due to frequent periods of below-average rains, there were fears in the 1990s that the next Arab–Israeli conflict would be over scarce water resources and Israel was often accused of "stealing" Palestinian water rights. This was complicated by the aquifers in the West Bank that run westwards towards the Mediterranean Sea. The falling water levels in the Sea of Galilee and the Jordan River meant that there was greater competition among the riparian states for diminishing water resources. Between 1920 and 2017, for example, the storage levels of the Sea of Galilee dropped to 9 million cubic metres below sea level. According to the Water Authority of Israel, the Sea of Galilee lost 15 centimetres of its water level in May 2017, which is recorded as the all-time low (*The Algemeiner*, 2017). Likewise, falling water levels led to the sudden emergence of sinkholes in and around the Dead Sea. As a result, Israel even contemplated "importing" water from its neighbours, especially the water-rich Turkey (Cohen, 2007).

Israel was able to arrest and reverse the process through technological intervention. Reduction of water evolution or the electrolysis of water during transmission was being practised since the early 1950s when the National Water Carrier was put in place to transfer the waters of the Sea of Galilee in the north, to population centres in central and southern Israel. The threat of water shortage was addressed through desalination and currently, there are five desalination projects in the country which produce 582 million cubic metres of water annually. There are another five desalination projects under construction which are likely to be functional by 2025. These projects produce about two-thirds of the total drinking water consumed in the country (Rinat, 2017). To minimize and reduce the requirement of freshwater nearly 85% of the requirements of agriculture have been met by recycled and brackish water (Frenkel, 2017). As a result, a large percentage of the tap water supplied throughout the country is potable. This, however, is not the case in India; it not only lacks running water but is also not potable.

These disparities have considerably undermined India's achievements in agriculture and allied sectors such as horticulture, floriculture, marine and aquaculture, animal husbandry and farming.

Despite the Green Revolution of the 1960s, India's food production is barely sufficient for its needs. India's total food grain production hovers around 275.68 million tonnes, which includes 98.38 million tonnes of wheat and 110.15 tonnes of rice, the two basic staple food items. Other items produced are coarse cereals (44.19 million tonnes), pulses (22.95 million tonnes). India also produces oilseeds (32.10 million tonnes), cotton (33.09 million bales), and sugarcane (306.72 million tonnes) in bulk (Press Information Bureau, 2017). Even though 2016–2017 recorded a higher production (by 7.27% or 18.67 million tonnes) than the previous five years, the self-sufficiency ratio is marginal and due to poor harvest and below-average rains, India often imports large quantities of its food items. Moreover, seasonal shortfalls of vegetables such as onions are political dynamites and often governments have been voted out of office because of soaring onion prices (Rai, 2013). Of late, farmer suicides due to mounting debts and financial hardship have become the major agenda of political parties and many otherwise "successful" governments have lost the trust of the voters, due to the agricultural crisis in some parts of the country.

The problems facing India's agricultural sector are diverse, ranging from institutional deficiencies to administrative inefficiencies. For the purpose of analyzing the role of Israel in addressing the food security challenges facing India, one can identify one major problem: the excessive reliance of agriculture upon monsoon. The monsoon which starts in Kerala around the first of June crosses Northeast India before it fizzles out in the north and north-western parts of India. This leads to dryness in parts of Rajasthan and Gujarat due to the deflection of the monsoon winds which finally retreat by November–December. This determines not only the fate of the farmers but also the state of the Indian economy. Normal and above-average rains often result in bumper harvests and contribute to a higher economic growth; while below-average rains correspondingly dent the official projections.

The monsoon not only determines the amount of water available for agriculture but also the water levels in lakes and wells for drinking purposes. Shortages of water, especially during the peak summer season, generate political controversies, tension and even violence between lower and upper riparian states over the waters of rivers that they share. While the country is not "water starved" as some of the countries in the Middle East and Africa, excessive rains in one part of the country are often accompanied by water shortages and even drought in other parts of India.

In other words, reducing the dependence upon the monsoon for agriculture and allied industries is a major challenge facing the country. India's transformation from being a water-deficient country into a water-surplus one, and in the process ensuring stable agricultural production, would depend upon two closely linked Israeli accomplishments, namely, technology-aided production and better management.

Agriculture as an engine of change

Following the normalization of relations in January 1992, India was rather cautious about reaching out to Israel and sought to balance its traditional support for the Palestinians with its new approach towards Israel. This meant that there were only limited political exchanges between the two. The visit of Foreign Minister Shimon Peres in May 1993 and the visit of President Ezer Weizman in December–January 1996–1997 were the only high-level contacts between the two in the 1990s. Despite the overwhelming international support for the Oslo process, New Delhi's approach towards Israel was one of cautious balancing.

This resulted in Israel looking at India's federal structure – wherein individual states have autonomy over developmental issues – as allies and state governments as partners. Unlike the union government, the state governments' mandate is different and their engagement with foreign countries is governed by economic, not political consideration. They wish to benefit from Israel's expertise in areas such as agriculture, water management and investments and are far removed from political issues such as the Middle East peace process and Palestinian statehood. In May 1993, Sharad Pawar, then with the Congress party, became the first Indian chief minister to visit Israel and he was followed by his counterparts in other states. Before long, one could notice a consensus. Irrespective of their political stance towards Israel and its policies concerning the Palestinians, state chief ministers adopted a non-discriminatory policy for seeking Israeli assistance. The crowning moment was the visit by West Bengal Chief Minister Jyoti Basu to Israel in the summer of 2000. The process of de-centralization has been the key component of Indo-Israeli relations (Kumaraswamy, 2017).

The primacy of agriculture has been visible since 1992 and one of the first visitors to Israel was the noted agricultural scientist M.S. Swaminathan, who visited Israel in June 1992, shortly after the embassy was opened in Tel Aviv. This was followed by the visit of Union Agricultural Minister Balram Jakhar, in July 1993, and since then, many union agricultural ministers have been visiting the Jewish state. Various state governments also have been sending delegations of farmers, agricultural experts and ministers to Israel to benefit from the latter's expertise.

The Indo-Israeli Agricultural Project (IIPA) which was concluded in 2006 between the Indian ministry of agriculture and the Israeli Agency for International Developmental Cooperation (MASHAV) under its foreign ministry was a major milestone. The primary objectives of this arrangement which has been operative since 2008 are: increasing crop diversity, productivity and resource use efficiency (MASHAV, n.d.). Conscious of the need for periodic monitoring and improvements, the project was extended and by January 2021, around 29 CoEs were established in 12 states and over 60,000 farmers were trained in floriculture, fruits and vegetable cultivation and in beekeeping. Around 17 new Israeli crop varieties of capsicum, tomatoes and cucumbers were introduced in the centres (Israel Ministry of Foreign Affairs, 2021; MASHAV, n.d.). Under the project, Israel has committed to establishing 30 Centres of Excellence (CoE) in different parts of the country through which its "technologies and know-how are disseminated" (Patil, 2016). As stakeholders, state governments are responsible for the allocation of "staff, land and budget" (MASHAV, n.d.: 25).Phase one and two of the project covered nine states, namely Bihar, Gujarat, Haryana, Karnataka, Maharashtra, Punjab, Rajasthan, Tamil Nadu and Uttar Pradesh.

As of December 2017, 15 out of the 26 CoEs that Israel had committed are fully operational in seven states, namely Andhra Pradesh, Chhattisgarh, Goa, Madhya Pradesh, Mizoram, Telangana and West Bengal. Thus, at present, the IIPA is in operation in 16 states ruled by the BJP, Congress and various regional parties, thereby indicating the non-partisan approach of the state governments from benefiting from Israel and its agricultural expertise (Table 8.1). Each CoE focuses on a specific area to maximize the results;

Table 8.1 List of CoEs in India

States	*Produce*	*Location*
Bihar	Mango and litchi	Vaishali
	Vegetables	Nalanda
Gujarat	Mango	Junagadh
	Vegetables – protected cultivation	Vadrad, Sabarkantha
	Date and banana-palm post-harvest management	Nani, Reladi, Bhuj
Haryana	Vegetables	Gharaunda, Karnal
	Fruits	Mangiana
	Beekeeping	Kurukshetra
	Animal husbandry and milk	Hisar
	Mango	Ladwa
	Flowers	Hisar
Karnataka	Mango	Kolar
	Pomegranate	Bagalkot
	Vegetables	Dharwad
Maharashtra	Alfonso mango	Dapoli
	Citrus	Nagpur
	Pomegranate	Rahuri
	Kesharmango	Aurangabad
Punjab	Fruits	Ghanora, Hoshiarpur
	Vegetables	Jalandhar
Rajasthan	Citrus	Kota
	Pomegranate	Bassi
	Date palm	Jaisalmer
	Vegetables	Bassi
Tamil Nadu	Flowers	Thally, Krishnagiri
	Vegetables	Reddiyar Chathram, Dindigul
Uttar Pradesh	Vegetables	Basti
	Mango	Basti
	Vegetables	Kannauj
West Bengal	Vegetables	Adi Saptagram, Hooghly District

Source: MASHAV, n.d. – Israel's Agency for International Development Cooperation

seven of them focus on mangoes and vegetables; four on citrus; three on pomegranates; two on dates; two on flowers; one each on beekeeping and dairy.

Israel's role includes imparting technologies through demonstration in CoEs; field training in micro-irrigation; planting of nurseries for sale and distribution to other farmers; plug-seeding technology, cultivation and distribution of hybrid seeds; protected cultivation; computerized irrigation and fertigation; and minimizing the use of fertilizers through better cultivation techniques. In addition to the activities under the IIPA, since the mid-1990s, a large number of farmers from rural India are taking part in the AgriTech exhibition held in Tel Aviv annually. Estimates suggest that over 20,000 farmers visit these CoEs and benefit directly through field demonstrations and interactions. While there are no nationwide estimates of the impact of the CoEs upon India's agriculture, reports indicate that there have been significant increases in yields per acre, often to the tune of six to ten times more than the yields under traditional cultivation methods. There is also a substantial decrease in the quantities of water, pesticides and fertilizers used (ibid.).

Besides the IIPA, both countries recognize the "strategic" importance of water for strengthening their bond and in the joint statement issued during Prime Minister Modi's visit to Israel, both countries agreed to:

> establish a "Strategic Partnership in Water and Agriculture". This will focus on water conservation, waste-water treatment and its reuse for agriculture, desalination, water utility reforms, and the cleaning of the Ganges and other rivers using advanced water technologies. It will also include the reinforcement and expansion of the existing Centres of Excellence (COE) under the stewardship of the Israeli Ministry of Foreign Affairs (MASHAV) and the Ministry of Agriculture of India to promote commercially viable business models involving Farmer Producer Organizations (FPOs); the provision of quality planting material; and the transfer of post-harvest technical know-how and market linkages involving the private sector through PPP, B2B & other models. The two leaders also agreed on the establishment of a Joint Working Group to steer this Partnership.
>
> (Ministry of External Affairs, 2017)

During their walkabout on the Mediterranean coast, Prime Ministers Modi and Netanyahu rode in the *Gal-Mobile*, a water desalinization and purification jeep which suggests that probably India would like to use this kind of option in its own fields. Another company has developed EWA (Extraction of Water from Air) technology and an operational model has been functioning in the Israeli embassy in New Delhi. This showcasing of new technologies which will be beneficial for the agriculture sector gives an indication that in years to come India might want to use such technologies to harness its agricultural yields.

All these have forced a fundamental shift in the media discourse on Israel. Until recently, security issues dominated the media and academic discussions and the de-centralization of the bilateral relations rarely evoked interests. Issues such as agriculture, water management, desalination, recycling and waste management were seen as being too trivial to merit academic or media attention. Much to the consternation and disappointment of many pundits and experts, both countries did not sign or announce any major defence deals during the visit of Modi to Israel in July 2017 (Ministry of External Affairs, 2017) or of Netanyahu to India in January 2018 (Ministry of External Affairs, 2018). While cyber security figured prominently during both visits, its application has been mostly directed at sensitive non-military areas such as bank transactions and the protection of biometric data under *Aadhaar* and similar other applications.

One could list some of the agricultural practices of Israel which would be beneficial for India if they were adapted to local conditions and demands. These include use of marginal, saline and recycled water for irrigation; micro-irrigation projects and fertigation methods to reduce water usage and maximize yields; development of disease-free nurseries of high-yielding vegetables and fruits; development of protected as against open cultivation to increase the cycle of cultivation beyond the *rabi* and *kharif* seasons and to increase agricultural production; controlled drainage and runoff to intensify and improve the productivity of horticultural crops such as fruits, vegetables and flowers; introduction of hybrid varieties of seeds and rootstocks; using post-harvest technologies to increase the shelf life and ensure a higher quality of the produce; and development of allied industries such as floriculture, horticulture, aquaculture, dairy and farming. However, given the diversity in soil type, salinity in the water, climatic and weather conditions and agricultural practices in the country, these methods need to be employed with utmost care.

In terms of allied sectors, water management acquires priority. For example, of the 160 million hectares of cultivable land in India, only about 65 million hectares or 41% is under irrigation and the rest is rain-fed. As of 2017, about 81% of the total area under cultivation in the country is dependent upon micro-irrigation. The distribution becomes problematic when one looks at the micro-irrigation in the country. The overall level of the efficiency of micro-irrigation through drip irrigation technology is 80–90% which drops to 50–70% through sprinklers but slips to 30–35% if traditional surface irrigation is adopted. Hence, water-surplus states such as Uttar Pradesh, Bihar, Punjab and Haryana, etc. could reduce their agricultural usage of water, if they were to shift from surface irrigation to drip irrigation techniques (NITI Aayog, 2017).

Challenges and opportunities

Some of the challenges facing bilateral relations for improving India's food security situation are institutional and systemic. Procedural delays and administrative inefficiency came to symbolize post-independent India's approach to state policies. Even though agriculture has emerged as the major issue of cooperation since the early 1990s, the IIPA came into force only in 2008. This pattern was reflected in the general focus of the bilateral relations which moved away from the hard-core security issues only during the visit of Prime Minister Modi in 2017, a quarter of a century after normalization.

Establishing – CoEs in a foreign country is not an insignificant achievement for Israel both in terms of size and scope. Since its establishment as a capacity building programme division – within the foreign ministry – MASHAV has been at the forefront of promoting Israeli foreign policy interests. With limited economic leverage and in spite of its non-membership in various Third World bodies such as the Non-aligned Movement and Group of 77, it has been working with various countries and communities to bring about a grassroots transformation and in the process improve Israel's relations with those countries. For example, even before political relations were established in 1992, India benefitted from cooperation in agriculture and allied industries.

At the same time, seen within the magnitude of the Indian problems and challenges, these CoEs are just a drop in the ocean. There is a need for hundreds of such centres in Indian states, which will help millions of farmers and agricultural workers. In other words, their scale and size are not adequate for Indian requirements. Asking Israel to multiply these numbers is unrealistic and unfair and therefore both sides have to work towards transforming these CoEs into incubators which would replicate their experience, expertise and methods through hundreds of clones without diluting their quality and impact. This would be a Herculean task for India, whose public and private sectors are not tuned to thinking big in terms of size and deliverables. Moreover, there are management issues with regard to types of crops given priority in the CoEs as most are cash crops which are good income generators but do not cater to securing India's food requirements.

The Israeli experience was imported but developed locally to meet its challenges and hurdles. Desalination, for example, was its response to water shortage along with drip irrigation techniques, when the amount of water available for agriculture was scarce. The same can be said about the high-yielding variety of vegetables and fruits which became necessary when domestic supplies were inadequate and imports costly. In other words, developing agricultural techniques and technologies for addressing domestic problems and challenges is the lesson India should learn from Israel. While Israel's willingness to help India through training, technology and transfers would considerably reduce its challenges, the long-term solution rests on the ability of India and its citizens, especially farmers, agricultural scientists and other stakeholders to invest their resources and attention in evolving timely and cost-effective responses to the challenges facing agriculture.

With the advent of the COVID-19 pandemic, it is projected that the global economy will be hampered drastically and various sectors of the economy in the country will be impacted. With the current pandemic, crisis in food sector looms large especially when India fares extremely low at both Global Hunger Index (102 out of 117 countries in 2019) (GHI, 2019) and Global Poverty Index (ranks 49th) wherein over more than 360 million Indians cannot afford a decent three square meals a day (Anthony, 2019; Singh, 2020). However, while professional services (–17.3%) and other sectors will be the worst hit by the pandemic, agriculture and allied sectors (–1.3%) will be among the least impacted (Keelery, 2020; Singh, 2020). Another estimate suggested that India produced 2,516.67 kgs of rice, wheat and coarse cereals per hectare of land on an annual basis prior to the outbreak of the virus and the plan was to double the produce by 2030 which may not be unachievable given that most of the migrant workers have returned to the villages and will probably be working in the agricultural sector (*The New Indian Express*, 2020). However, to yield optimum results will require well-structured planning. Additionally, according to an April 2020 report by the NITI Aayog, "the farm sector is poised to grow" by 3% despite the disruption in the economy by COVID-19 and continues to be the "beacon of hope" amidst the crisis (Haq, 2020). The report noted that there has been an increase in rice plantation areas by 37%, and owing to larger summer crop areas being planted and higher sales of fertilizers and seeds, the sector has flourished and food production has increased by 3.7% (Singh, 2020; Haq, 2020). There is still a need for advanced technologies, fertilizers and capital for the farmers to perform adequately and to contribute decently to the GDP, especially when other sectors of the economy have suffered. This can be facilitated by further cooperation and collaboration with Israel.

While increasing the *availability* aspect of food security, India should pay equal attention to the other three components of the food security debate, namely, *accessibility*, *utilization* and *stability* of food. These are independent of Israel and its expertise and cannot be addressed by external intervention or help. In other words, Israel's expertise and its willingness to share its experience and expertise in meeting its food security demands, though helpful, will be insufficient for solving India's long-term problems. Rather than "importing" Israeli successes, India should be learning from the Israeli experience and apply its approaches to its problems and develop its own responses to food security challenges. This, however, will need decades of persistent endeavour and, above all, innovation and mental transformation.

References

Algemeiner, 2017. "Sea of Galilee Hits All Time Low Recorded Water Level", June 7, 2017, URL: https://www.algemeiner.com/2017/06/07/sea-of-galilee-hits-all-time-low-recorded-water-level/, Accessed on 20 October 2017.

Cohen, Amiram, 2007. "Israel to Import Water from Turkey", *Ha'aretz*, August 7, 2007, URL: https://www.haaretz.com/1.5038640, Accessed on 20 October 2017.

Community data.gov.in, 2016. "Average Milk Yield from Indigenous/Non-Descript Cows in India During 2014–15", October 14, 2016, Government of India, URL: https://community.data.gov.in/average-milk-yield-from-indigenousnon-descript-cows-in-india-during-2014-15/, Accessed on 15 October 2017.

Directorate of Economics and Statistics, 2011. "Agricultural Statistics at a Glance 2011",Department of Agriculture, Cooperation of Farmers Welfare, Ministry of Agriculture and Farmers Welfare, Government of India, URL: http://eands.dacnet.nic.in/latest_20011.htm, Accessed on 15 October 2017.

FAO, 1996. "Rome Declaration of World Food Security and World Food Summit Plan of Action", FAO, Rome, 1996, URL: www.fao.org/docrep/003/w3613e/w3613e00.HTM, Accessed on 15 October 2017.

FAO-IFAD-UNICEF-WFP-WHO, 2017. *The State of Food Security and Nutrition in the World 2017*, Building Resilience for Peace and Food Security, FAO, Rome, 2017, URL: http://www.fao.org/3/a-I7695e.pdf, Accessed on 15 October 2017.

FAO-IFAD-WFP, 2015. *The State of Food Insecurity in the World*, Meeting the 2015 International Hunger Targets: Taking Stock of Uneven Progress, FAO, Rome, 2015, URL: http://www.fao.org/3/a-i4646e.pdf, Accessed on 15 October 2017.

Frenkel, Elad, 2017. "The Effects of Water Quality Treatment on Agriculture", Israel Agriculture International Portal, *Israel Agri*, August 7, 2017, URL: http://www.israelagri.com/?CategoryID=395&ArticleID=1459, Accessed on 23 October 2017.

Global Hunger Index, 2019. "2019 Global Hunger Index by Severity", URL: https://www.globalhungerindex.org/results.html, Accessed on 26 May, 2020.

Haq, Zia, 2020. "https://www.hindustantimes.com/india-news/farm-sector-a-beacon-of-hope-in-economic-gloom/story-YEsFZcYnq76VGI41ic5zzM.html", *The Hindustan Times*, 24 May 2020, , Accessed on 30 May 2020.

Indexmundi, 2018. "Israel Economy Profile 2018", URL: https://www.indexmundi.com/israel/economy_profile.html, See Also: Israeli Ministry of Economy and Industry, 2016. *The Israeli Economy at a Glance, Research and Economic Administration*, 2016. URL: http://www.economy.gov.il/Research/Documents/The%20Israel%20Economy%20At%20a%20Glance%202016.pdf, Accessed on 23 May 2018.

ISHITECH, *Israel Hi-Tech and Investment Report*, 2012. "12,000 Litres Milk per Cow!" January 2012, URL: http://www.ishitech.co.il/0112ar9.htm, Accessed on 15 October 2017.

Israel Ministry of Foreign Affairs, 2021. "The Indo-Israel Agriculture Project in India", *MASHAV, Israel*, January 18, 2021, URL: https://mfa.gov.il/mfa/mashav/latest_news/pages/the-indo-israel-agriculture-project-in-india.aspx, Accessed on 4 November 2021.

Keelery, Sandhya, 2020. "Estimated Economic Impact from the Coronavirus (Covid-19) on India between April and June 2020, by Sector GVA", *Statista*,

14 May 2020, URL: https://www.statista.com/statistics/1107798/india-estimated-economicimpact-of-coronavirus-by-sector/, Accessed on 30 May 2020.

Kumaraswamy, P. R., 2017. "Redefining 'Strategic Cooperation'", *Strategic Analysis*, Vol. 41, Issue 4, July–August, 355–368.

—2018. "Reading Modi's Visit to Israel", *India Quarterly*, Vol. 74, Issue 1, March 18, 2018, 1–16, URL: http://journals.sagepub.com/doi/abs/10.1177/0974928417749644.

—2010. *India's Israel Policy*, New York: Columbia University Press, July 2010.

Kumaraswamy, P. R. and Singh, Manjari, 2018. "Jordan's Food Security Challenges", *Mediterranean Quarterly*, Vol. 29, Issue 1, 2018, 70–95, URL: https://read.dukeupress.edu/mediterranean-quarterly/article-abstract/29/1/70/134105/Jordan-s-Food-Security-Challenges, Accessed on 19 December 2019.

MASHAV, n.d. "The Indo-Israeli Agricultural Project", Israel's Agency for International Development Cooperation, Israeli Ministry of Foreign Affairs, URL: http://www.mfa.gov.il/MFA/mashav/Publications/Subject_Publications/Documents/Indo-Israeli%20Agricultural%20Project.pdf, Accessed on 4 November 2021.

Ministry of External Affairs, 2017. "India-Israel Joint Statement during the Visit of Prime Minster to Israel", July 5, 2017, URL: http://www.mea.gov.in/bilateral-documents.htm?dtl/28593/IndiaIsrael_Joint_Statement_during_the_visit_of_Prime_Minister_to_Israel_July_5_2017, Accessed on 23 October 2017.

—2018. "India-Israel Joint Statement during Visit of Prime Minister of Israel to India", January 15, 2018, URL: http://www.mea.gov.in/bilateral-documents.htm?dtl/29357/IndiaIsrael+Joint+Statement+during+visit+of+Prime+Minister+of+Israel+to+India+January+15+2018, Accessed on 26 February 2018.

Navin, Anthony, 2019. "Poverty Index: India Rank 49", *The Week*, 17 August 2019, https://www.theweek.in/theweek/cover/2019/08/17/poverty-index-indiarank-49.html, Accessed on 26 May 2020.

Newmann, Marissa, 2017. "1.8 Million Israelis, 842,000 of Them under Poverty Line – Report", *The Times of Israel*, Jerusalem, December, 6, 2017, URL: https://www.timesofisrael.com/1-8-million-israelis-842000-of-them-children-under-poverty-line-report/, Accessed on 7 January 2018.

NITIAayog, 2017. "From the Source to the Roots", Guidelines for Micro Irrigation Through Public-Private Partnership, Draft Concept Note, Government of India, October 2017, URL: http://niti.gov.in/writereaddata/files/document_publication/Draft%20Concept%20Paper%20on%20PPP%20in%20Microirrigation_Oct%202017.pdf, Accessed on 7 January 2018.

Patil, Vijay Kumar, 2016. "Israel Plans to Setup 30 Centres of Excellence in India to Train Farmers", September 6, 2016, URL: http://www.thehindu.com/news/national/karnataka/israel-plans-to-set-up-30-centres-of-excellence-in-india-to-train-farmers/article6923728.ece, Accessed on 23 October 2017.

PHDCCI (PHD Chamber of Commerce and Industry), 2019. "India Ranks at 102nd place in Global Hunger Index 2019", URL: https://www.phdcci.in/wp-content/uploads/2019/10/India-ranks-at-102nd-place-in-Global-Hunger-Index-2019.pdf, Accessed on 4 November 2021.

Press Information Bureau, 2017. Ministry of Agriculture and Farmers Welfare, Government of India, August 16, 2017, URL: http://pib.nic.in/newsite/PrintRelease.aspx?relid=170036, Accessed on 23 October 2017.

Rai, Saritha, 2013. "Soaring Onion Prices in India Catch a Government Napping", *Forbes*, October 25, 2013, URL: https://www.forbes.com/sites/saritharai/2013/10/25/soaring-onion-prices-in-india-catch-a-government-napping/#6f18f51a38db, Accessed on 15 October 2017.

Rinat, Zafrir, 2017. "Desalination Problems Begin to Rise to the Surface in Israel", *Ha'aretz*, February 6, 2017, URL: https://www.haaretz.com/israel-news/.premium-desalination-problems-begin-to-rise-to-the-surface-in-israel-1.5494726, Accessed on 21 October 2017.

Shaked, Oren, 2016. "Israel: Grain and Feed Annual", USDA Foreign Agricultural Service, May 4, 2016, URL: https://gain.fas.usda.gov/Recent%20GAIN%20Publications/Grain%20and%20Feed%20Annual_Tel%20Aviv_Israel_4-5-2016.pdf, Accessed on 15 October 2017.

Singh, Manjari, 2020. "India's Alarming Call: Need for Greater Sustainability", pp. 25–44, in Ahluwalia, V. K. and Jash, Amrita (eds), *COVID-19 & Its Challenges: Is India Future Ready?*, Pentagon Press, New Delhi.

UNDP, 2016. "Zero Hunger: Why It Matters", 2016, URL: http://www.un.org/sustainabledevelopment/wp-content/uploads/2016/08/2_Why-it-Matters_ZeroHunger_2p.pdf, Accessed on 15 October 2017.

United Nations in India, 2016. "SDG 1: No Poverty", 2016, URL: http://in.one.un.org/page/sustainable-development-goals/sdg-1/, See Also: Bahri, Charu, 2017. "Can India Meet Sustainable Development Goals on Poverty, Hunger, Despite Sluggish Economy?" Odhisa, October 14, 2017, URL: https://www.hindustantimes.com/india-news/can-india-meet-sustainable-development-goals-on-poverty-hunger-despite-sluggish-economy/story-8NlIxkeBpS2pcm420YjN7O.html, Accessed on 15 October 2017.

Weatheronline, n.d. "Israel and Palestine", URL: https://www.weatheronline.co.uk/reports/climate/Israel-and-Palestine.htm, Accessed on 4 November 2021.

Chapter 9

The G20 and India's food security concerns

Arpita Anant

Sustainable Development Goal 2 aims to eliminate hunger, achieve food security and improve nutrition by the year 2030. The Global Hunger Index (GHI) 2019, however, points out that going by the current trends of progress, 45 countries will fail to achieve these targets (Von Grebmer et al., 2019). On the GHI severity scale of 100 points, 0 is the best score and 100 is the worst. A score of less than, or equal to, 9.9 is regarded as low, 10.0–19.9 moderate, 20.0–34.9 serious and 35.0–49.9 alarming (ibid.).

According to the GHI 2020, nine of the G20 countries, namely Australia, Canada, France, Germany, Italy, Japan, South Korea, the United Kingdom and the United States, have no serious food security issues. Among the remaining ten, India, Indonesia and South Africa are the only three countries that have double-digit scores on the GHI; only India falls in the "serious category" of hunger scores, with a score of 27.2. (Von Grebmer et al., 2020). This illustrates the importance, as well as limitations, of focusing on the G20 to address issues relating to food security. Going by the GHI scores there are those, among the G20 countries, that have completely resolved their own food-related issues, there are others that have done well over the years as their economies improved, and still others that still have substantial issues to address. More importantly, these are economically significant countries that have taken upon themselves, the responsibility of reforming the global governance of issues other than finance, food being one among them. They are therefore collectively responsible for setting the right norms that would ameliorate food security issues for the vulnerable people, in their own countries and other more vulnerable ones. While the GHI scores highlight the geographical areas of concern for hunger-related issues, they do not tell the whole story. The story is incomplete without an understanding of the domestic issues of a country, the global politics and economics of food production and distribution, and the resultant regime of the global governance of food.

This chapter focuses on food security issues in India and seeks to understand whether the evolving G20's norms on food security are in line with India's food security concerns. It argues that being a part of the

DOI: 10.4324/9781003272656-9

G20 allowed a developing country narrative, in this case that of India, to become the big powers' narrative. Moreover, several concerns that date back to the earliest UN development decades came back on the agenda of food security.

The first section examines the narrative of food security and the complex terrain it has had to traverse. The second section highlights the features of the global governance of food security since the end of World War II and identifies the lingering lacunae in the global governance of food-related issues. The third section looks at the role of the G20, as an informal institution of global governance and investigates how it has sought to address issues of food security. The fourth section dwells on India's concerns and position on food security in multilateral forums. The conclusion combines the findings of the preceding sections to posit whether the G20 norms on food security are in line with India's food security concerns.

The global food security narrative

As it evolved, the narrative on food security has traversed a complex terrain. The post-World War II years witnessed the rise of the contemporary international system, which inherited a world that was steeped in an agricultural division of labour. Colonial powers such as the United Kingdom were dependent on their colonies for some food items, while the former colonies were dependent on importing other items. As the colonies started becoming independent, both encountered food shortages of various kinds. Meanwhile, the United States and some other countries in the Commonwealth, mainly Canada and Australia, had huge surpluses of staple grains. The transfers of staple food grains, through trade or as aid, became an important component of international relations. They were, however, largely unregulated, since agriculture did not fall within the purview of any multilateral institutional arrangement. The first food crisis in the 1970s, in the wake of the rising oil prices and the consequent increase in fertilizer prices that led to reduced production of food in many developing countries, made food security an important issue in multilateral forums. In 1974, the World Food Summit was held and defined food security as "availability at all times of adequate world food supplies of basic foodstuffs to sustain a steady expansion of food consumption and to offset fluctuations in production and prices" (Chang et al., 2013). By the 1980s, the path-breaking study of Amartya Sen on world hunger shifted the focus to access and distribution of food (Clapp, 2014). The World Food Summit in 1996 offered a holistic definition of food security that consisted of four dimensions: availability, stability, access and utilization of food. Thus, "food security exists when all people at all times have access to sufficient, safe, nutritious food to maintain a healthy and active life" (Chang et al., 2013).

Come the 1990s, in order to deal with the rising debt of developing countries, the IMF and the World Bank rolled out loans conditional on structural adjustment (Burnett, 2014). This exacerbated the global agricultural division of labour which forced developing countries to export cash crops to pay their debts, thereby taking them further away from the production of food crops (Parra et al., 2015). This and the WTO's Agreement on Agriculture compelled the withdrawal of governments in developing countries from their agriculture sector and led to the monopoly of large multinational corporations and businesses in agriculture, spearheaded by initiatives such as the Sustainable Agriculture Initiative of Danone, Nestle and Unilever, joined by Kellogg's, Kraft, McDonald's, PepsiCo and Sara Lee in 2008 (Lang and Barling, 2012). Corporations such as Monsanto and Syngenta used this situation to push their case for the sale of technologically improved varieties of crops to developing countries, even when these were not staple food crops like cowpea, millet, sorghum/cassava, or quinoa. Studies have shown that the nutritional value of food crops had diminished due to a combination of biophysical factors associated with changing agricultural practices, which had also brought the widespread loss of farmland to other uses, a shortfall in freshwater for irrigation, erosion and degradation of soils, decreasing returns from the use of fertilizers, issues associated with chemical control of pests, declining genetic diversity of crops, low yields due to exposure to ultraviolet-B radiation, air pollutants and rapid climate change (Ehrlich et al., 1993). The end result was an increase in the vulnerability of small farmers in rural areas of developing countries. In urban areas, informal retailers outside of government regulation and supermarkets also started to play a larger role in making food available (Parra et al., 2015).

Approximately a decade ago, many countries experienced rapid increases in the price of food, despite high levels of production. This triggered yet another food crisis in 2007–2008. Some argued that the price rise occurred due to increased demand for protein-rich food in Asia (Collier, 2008: 69). Contrarily, it was posited that the high demand for energy in Asia led to the rise in the price of fuels, which in turn raised the cost of transporting the food and fertilizers that were produced by using the over-priced fossil fuels (Naim, 2008: 96). Yet others argued that shortages in food and rise in food prices were triggered by the world financial crisis in 2007–2008 (Sundaram, 2011). The crisis led to a rise in the production of biofuels (Collier, 2008; Naim, 2008), increased investment in commodity futures with raised spot prices, increased speculation, asset diversification from financial markets to new areas of investment, reduced government investment in agriculture research leading to private TNCs taking control over innovative research, economic deregulation favouring cheaper food imports from EU countries that subsidize agriculture over domestic production, further loss of cropland due to urbanization and further environmental degradation associated with the preference for meat over vegetarian diet (Sundaram, 2011). It was also argued that the 2007–2008 food crisis was triggered by a system under stress, which also included, among other causes, the FAO's three-pronged approach to food security consisting of the three As of accessibility, affordability and availability, rather than the five As of availability, adequacy, accessibility, acceptability and agency to produce sustainable food systems (Lang and Barling, 2012: 317). In these circumstances, there was a resurgence of the idea of creating reserves of grains. Despite a strong push for this from some quarters, this had not previously materialized, since it was felt that food prices were quite stable and buying food in the world market was an equally viable option (Mousseau, 2009). The World Bank endorsed a proposal put forward by the International Food Policy Research Institute (IFPRI) to create a global food reserve with virtual and physical components. As described by Mousseau (ibid.: 79):

> The "virtual" system would be a fund supported by pledges from big exporting countries, which would be used to intervene in grain futures markets and discourage speculation, when prices rise. The notion of a virtual reserve is based on the idea that speculation on futures markets for grain and other commodities, is a key factor in price increases, which would be curbed by such a mechanism.

It was also posited that the shift towards sustainable food systems would require integrity and competence in public administration, security, stability and order, property rights, competition through trade rather than parastatals (state-owned enterprises), sound macroeconomic policies such as fiscal responsibility, monetary restraint, appropriate tax policies to attract investments, a good trade policy with protection for infant industries, investment in research, environment, sanitation, health and infrastructure and a sound public income and food safety net supported by the private sector and religious organizations (Tweeten, 1999: 479).

Global governance of food

The governance of food-related issues at the global level has been subject to the vagaries of the geopolitics of food aid bilaterally as well as in various multilateral institutions that were set up in the post-World War II world to address food-related issues, such as the Food and Agriculture Organization (FAO), the IMF, the World Bank and the WTO (Hopkins, 1992).

In the realm of food aid, there were important changes, from aid being seen as a bilateral mechanism for the disposal of agricultural surpluses, or export promotion or being sent to "friendly countries" during the Cold War (Nau, 1978), to being characterized as a strategy for attaining world food security and for serving humanitarian causes in conflicts (Unvin, 1992). Several multilateral institutions too were created for disbursal of aid, prominent among them being the World Food Programme, created jointly by the UN General Assembly and the FAO in 1963, through which nearly 25% of the food and emergency aid was channelled (ibid.: 303). This was a result of the world food crisis of the 1970s, as well as ideological changes in the donor countries, especially the United States, where in 1977, the PL480 legislation was given the additional nomenclature of "Food for Development" in recognition of the need for food aid (ibid.). In the 1980s, the EEC, new OECD countries, as well as China, Saudi Arabia, India, Turkey and the OPEC countries became aid givers, even though they were not themselves surplus producers yet.

The FAO, which was set up in 1954 under the aegis of the UN, was the first among the multilateral institutions to address the issue of food shortages. It was, however, not very successful in doing so, since this was the era when the United States as one of the two superpowers was determined to continue to use its increased agricultural productivity as a foreign policy tool, rather than allow the FAO to emerge as a strong actor. There was thus a tussle between those who believed that world trade and the ability to buy food in the world market were the best ways to deal with food shortages and those who felt that reducing world hunger was "a collective moral, ethical and social responsibility, and that people have right to food" (Jarosz, 2009: 38) This also generated other tensions between those who wanted the FAO to be a governing institution that would set the norms for dealing with food shortages, and others, mostly those appointed with the support of the United States, feeling that it should just be a forum for discussion of statistics.

The third fault line was between food technologists who dominated the work of the FAO and favoured the transfer of green revolution technologies from the North to the South versus those wanting to address the issue of food holistically by looking into issues of energy, trade, aid, food pricing. While the former idea won out at the FAO, its concurrent idea of developing locally resistant varieties and food reserves did not materialize. The FAO was further weakened by the setting up of the World Food Programme (WFP) in 1963 to steer emergency food aid deliveries, and the formation of the International Fund of Agricultural Development (IFAD) in 1977 and the World Food Council (WFC) in 1975 to create food reserves. IFAD and WFC were outcomes of the World Food Conference, held to deliberate upon the issue of food shortages in developing countries in the wake of the oil crisis (see Nau, 1978: 799). As issues of food price volatility began affecting developing countries, they demanded the conclusion of an International Grain Price Agreement, which did not materialize due to the lack of consensus. Nothing could be done about the structural adjustment programmes of the World Bank which forced developing countries to produce cash crops to repay their debts, at the cost of producing grains for their domestic food requirements. By the 1990s, the discourse on liberalization of trade as a panacea for food security came to dominate. The FAO became even more powerless to bring about any change in the stock and pricing policies of the developed countries.

The inter-relatedness of food-related issues, characterized by chronic food shortages in South Asia and Africa, instability in supply, together with price fluctuations, unpredictable markets and undependable trade flows, insecurity vis-à-vis food imports, low productivity of agriculture in LDCs and chronic malnutrition, made it, what was termed as, a "complex regime" (Hopkins and Puchala, 1978). The weakness of this complex regime stemmed from the fact that it was a coming together of national policies, internationally coordinated, with no involvement of the rural poor of the Third World either in the regime or in other specific issues such as production, storage and stockpiling or dis-incentivization of agriculture (ibid.: 600–601).

In more recent theoretical renderings, the complicated terrain of food issues has been characterized as a "regime complex" where divergent regimes overlap, deal with subjects rather than issue areas, and are narrower in scope (Orisini et al., 2013). This means that a regime complex can bring together a set of regimes linked by distinct and sometimes incompatible hierarchies. The global food security complex, it is argued, combines the international trade and finance, human rights and agriculture regimes (Margulis, 2013). On the one hand, the WTO's requirements made it imperative to liberalize agriculture, with some special safeguard measures permissible for a specific time, while at the same time, enforcing sanitary and phytosanitary measures, for ensuring food safety. These measures that favoured the Northern countries were opposed by the developing country coalition G-20 (distinct from the G20 that is the focus of this study) in the WTO. The human rights regime (the Office of the High Commissioner for Human Rights; the Committee on Economic, Social and Cultural Rights; and the Human Rights Council) together with the FAO seeks to take the discourse on food security to a higher level, by characterizing it as right to food. This normatively contradicts what the trade regime dictates. According to Burnett (2014: 360):

> When the WTO emerged as a central site of governance of global food security with the negotiations of the Agreement on Agriculture (AoA), it sought to govern using market forces. In response, the UN system, traditionally the location of international governance over hunger and food issues, launched a counter-movement within the negotiations to defend developing countries from sweeping liberalization policies.

In the same vein, Margulis (2013: 65) argues that: there is a strong divergence of views between the United States, international financial institutions and private actors (which are resistant to new public forms of regulation of commodities trading) and France, and most net food-importing developing countries, the UN system, and global civil society (which strongly support greater regulation of financial markets).

In the wake of the food crisis of 2007–2008, the Secretary-General of the UN set up a High-Level Task Force on the Global Food Crisis which prepared a Comprehensive Framework for Action (CFA) aimed particularly at addressing the food security issues of least developed countries. As a result, a four-pronged approach to food security was formulated at the multilateral level (Lang and Barling, 2012: 315). It consisted of ensuring a better emergency response for hunger relief and food aid, better management of information on food, harvests and national food stocks on an annual basis, increasing production by using high and low technology and finally reforming the FAO's Committee on Food Security (CFS), by involving members of civil society (ibid.: 315). The Framework arranged for more investments in safety nets, and for some structural adjustment including increasing investment in agriculture and, "connecting producers with access to essential agricultural resources" (Burnett, 2014: 358). It was supported by the G8 La Aquila Summit of 2008. In 2009, the World Bank initiated a trust fund called the Global Agriculture and Food Security Programme.

The present predicament of the global governance of food is described by some as a crisis in food-related multilateralism (Burnett, 2014) while others assert that it makes food security less amenable to governance outcomes (Margulis, 2013: 54).

The G20 and the governance of food

Within a neoliberal framework, the G20 is seen as a "network (that) is helping to produce modified variants of hegemony and collectivism within the system" (Beeson and Bell, 2009) thereby attempting to include new norms in some arenas of global governance. It is argued that after the gold standard was given up in 1971, there was space for revision of global economic governance, through informal multilateral forums such as the G5 which were formed in 1973. These were termed "multilateralism light". Many years later, in 1999, the G5 became the G20 (Madhur, 2012). The G20 has indeed played an important role in issues relating to global finance (Woods et al., 2013) – instituting reforms in the IMF governance system (Beeson and Bell, 2009), and the Financial Stability Board being among its most notable achievements (Cooper, 2010: 741). It has also played an advisory and intermediary role in the institutional division of labour in the taxation and energy regime complexes (Orsini et al., 2013: 37).

The alignment of emerging developing countries in the WTO managed to stall the Doha negotiations in Cancun in 2003 by forcing OECD countries to reduce agricultural subsidies before liberalizing trade in other sectors (Compagnon, 2012: 712). They were able to gain substantially in the framework agreement on agriculture against a combined US–EU draft (Kanth,

2004: 3796). Their eventual membership of the G20 has also been influential (Gallagher, 2015). On investment regulation, renamed investment protectionism, the OECD-UNCTAD were made to submit regular monitoring reports to the G20 to ensure liberalization, especially of the capital account. It is to the credit of the G20 that they have done so despite "the degree of the divergence in comparative historical experiences (including the scars of colonialism), regime types and conceptualization of global order" (Cooper, 2010: 743).

Once the urgent task of dealing with the financial crisis of 2008–2009 was addressed, the G20 added several developmental issues to its agenda. The G20 in its Pittsburgh Summit in 2009 urged the World Bank and multilateral development banks to revise their mandate to include the thrust on food security and other human development requirements. They urged the various UN agencies to coordinate with each other to help overcome food insecurity (G20, 2009). The Seoul Development Consensus for Shared Growth of 2010 included a Multi-Year Action Plan for Development. Its food security component had a two-point action plan for enhancing policy coordination and approach to mitigate the risks arising from price volatility to protect the vulnerable sections of the population (small farmers) against it (Margulis, 2013: 37). The various stakeholders in the process were FAO, IFAD, IMF, OECD, UNCTAD, WFP, the World Bank and WTO. It was agreed that from 2012, food security should be on the agenda of the G20 (Heap, 2011). The G20, at its France Summit in 2011, decided to focus on agriculture. The agriculture ministers of G20 countries created the Agricultural Market Information System (AMIS) for transparency in the agricultural commodity markets within the FAO, managed by the already experienced International Grains Council (G20, 2011). They also launched the International Research Initiative for Wheat Improvement (ibid.: Annex 1), the Global Agricultural Geo-monitoring Initiative, a Rapid Response Forum within AMIS, an Agriculture and Food Risk Management Toolbox, Emergency Humanitarian Food Reserves, on a small scale at the regional level. Meanwhile, the G20 ministers of agriculture provided assistance for food security measures in developing countries along with the expertise for solving food security-related problems (IFPRI, 2012: 69–78). The 2012 G20 Summit, which was held in Mexico, turned the focus on small family farms. An interagency report on the food crisis was prepared for the Mexican presidency of G20 (Biodiversity International et al., 2012). The Mexico Summit supported the work of the UN World Food Committee on better use of fisheries, land and forests programmes, for small farm holders. and for improving the Agriculture Innovation Systems (G20, 2012).

The 2013 St Petersburg Action Plan made no reference to food security, while the Leaders' Declaration emphasized the importance of agricultural productivity, investment and trade to ensure food security and job creation (G20, 2013). As requested by the G20, the FAO and OECD prepared a "G20

Food Security and Nutrition Framework". The framework was endorsed by the G20 in 2014 (G20, 2014). The framework has a food system's approach that goes beyond the agriculture sector (FAO et al., 2014). The framework was geared to benefit low-income countries as well. Its main concern was human nutrition with a focus on women, youth and small farm holders. Its first priority was to increase responsible investment in the food systems; the second was to raise incomes and quality employment in food systems; while the third priority was to increase productivity sustainably to improve food supply. All of this was to be overseen by the Development Working Group and steps were to be taken to ensure that there was no duplication of the work that other organizations were engaged in.

The Istanbul Summit of the G20 in 2015 stated that the Development Working Group which coordinates action on food security had identified poverty as the main cause of food insecurity. Listed among the achievements on the food security front were:

> the 2011 Action Plan on Food Price Volatility and Agriculture and included the Agricultural Market Information System (AMIS), support to sustainable productivity improvement in particular through the Global Agriculture and Food Security Programme (GAFSP), support to the development and voluntary implementation of Principles for Responsible Agricultural Investment (RAI), the promotion of innovation through an annual Meeting of Agricultural Chief Scientists (MACS) and the Platforms for Agricultural Risk Management (PARM) and for Tropical Agriculture (TAP).
>
> (G20, 2015)

The Summit also resolved to support the Rome Declaration on Nutrition, adopted by the Second International Conference on Nutrition; Expo Milano 2015, on the theme of "Feeding the Planet: Energy for Life", and its many related events on food security and nutrition; voluntary Principles for Responsible Investment in Agriculture and Food Systems endorsed by the CFS in 2014 and the OECD policy framework for Investment in Agriculture; Voluntary Guidelines on the Responsible Governance of Tenure of Land; Fisheries and Forests in the Context of National Food Security (VGGT); recognition of the fundamental role of the multilateral trading system in global food security; and successful completion of WTO negotiations with a view to promptly conclude the Doha Development Agenda and ensure the success of the WTO Tenth Ministerial Conference at Nairobi, as also the Global Initiative for Food Loss and Waste Reduction (SaveFood) of FAO and IFPRI. It sought the guidance of FAO, IFAD, UNCTAD, the World Bank Group and OECD to operationalize these initiatives in interested countries and to improve the capacities of the standard-setting bodies such as CODEX Alimentarius, International Plant Protection Convention

(IPPC) and World Organisation for Animal Health (Office International des Epizooties, OIE) to provide scientific advice and guidance to all countries. In addition, the G20 Technical Platform for Measurement and Reduction of Food Loss and Waste was adopted in 2015.

The G20 agriculture ministers meeting of 2016 in China, supported the Addis Ababa Action Plan for North-South, South-South and trilateral cooperation to address food security issues (G20, 2016). It also committed itself to the SDGs' economic, social and environmental targets linking agriculture and inclusive rural development, poverty reduction and environmental protection. It pledged support for FAO's Globally Important Agricultural Heritage Systems (GIAHS) and WHO's global action plan on microbial resistance. It emphasized the importance of innovation and research and development and ICT platforms. It sought to set up Global Agriculture Research Platforms (GARPs) and a China-led working group on Agricultural Technology Sharing. It envisaged collaborating with the Global Forum of Leaders for Agricultural Science and Technology (GLAST), Global Conference on Agricultural Research for Development (GCARD) and the Tropical Agriculture Platform. Finally, it announced its support for the Global Partnership on Financial Inclusion, SME financing and remittance-based rural financial inclusion.

The Berlin Agriculture Minister's Meeting 2017 stressed upon food security for cities (G20, 2017). The G20 Agriculture Entrepreneurs Forum (AE20) was also set up. Support was extended for responsible investment in agriculture through Voluntary Guidelines on Responsible Governance of Tenure of Land, Fisheries and Forests in the Context of National Food Security and Principles for Responsible Investment in Agriculture and Food Systems endorsed by the CFS (CFS-RAI). It sought to build synergies between the Agriculture Deputies, the Development Working Group and the Trade and Investment Working Group. The Berlin declaration emphasized the implementation of the SDG agenda, UNFCCC and the Paris Agreement of 2015, and for engaging actively with the Subsidiary Body for Scientific and Technological Advice (SBSTA) to the UNFCCC on issues of agriculture. It established the discursive link between agriculture SDG 2 on agriculture and SDG 6 on water as part of "one health" (including building anti-microbial resistance).

The 2018 G20 agriculture ministers' meeting in Argentina acknowledged the importance of agriculture for climate change and reiterated its commitment to the Paris Agreement, in the light of the US withdrawal from it (G20, 2018). They aligned the G20 Food Security and Nutrition Framework with the Global Strategic Framework for Food Security and Nutrition of the Committee on World Food Security, to ensure a sustainable food future. They also committed to support international and national initiatives for ending hunger and malnutrition. The G20 also recognized the importance of small farmers and women in food security and outlined nine measures of support for these vulnerable groups engaged in agriculture. They urged the G20 Meeting of Agricultural Chief Scientists (MACS) to improve agricultural risk assessment. In addition, they reiterated their commitment to sustainable soil management; application of ICTs to agriculture; prevention of food loss and wastage; improving trade in agriculture though the WTO and creating responsible investment and supply chains; cooperation in building anti-microbial resistance in people, animals and the environment; as part of the "One Health" initiative. The 2019 G20 Agricultural Ministers' Declaration highlighted the need for creating a sustainable agro-food sector with the use of digital technology for creating better food value chains (G20, 2019). Finally, the 2020 Communique of Agriculture and Water Ministers endorsed the importance of Responsible Investment in Agriculture and Food Systems to help end world hunger (G20, 2020). It also reinforced the need for minimizing wastage of food.

Yet, to date, in the view of Basant Kumar Gupta, former permanent representative of India to the FAO, IFAD and WFP, the initiatives of the G20 have not been very significant and are at best the duplication of efforts of the FAO.[1] Critics have pointed out several shortcomings in the G20's action on streamlining food security-related issues. To begin with, the AMIS set up in 2011, has been dubbed as a minimalist step, considering the very serious lacunae in the regimes related to food such as commodity speculation, biofuel policies and the agricultural trade practices followed by the G20 countries themselves (Clapp et al., 2011; Clapp 2012a). The EU, the US, Brazil, Canada, China and Australia themselves invest heavily in biofuels and subsidize them, which distorts markets and diverts them from being used as food (Clapp, 2011). This is not very useful, since this function is already being performed by the FAO and the International Grains Council. Further, it is disheartening that the G20's agenda is now dictating the work of the UN Committee on Food Security (ibid.). Some other issues it could have delivered on are: reduction of biofuel subsidies; reduction of other harmful fossil fuel, producer as well as consumer subsidies and subsidies of fisheries (MacDonald, 2011) or even limiting itself to coordination among countries, to ensure a political commitment to development; and breakout technology, at the national level.

The Mexico Summit focused on issues of agricultural productivity like agricultural biotechnology, GM plants and private sector investment, but did not address any structural issues (Clapp, 2012b). Such a discourse is hence described as "neoliberal geopolitics", that provides "a securitized framing of food insecurity, where hunger is seen not only as a politically revolutionary force but also as a fount of secondary problems such as disease, terrorism, illicit drugs and refugees" (Sommerville et al., 2014: 242), and in which the "discourses on food security are constitutive of the very political economy that causes the food insecurity" (ibid.: 250).

The declarations of the G20, while somewhat indicative of the common thinking and evolving norms of the G20, do not indicate the individual preferences of the G20 countries, in other forums. For instance, at the WTO, India and the G33 group of 62 developing countries, insisted on subsidies for public stockholding, while several G20 countries such as Brazil, Canada, the US and the EU opposed them (Sen, 2017). The green box provisions of WTO similarly provide high subsidies to farmers of industrialized countries, which is not suitable for developing countries (Swaminathan, 2015c: 163). It is to this aspect that this study now turns, with a section focused on India.

India's food story in the global context

Currently, India has 17.3% of the world's population and 23.4% of the world's undernourished population (WFP India, 2017; 2018). In actual numbers, this means 190 million people and ranks India at number 100 out of 119 countries in the GHI of 2017. Issues of food security, however, have dogged the country since pre-independence times (Itteyerah, 2013). Interestingly, the story of food security in India is intertwined with that of several individual G20 countries. Colonial India was a crucial supplier of cereals to the United Kingdom. Independent India's food narrative would be incomplete without reference to some significant external engagements. They include food imports from the United States under the PL 480 regulation in the 1970s; the serious consideration accorded to Japan's Norin Experiment Station's semi-dwarf varieties of wheat (called Gaines) that could kick-start the Green Revolution in India; and the contact with Dr Orville Vogel in Pullman, Washington, and through him with Dr Norman Borlaug in Mexico, whose semi-dwarf varieties grown in tropical conditions were used to produce the *Kalyan Sona* and *Sonalika*, the Indian variants of the wheat (Swaminathan, 2015a: 3). To ensure that supply of wheat meets the demand, the minimum support price for the Mexican red coloured wheat, *Var Lerma Rojo* and its amber-coloured Indian variant were kept equal, at INR 65 per quintal, so as not to discourage imports. Notable also was the contribution of Dr Glen Anderson of Canada, who was associated with the All India Coordinated Wheat Improvement Project through the Rockefeller Foundation (ibid.: 6).

India's food security concerns were initially largely related to under-production. However, since India achieved self-sufficiency (Suryanarayan,1997), the narrative on food security is dominated by two issues: access or distribution, and the distress of small farmers (Vyas, 2003: 105). In the context of the former, the National Food Security Act (NFSA) was enacted in 2013, to address the ills of the system. According to government estimates, the law will cost the treasury at least $1.9 billion, which is $633 million above the current subsidy provided to the poor in various food rationing programmes. The programme offers a legal entitlement to cheap grain and millets, to

63.5% of the total population of India, 75% of whom live in rural India and 50% in urban India. About 46% of rural coverage will be for the benefit of "priority households", those which are below the poverty line, while 28% of the urban 50% will be allotted for such households. The rest will be for the general public, from households above the poverty line. A total of 7 kg of food grain per person, or 35 kg per family per month will be allotted for priority households and 3 kg per person per month for general households. General households will have to pay 50% of the minimum price. To ensure supply, production of food grains has to be increased from the present 54 million tonnes to 62 million tonnes (Hossain, 2014: 148). To ensure the fiscal viability of the Act, it was important to maintain the primary deficits/ GDP ratio below 1.5%, by way of a periodic upward revision of issue price of food grains, as envisaged in the Act, coupled with higher productivity and lower interest on government debt (Pradhan, 2014).

The nutrition aspect was further endorsed as a distinct aspect, when the NITI Aayog spelt out the National Nutrition Security Strategy in September 2017, to end malnutrition among children, women and men by 2030 (Rao, 2017). Issues related to setting up a suitable mechanism for the implementation of the NFSA and how best to achieve fortification of food are ongoing (The Hindu, 2017) The NFSA is also not without its share of weaknesses since it does not address the lack of drinking water, sanitation, primary healthcare and nutritional literacy that are essential components of food security (Swaminathan, 2015: 17). It neglects the farmer and lacks an institutional structure comprising representatives from all political parties and chief ministers of food-surplus and food-deficit states headed by the Prime Minister (ibid.: 18). Finally, the right to food is not enforceable, such that the state can be penalized for not being able to provide adequate food to people, despite a Supreme Court ruling in November 2001 (Ansari, 2017).

In the context of the latter, the role of the state is still very crucial for ameliorating small farmer distress in India. This includes the development of high-yielding varieties, setting up infrastructure and marketing facilities in remote areas, ensuring food availability and prices stability by insuring crops, establishing forward markets, strengthening storage and warehouse facilities (Vyas, 2003: 108–109). Recent initiatives have focused on doubling farming income, providing credit to small landholders and a Kisan Bima Yojana that aims to provide better insurance to small farmers.[2] The Indian state has also played some role in the domestic food market to ensure that both the producer and consumer are buffered against the fluctuations in prices of food items (Mousseau, 2009: 77). International support too is important. The Country Strategic Plan of the WFP for India has transitioned since 2015 as India has surplus cereal production. Based on a mid-term assessment in 2011, it was decided to take food delivery off the list and to focus on technical assistance and policy and advocacy support in the period 2015–2018. The WFP also supports the three main programmes for food security that are part of the NFSA, namely, the targeted public distribution scheme (TPDS), the mid-day meal scheme, and the Integrated Child Development Scheme (ICDS). It operates in Odisha, Kerala and on the TPDS in Jharkhand (WFP, 2017).

However, it is in the context of small farmer distress that the India story gets aligned with the global counter-narrative against the neoliberal "geo-politics of food". The domestic impact of the Uruguay Round of trade negotiation, that put in place TRIPS, the multilateral patent regime, became applicable to India in 2005 after some grace years, has not been very positive since it allowed product patenting in the agriculture sector, nearly 70% of which were claimed by foreign companies (Plahe, 2009: 1205). The major beneficiaries were the global majors such as Monsanto, Dupont, Syngenta, Dow/Mycogen/Agrigentics/Phytogen and Bayer/Aventis. It has also been argued that for tropical countries including India, trade has been harmful because of the inelastic supply of tropical land and limited investment. The export of tropical products would necessarily reduce the domestic availability of such products and food grains, and leave the mass of the population worse off, for which manufactured imports from the north, no matter how cheap, cannot compensate (Patnaik, 1996).

Another issue that is increasingly linking India with the global narrative is the urban food security issue. Comparative studies that are India-focused have highlighted that rising numbers of urban poor who migrate from rural areas requires, that the public distribution system that was hitherto focused on rural areas, must now be extended to urban areas. This is because the numbers of wet markets are on the decline and the supermarkets do not cater to the requirements of the urban poor. Simultaneously, the informal economy, infrastructure, travel costs, etc. must become part of food security planning in India (Parra et al., 2015). The third point of linkage with the global narrative is the water-food-energy nexus. The developing world is also losing precious water resources because of the virtual water trade taking place through food imports from water-rich countries. Hence the decentralised water management techniques adopted at the local level, do not help in the sustainable development of groundwater sources (Kumar et al., 2014: 3). Nor do they address the drinking water requirements of the rural poor.

Multilaterally, as a member of the G20, India has supported the G20 action plan and the AMIS under FAO. India has, in addition, stressed the importance of increasing agricultural productivity (Ministry of Agriculture, 2011). At the G20 Summit in Paris, the Indian finance minister emphasized that the excess finance available, for capitalizing multilateral and regional development banks should be so that the excess finance can be used to develop infrastructure and simultaneously prevent price volatility, to reduce food insecurity (DEA, 2011).

Historically too, India has been an active member of the FAO. India's Binay Ranjan Sen was the third director-general of the FAO and played a seminal role in launching the Freedom from Hunger campaign that sought to build capacities in developing countries by focusing on women. He also sought a governance role for the FAO (see Jarosz, 2009: 44–45). India has been a part of the Board of Governors of the FAO which consists of 22 countries today and hence has been party to decision making in this institution. An analysis of India's interventions in food-related issues since the 1980s, reveals the importance it attaches to the strengthening of the IFAD and the maintaining of food stocks. For instance, in 1984, the Indian representative, while participating in a discussion on international development in the context of shortage of food in Africa, emphasized the importance of industrialization for agriculture, but also made a case for expanding the sources of funding for the IFAD and the FAO's definition of food security. He also said that although the costs of maintaining food stocks were high, they were a valuable source of food security for Asia, which led India to maintain 17 million tonnes of stocks of cereals. India also has favoured self-sufficiency over aid. For example, in the wake of the food shortages in 2004–2005, when there was an overwhelming international mood in favour of providing humanitarian assistance, the Indian representative stressed on the simultaneous development of institutions in respective countries, so as to reduce the need for aid.

According to Indian authorities, the 2008 food crisis was caused by the diversion of food grains for biofuel production by prominent food exporters, to reduce their dependence on the high price fossil fuels that they were importing. India also felt that the rise in food prices was due to international speculators investing in food futures. India supported the position of the FAO, WFP and UNDP that encouraged increasing domestic production of food, rather than that of the Bretton Woods institutions, that encouraged the production of cash crops. India felt the IFAD could be used for protecting small and marginal farmers, and other international bodies could take care of other important aspects such as land development, water management and seed technology. It also felt that open domain intellectual property rights had enabled the green revolution through the transfer of high-yielding seeds, which the TRIPS agreement of the later years denied, resulting in the rise in food price rise. So, TRIPS needed to be revised, as did the levels of subsidies given to agricultural products in developed countries. India, therefore, called for a new global compact, a compact between the developed and developing countries, between the land surplus and labour surplus economies and between food exporters and food importers. India is the largest donor to IFAD from the Group A list of countries.[3]

India also supported the L'Aquila initiative of the G8 and the World Bank's Global Food Crisis Response Programme. At the same time, it also actively contested the discourse that blamed increasing consumption levels in developing countries, for the rise in food prices and said the food crisis was caused by the diversion of food crops for fuel production among other factors such as:

> environmental degradation and stagnant agricultural productivity had led to a mismatch between global food supply and demand, while the flow of speculative capital into global commodity markets and an increase in futures trading in developed countries had contributed to price hikes and volatility. That situation could be corrected only by improved regulation of commodity markets.
>
> (UN General Assembly, 2012)

India has committed itself to sharing technical expertise in food technology with other developing countries. The connection between ending hunger in the developing world and sustainable consumption and wastage in the developed world was re-emphasized during the formulation of the SDG Goals 2 and 12, respectively. A special focus on women in terms of economic opportunities and access to resources, especially in rural areas was also, emphasized.

Conclusion

The preceding sections lend themselves to interesting conclusions. The analysis of the narrative on food security in Section I reveals the complex terrain the idea has had to traverse. The analysis of the global governance of food in Section II reveals, that although much has been attempted by UN-related bodies that were created to deal with food-related issues, the unequal position of developed and developing countries in agriculture and food continues to stall the fundamental changes that will ease food security issues for them. This context makes the G20 an interesting forum for study, as it brings together countries that have historically been on opposite sides of the food debate.

An analysis of the G20's engagement with food issues in Section III reveals that the G20 narrative takes on board several concerns that are part of the developing country narratives. While critics deride it for not addressing structural issues such as trade reform and reducing biofuel production, successive G20 summits have been credibly able to expand the remit of several aspects related to food security in the developing world. Developing country concerns that required global policy changes and were not discussed in UN-related forums, have been sequentially brought on the agenda of the G20. The forum has also ensured that developed countries take the UN-related forums more seriously and are accountable to them. Historically, these forums were shunned by developed countries as they were seen as representing the interests of the developing and LDC countries. The G20's efforts have brought them centre-stage, apart from adding to their mandates. If pursued with sincerity, these policies have the potential to change the very fundamentals of international agricultural economics by strengthening the agriculture sector in developing countries. Developing countries, thus empowered may, in the long term, have a substantially different take on rules for agricultural trade and TRIPS.

The case of India fits this paradigm, as Indian policymakers have viewed the G20 as a forum for change, and, quite unambiguously stated that India supports the UN bodies' narrative on food security, rather than those of the Bretton Woods institutions. An analysis of India's narrative on food security in Section IV reveals that it has pinned its bets on increased funding for the protection of its small farmers through the IFAD. It has also emphasized self-sufficiency through the creation of institutions as well as for providing humanitarian food aid. It has been critical of the IPR regime that was put in place after the Uruguay Round of trade negotiations, which ceased to exist in 1994. The Indian narrative in the UN does not focus much on agriculture trade reforms and the Doha Development Round, perhaps because these issues are outside their remit. Finally, in the context of the SDGs, India has been focusing on the unsustainable consumption patterns of the developed world, an argument that has been central to its climate and environment diplomacy.

If one compares the Indian narrative with what has been attempted normatively and put in place concretely by the G20 thus far, it is apparent that while issues of small farmers that are crucial for India have been taken up, issues of IPR have not figured in the G20. On the former issue, the G20 thus has been able to incorporate, some concerns of the critics of neoliberal international economics, into its agenda. On the latter, the gap between India's narrative in the UN and the G20s efforts need not be taken too seriously, given that India's own domestic IPR laws that were adopted post-Uruguay, have been assessed as having failed in taking advantage of the leeway given to the farm sector in developing countries.

The most important takeaway from this analysis is that being a part of the G20 allowed the developing country narrative, to become the big powers' narrative. Many of the issues reflected in the G20 declarations, are much larger than the narrative of any one country – in this case India's. Moreover, several concerns that date back to the earliest UN development decades are back on the agenda. More discussions and deliberations may lead to even greater structural reforms in the future.

Notes

1 Author's telephonic interview, held on 20 March 2020, with Ambassador Basant Kumar Gupta, Permanent Representative of India to FAO, IFAD and WFP, 2013–2016.
2 Ibid.
3 Ibid.

References

Ansari, Adnan, 2017. "The Deja-Vu of Food Security and the Right to Food in India", *World Affairs*, Vol. 22, No. 4, Winter 2017, pp. 82–97.

Beeson, Mark and Stephen Bell, 2009. "The G-20 and International Economic Governance: Hegemony, Collectivism, or Both?", *Global Governance*, Vol. 15, No. 1 (January–March 2009), pp. 67–86. Online at: http://www.jstor.org/stable/27800739, pp. 68–69.

Biodiversity International, CGIAR Consortium, FAO, IFAD, IFPRI, IICA, OECD, UNCTAD, Coordination team of UN High Level Task Force on the Food Security Crisis, WFP, World Bank, and WTO, 2012. *Sustainable Agricultural Productivity Growth and Bridging the Gap for Small Family Farms*, Interagency Report to the Mexican G20 Presidency, June 12, 2012. Online at: http://g20india.gov.in/pdfs/2012-B-June_sustainable-agricultural-productivity.pdf (accessed 24 October 2017).

Burnett, Kim, 2014. "Trouble in the Fields: Fair Trade and Food Sovereignty Responses to Governance Opportunities after the Food Crisis", *Geopolitics*, Vol. 19, No. 2, pp. 351–376, DOI:10.1080/14650045.2012.752356.

Chang, Ching-Cheng, Huey-Lin Lee and Shih-Hsun Hsu, 2013. "Food Security: Global Trends and Regional Perspective with Reference to East Asia", *The Pacific Review*, Vol. 26, No. 5, pp. 589–613.

Clapp, Jennifer, 2011. "Taking Action for Food Security: The Responsibilities of G20 leaders", September 13, 2011. Online at: https://www.cigionline.org/publications/taking-action-ensure-food-security-responsibilities-g20-leaders (accessed 24 May 2017).

Clapp, Jennifer, 2012a. "The G20s Food Security Agenda: Making Positive Change or Passing the Buck", May 1, 2012. Online at: https://www.cigionline.org/articles/g20s-food-security-agenda-making-positive-change-or-passing-buck (accessed 25 May 2019).

Clapp, Jennifer, 2012b. "G20 and Food Security: Better to Keep the Focus on Economic Policy Reform", May 28, 2012. Online at: https://www.cigionline.org/articles/g20-and-food-security-keep-focus-economic-policy-reform (accessed 24 May 2019).

Clapp, Jennifer, 2014. "World Hunger and the Global Economy: Strong Linkages, Weak Action", *Journal of International Affairs*, Spring/Summer, Vol. 67, No. 2, 2014, pp. 1–18.

Clapp, Jennifer and Tim Wise, 2011. "G20 ignores Food Security", *The Real News Network*, November 2, 2011. Online at: http://therealnews.com/t2/index.php?option=com_content&task=view&id=31&Itemid=74&jumival=7536 (accessed 10 May 2020).

Collier, Paul, 2008. "The Politics of Hunger: How Illusion and Greed Fan the Food Crisis", *Foreign Affairs*, Vol. 87, No. 6, Nov-Dec 2008, pp. 67–79.

Compagnon, David, 2012. "Global Governance and the South: Blind Spot or Terra Incognita", *International Studies Review*, Vol. 12, No. 4, December 2012, pp. 710–719.

Cooper, Andrew F., 2010. "G20 as an Improvised Crisis Committee and/or a Contested 'steering committee' for the World", *International Affairs*, Vol. 86, No. 3, May 2010, pp. 741–757.

Ehrlich, Paul R., Anne H. Ehrlich and Gretchen C. Daily, 1993. "Food Security, Population and Environment", *Population and Development Review*, Vol. 19, No. 1, March 1993, pp. 1–32.

FAO, IFAD and WFP, 2014. *The State of Food Insecurity in the World*, 2014, G20 Food Security and Nutrition Framework, Rome. Online at: http://www.fao.org/3/a-i4030e.pdf (accessed 31 October 2017).

DEA, 2011. Finance Minister's Intervention Statement on Development Agenda (Infrastructure and Food Security) for G20 Development and Finance Ministers' Meeting on 23rd September 2011. Online at: https://dea.gov.in/sites/default/files/FM_statement_G20_FMMeeting.pdf (accessed 31 October 2019).

Gallagher, Kevin P., 2015. "Good Talk, Little Action: The Limits of G20", in Gallagher, Kevin P. (ed.), *Ruling Capital: Emerging Markets and the Regulation of Cross-Border Finance* (1st ed), Ithaca, NY: Cornell University Press, 2015, pp. 161–162. Online at: www.jstor.org/stable/10.7591/j.ctt1287ds5.11 (accessed 12 February 2018).

G20, 2009. *Pittsburgh Summit, Leaders Statement*, September 24–25, 2009. Online at: http://www.g20.utoronto.ca/2009/2009communique0925.html (accessed 11 October 2017).

G20, 2011. *Paris Summit, Ministerial Declaration: Action Plan on Food Price Volatility and Agriculture*, Meeting of G20 Agricultural Ministers, Paris, June 22–23, 2011. Online at: http://www.g20.utoronto.ca/2011/2011-agriculture-plan-en.pdf (accessed 11 October 2017).

G20, 2012. *Agriculture Vice Ministers/Deputies Meeting Report*, Mexico City, May 18, 2012. Online at: http://www.g20.utoronto.ca/2012/2012-0518-agriculture.pdf (accessed 31 October 2017).

G20, 2013. *G20 Leaders' Declaration*, St. Petersburg, September 6, 2013. Online at: http://www.g20.utoronto.ca/2013/Saint_Petersburg_Declaration_ENG.pdf (accessed 11 October 2017).

G20, 2014. *G20 Food Security and Nutrition Framework*, November 2014. Online at: http://www.g20.utoronto.ca/2014/g20_food_security_nutrition_framework.pdf (accessed 11 October 2017).

G20, 2015. *Agriculture Ministers Meeting*, Istanbul, Final Communique, May 7–8, 2015. Online at: http://www.g20.utoronto.ca/2015/150508-agriculture.pdf (accessed 11 October 2017).

G20, 2016. *Agriculture Ministers Meeting Communiqué*, Xi'an, June 3, 2016. Online at: http://www.g20.utoronto.ca/2016/160603-agriculture.pdf (accessed 30 October 2017).

G20, 2017. *Agriculture Ministers' Declaration 2017*, Towards Food and Water Security: Fostering Sustainability, Advancing Innovation, January 22, 2017, Berlin, Online at: http://www.g20.utoronto.ca/2017/170122-agriculture-en.pdf (accessed 30 October 2017).

G20, 2018. *Declaration*, G20 Meeting of Agriculture Ministers, Buenos Aires, July 27–28, 2018. Online at: http://www.g20.utoronto.ca/2018/2018-07-28-g20_agriculture_declaration_final.pdf (accessed 12 February 2019).

G20, 2019. *Agriculture Ministers' Declaration 2019*, Niigata, Japan, May 12, 2019. Online at: http://www.g20.utoronto.ca/2019/2019-G20_2019_AMM.pdf (accessed 21 May 2020).

G20, 2020. *Communiqué*, G20 Agriculture and Water Ministers, November 22, 2020. Online at: http://www.g20.utoronto.ca/2020/2020-g20-agriculture-0922.html (accessed 10 June 2021).

Heap, Peter, 2011. *CIGI Conference Report, The New Geometry of Global Summitry: The Future of the G20 (and the G8)*, 2011. Online at: https://www.cigionline.org/sites/default/files/conference_report_1.pdf (accessed 23 May 2019).

The Hindu, 2017. "Food for Action: On Food Security India", *The Hindu*, 9 August 2017. Online at: http://www.thehindu.com/opinion/editorial/food-for-action-on-food-security-in-india/article19452387.ece (accessed 15 November 2017).

Hopkins, Raymond, 1992. "Reform in the International Food Aid Regime: The Role of Consensual Knowledge", *International Organisation*, Vol. 46, No.1, Winter 1992, pp. 225–264.

Hopkins, Raymond F. and Donald J. Puchala, 1978. "Perspectives on the International Relations of Food", *International Organisation*, Vol. 32, No. 3, Summer 1978, pp. 581–616.

Hossain, Moazzem, 2014."Building Responsible Social Protection in South Asia: India's Food Security Act as a New Direction", *South Asia Research*, Vol. 34, No. 2, pp. 133–153.

IFPRI, 2012. *Global Food Policy Report*, April 2012, Chapter 8, pp. 69–78.

Itteyerah, Anil Chandy, 2013. *Food Security in India: Issues and Suggestions for Effectiveness*, Indian Institute for Public Administration, Theme Paper for 57th Members' Annual Conference, New Delhi, 2013, pp. 1–37. Online at: http://www.iipa.org.in/upload/Food%20Security%20Theme%20Paper-2013.pdf (accessed 15 November 2017).

Jarosz, Lucy, 2009. "The Political Economy of Global Governance and the World Food Crisis: The Case of the FAO", *Review (Fernand Braudel Center)*, Vol. 32, No. 1, Political Economic Perspectives on the World Food Crisis, 2009, pp. 37–60, Stable URL: http://www.jstor.org/stable/40647788.

Kanth, Ravi, 2004. "WTO: Advantage G20", *Economic and Political Weekly*, Vol. 39, No.34, August 21–27, 2004, pp. 3795–3797.

Kumar, M. Dinesh, Nitin Bassi, A. Narayanamoorthy and M.V.K. Sivamohan, 2014. "Water-food-energy Nexus: Global and Local Perspectives", in Kumar, M. Dinesh, Nitin Bassi, A. Narayanamoorthy and M.V.K. Sivamohan (ed.), *The Water, Energy and Food Security Nexus: Lesson from India for Development*, Routledge, London and New York, 2014, pp. 1–18.

Lang, Tim and David Barling, 2012. "Food Security and Food Sustainability: Reformulating the Debate", *The Geographical Journal*, Vol. 178, No. 4, December 2012, pp. 313–326.

Macdonald, Lawrence, 2011. CIGI'11: Development/Food Security Session, Gaps in Global Governance. Remarks, at the Presentation of Jennifer Clapp, November 4, 2011. Online at: https://www.cigionline.org/multimedia/cigi11-developmentfood-security-session (accessed 11 May 2019).

Madhur, Srinivasa, 2012. "Asia's Role in Twenty-first-Century Global Governance", *International Affairs*, Vol. 88, No. 4, July 2012, pp. 817–833.

Margulis, Matias E., 2013. "The Regime Complex for Food Security: Implications for the Global Hunger Challenge", *Global Governance*, Vol. 19, 2013, pp. 53–67.

Ministry of Agriculture, 2011. "India Seeks Global Action to Achieve Higher Agriculture Production", Shri Pawar Participates in G-20 Agriculture Ministers' Meet, PIB, June 24, 2011, http://g20india.gov.in/pdfs/2011-C-India's-Participation-in-Agriculture-Ministrers.pdf (accessed 25 May 2019).

Mousseau, Frederic, 2009. "Toward a Future without Want", *World Policy Journal*, Vol. 26, No. 2, 2009, pp. 73–81.

Naim, Moises, 2008. "Missing Links: The Global Food Fight", *Foreign Policy*, No. 167, July-August 2008, pp.94–95.

Nau, Henry, 1978. "The Diplomacy of World Food: Goals, Capabilities, Issues and Arenas", *International Organisation*, Vol. 32, No. 3, Summer 1978, pp. 775–809.

Orsini, Amandine, Jean-Frédéric Morin and Oran Young, 2013. "Regime Complexes: A Buzz, A Boom or a Boost for Global Governance", *Global Governance*, 19, 2013, pp.27–39.

Parra, David Celis, Krista Dinsmore, Nicole Fassina and Charlene Keizer, 2015. "Toward SDG 2: Food Security and Urbanization in the Global South", *Policy Brief*, No. 8, 2015. Online at: https://www.cigionline.org/sites/default/files/graduate_fellows_pb_no.8.pdf (accessed 25 May 2019).

Patnaik, Utsa, 1996. "Export-Oriented Agriculture and Food Security in Developing Countries and India", *Economic and Political Weekly*, Vol. 31, No. 35/37, Special No. (September 1996), pp. 2429–2431+2433–2437+2439+2441–2449. Online at: http://www.jstor.org/stable/4404563.

Plahe, Jagjit Kaur, 2009. "The Implications of India's Amended Patent Regime: Stripping Away Food Security and Farmer's Rights", *Third World Quarterly*, Vol. 30, No. 6, pp. 1197–1213.

Pradhan, Krishanu P., 2014. *Fiscal Sustainability of the National Food Security Act, 2013 in India*, Working Paper 332, The Institute of Social and Economic Change, Bangalore, 2014.

Rao, Nivedita, 2017. "Malnutrition in India: The National Nutrition Strategy Explained", *PRS Comment*, September 8, 2017. Online at: https://www.prsindia.org/theprsblog/malnutrition-india-national-nutrition-strategy-explained (accessed 21 January 2020).

Sen, Amiti, 2017. "India Faces "food security" Hurdle in WTO", *The Hindu*, November 14, 2017. Online at: http://www.thehindubusinessline.com/economy/agri-business/india-faces-food-security-hurdle-in-wto/article9960550.ece (accessed 15 November 2019).

Soederberg, Sussane, "The Politics of Representation and Financial Fetishism: The Case of G20 Summits", *Third World Quarterly*, Vol. 31, No. 4, pp. 523–540.

Sommerville, Melanie, Jamey Essex and Philippe Le Billon, 2014. "The Global Food Crisis and the Geopolitics of Security", *Geopolitics*, Vol. 19, No. 2, 2014, pp. 239–265, DOI:10.1080/14650045.2013.81164.

Sundaram, Jomo Kwame, 2011. "A Global Green New Deal for Economic Recovery: Addressing the Financial, Climate, Food, Jobs and Development Crises Together", *The Pakistan Development Review*, Vol. 50, No. 4, Winter 2011, pp. 295–303.

Suryanarayan, M.H. 1997. "Uruguay Round and Global Food Security", *Economic and Political Weekly*, Vol. 32, No. 43, Oct. 25–31, 1997, pp. 2821–2828. Online at: http://www.jstor.org/stable/4406015.

Swaminathan, M.S., 2015a. "Genesis and Growth of the Yield Revolution in Wheat", in Swaminathan, M.S. (ed.), *Combating Hunger and Achieving Food Security*, Cambridge University Press, 2015, pp. 1–9.

Swaminathan, M.S., 2015b. "Shaping Our Agricultural Destiny", in Swaminathan, M.S. (ed.), *Combating Hunger and Achieving Food Security*, Cambridge University Press, 2015, pp. 15–19.

Swaminathan, M.S., 2015c. "The Future of Indian Agriculture", in Swaminathan, M.S. (ed.), *Combating Hunger and Achieving Food Security*, Cambridge University Press, 2015, pp. 162–164.

Tweeten, Luther, 1999. "The Economics of Global Food Security", *Review of Agricultural Economics*, Vol. 21, No. 2, Autumn-Winter 1999, pp. 473–488. Online at: http://www.jstor.org/stable/1349892, pp. 474–475.

UN General Assembly, 2012. *Agenda Item 26: Agriculture Development and Food Security*, A/C.2/67/SR.19, December 24, 2012.

Unvin, Peter, 1992. "Regime, Surplus and Self-Interest: The International Politics of Food Aid", *International Studies Quarterly*, Vol. 36, No. 3, September 1992, pp. 293–312.

von Grebmer, Klaus, Jill Bernstein, Fraser Patterson, Miriam Wiemers, Réiseal Ní Chéilleachair, Connell Foley, Seth Gitter, Kierstin Ekstrom, and Heidi Fritschel, with Guest Author,Rupa Mukerji, 2019. *Global Hunger Index 2019: The Challenge of Hunger and Climate Change*, Welthungerhilfe and Concern Worldwide, Dublin/Bonn, October 2019. Online at: https://www.globalhungerindex.org/pdf/en/2019.pdf (accessed 21 May 2020).

von Grebmer, K., J. Bernstein, R. Alders, O. Dar, R. Kock, F. Rampa, M. Wiemers, K. Acheampong, A. Hanano, B. Higgins, R. Ní Chéilleachair, C. Foley, S. Gitter, K. Ekstrom, and H. Fritschel. 2020. *2020 Global Hunger Index: One Decade to Zero Hunger: Linking Health and Sustainable Food Systems*. Bonn: Welthungerhilfe; and Dublin: Concern Worldwide.

Vyas, Vijay S., 2003. "Economic Policies for Ensuring Food Security", in Dev, S. Mahendra, K.P. Kannan and Nira Ramachandran (eds.), *Towards a Food Secure India: Issues and Policies*, Institute for Human Development/Centre for Economic and Social Studies, New Delhi/Hyderabad, 2003, pp. 105–112.

Woods, Ngaire, Alexander Betts, Jochen Prantl and Devi Sridhar, 2013. "Transforming Global Governance for the 21st Century", Human Development Report Office, Occasional Paper, 2013.

WFP India, 2017. *Country Brief*, September 2017.

WFP India, 2018. *Country Brief*, October 2018.

Chapter 10

Climate change and food security in India

Domestic and global solutions

Malancha Chakrabarty

Food insecurity continues to be the most pressing challenge facing the world today. After a period of sustained decline, global hunger began to increase from 2014 onwards – the number of people affected by chronic food deprivation increased from 777 million in 2015 to 815 million in 2017 (FAO, 2017). The sub-Saharan African region has the highest prevalence of undernutrition, affecting about 22.7% of the population. The situation is particularly severe in East Africa where over one-third of the population suffers from undernutrition. However, in terms of absolute numbers, Asia heads the list with almost 520 million undernourished persons followed by 243 million in Africa and 42 million in Latin America and the Caribbean. The increase in the prevalence of undernourishment can be traced to the decline in food availability and high food prices due to the El Niño /La Niña phenomena in Eastern and Southern Africa and in South-East Asia. A rise in the number of conflicts also contributed to food insecurity in several countries such as Yemen, South Sudan, Nigeria and Somalia. The world population is predicted to reach 8.6 billion in 2030, and to rise further to 9.8 billion in 2050 and 11.2 billion in 2100 (United Nations, 2017). As a result, meeting the food needs of the world will be a greater challenge in the years to come.

Climate change has become a central issue in the global political arena. The current trajectory of greenhouse gases poses a huge threat to economic development, environmental sustainability and human well-being. Sadly, international agreement on the measures required to reduce greenhouse gas emissions has been elusive. The scientific community predicts that average temperatures will rise by 2–4°C by the end of the century, posing multiple threats to human beings. One of the most severe impacts of climate change will be on food security. The relationship between climate change and food security is complex, with climate change affecting all aspects of food security: availability, access, utilization and stability. Moreover, with disproportionate impacts on those who have contributed the least to global warming, climate change will gravely undermine the right to food (United Nations, 2015). Developing countries like India will be most severely affected, not

DOI: 10.4324/9781003272656-10

only because of their geographical location but also, because the bulk of the population depends on small-scale agriculture for its livelihood or is engaged in the urban informal sector.

This chapter highlights the challenges that climate change poses for India's food security and argues for significant changes in global and national policies for an effective solution. The chapter is organized as follows. The section "India's challenges" presents an overview of India's agricultural crisis and the nutritional challenges that the country faces and argues that the deep crisis in agriculture and the poor nutritional status of its people and a growing population render the country extremely vulnerable to the impacts of climate change. The following section discusses the impacts of climate change on four aspects of food security in India – food availability, access, utilization and stability. The sections on "domestic policy" and "global governance" recommend actions that India can adopt to address the challenges that climate change poses to its food security and discuss key areas for international action. The last section concludes.

India's challenges

Despite the high rates of economic growth in the period after liberalization, the incidence of undernutrition is very high in India. India's performance in tackling undernutrition has been particularly disappointing. The prevalence of undernutrition declined marginally from 210.1 million in 1990 to about 194.6 million in 2014. The country also failed to meet the Millennium Development Goal of halving the proportion of people who suffer from hunger. More than one-fourth of the children in Gujarat, Jharkhand, Karnataka, Madhya Pradesh and Maharashtra are stunted and over 40% of the children are underweight in states such as Jharkhand (47.8%), Bihar (43.9%) and Madhya Pradesh (42.8%). India continues to lag behind in the United Nations Human Development Index (HDI) and the Global Hunger Index published by the International Food Policy Research.

While large sections of the Indian population suffer from undernutrition, due to rising incomes, the rich and the middle classes are increasingly demanding a more diversified diet which is rich in proteins. Thus, the composition of the food basket in urban areas is increasingly shifting away from cereals to high-value agricultural commodities such as fish, eggs, milk and meat (Mittal, 2006). As a result, in the coming years, the indirect demand for food grains as livestock feed will also grow rapidly in India. According to projections by Kumar et al. (2016), India will not remain rice surplus and may even face a net deficit of 3 to 5 million tonnes by 2030. With regard to wheat, India's production will be sufficient to meet domestic needs and there may even be a marginal surplus but the deficit in pulses and oilseeds will widen and the country will become more dependent on imports for these commodities. Mittal (2006) and Kumar et al. (2009) also reached the same conclusion. Thus, without significant efforts by the government to increase productivity in agriculture through public investments in irrigation, rural infrastructure, agricultural research and efficient use of water, India will not be able to meet its long-term food requirements, with domestic production alone.

Low agricultural productivity is one of the biggest challenges confronting Indian agriculture today. India's cereal yields are substantially lower than those of developed regions such as North America (7,318.4 kg per ha), East Asia and Pacific (5,401.4 kg per ha), Euro Area (5,362.6 kg per ha) and Central Europe and the Baltics (4,453.2 kg per ha) (Table 10.1).

Further, as shown in Table 10.2, yields per hectare of major food grains such as rice, wheat and coarse cereals have stagnated in India since the 1980s.

Rapid economic growth has failed to bring about a structural change in the Indian economy, in terms of the ability to shift labour out of low productivity activities, especially in agriculture, to higher productivity manufacturing jobs (Ghosh, 2014). Agriculture continues to employ about 49% of the labour force even though its share in GDP is just about 16% (Ministry of Finance, 2018). This is despite the fact that farming is increasingly becoming an unviable occupation and is not the occupation of choice for a majority of the persons engaged in agriculture.

Table 10.1 Cereal yields (kg per ha, 2016)

Country/Region	*Region (kg per hectare)*
East Asia and Pacific (IDA and IBRD countries)	5,401.4
Central Europe and Baltics	4,453.2
Sub-Saharan Africa	1,394.7
Europe and Central Asia (IDA and IBRD countries)	3,079.6
Euro Area	5,362.6
North America	7,318.4
India	2,992.8
World	**3,966.8**

Source: World Bank

Table 10.2 Growth rate of yield per hectare grain (per cent)

Year	*Rice*	*Wheat*	*Coarse cereals*	*Pulses*	*Total food grains*
1970–1971 to 1980–1981	1.8	2.2	0.4	−1.0	1.6
1980–1981 to 1990–1991	2.7	3.4	2.6	2.0	3.0
1990–1991 to 2000–2001	0.9	1.7	1.3	−0.6	1.7
2000–2001 to 2010–2011	1.6	1.0	4.1	2.4	1.7
2010–2011 to 2016–2017	2.2	1.2	2.6	2.0	1.8

Source: Reserve Bank of India, *Handbook of Statistics on Indian Economy*

According to Despande and Prabhu (2005), about one-third of Indian farmers do not like farming because it is not a profitable activity and 40% are willing to give it up if they could find a better source of livelihood – in short, nearly 70% of the farmers in India are farming out of compulsion. This is largely because the period of high growth in India was marked by a massive crisis in agriculture, the most extreme manifestation of which has been the rising number of farmer suicides in India. Farmer suicides have now become a regular feature and can no longer be brushed aside as stray incidents. Most studies indicate that household indebtedness is the main reason for farmer suicides in India. About 52% of the agricultural households in India are indebted, with an average outstanding loan of Rs 47,000 per household (Ministry of Statistics and Programme Implementation, 2014). Among states, Andhra Pradesh has the highest share of indebted households (92.9%) followed by Telangana (89.1%) and Tamil Nadu (82.5%). India's agrarian distress is the cumulative effect of a number of factors: technological, sociocultural, ecological and policy-induced (Reddy and Galab, 2006).

In a nutshell, India is a particularly vulnerable country with regard to climate change. In the following section, we explore the impact of climate change on four aspects of food security: availability, access, utilization and stability.

Impact of climate change on India's food security

Impact on food production and availability

Given India's growing population and the rising demand for a diet rich in proteins among the affluent sections of the population, combined with low agricultural productivity, it will be difficult for India to meet the consumption needs of the population, through domestic production in the next few decades. In this context, climate change constitutes additional stress for India's long-term food security, because it affects food production in complex ways. The most significant impact of climate change on India's food production is likely to occur because of its impact on the country's water resources. Several studies indicate that climate change is likely to cause significant changes in the inter-annual and intra-seasonal variability of the monsoon rainfall. Significant changes have already been observed in India's rainfall pattern. The Economic Survey 2017–2018 finds that the number of dry days (rainfall less than 0.1 mm per day) and wet days (rainfall greater than 80 mm per day) have steadily increased from 1970 onwards (Ministry of Finance, 2018). Uttar Pradesh, Kerala, Jharkhand, Chhattisgarh, parts of Madhya Pradesh and the north-eastern states are regions that have extreme deficiencies in rainfall. According to a World Bank report, with a global mean warming of 4°C, a 10% increase in annual mean monsoon intensity and a 15% increase in the year-to-year variability of Indian monsoon precipitation can be projected (World Bank, 2013).

Fluctuation in rainfall will also adversely affect India's groundwater resources which provide for more than 60% of the irrigated land because groundwater resources are mainly recharged through rainfall. India's groundwater resources are already stressed due to over-exploitation for agricultural purposes. About 54% of the groundwater wells are receding with 16% of them receding by more than one metre per year. The north-western part of the country is most vulnerable to this because 58% of the 550 wells are declining in this region (Shiao et al., 2016). Given the prolonged dry spells and poor precipitation, groundwater will become more important for irrigation purposes, leading to greater pressure on water resources. The World Bank predicts that with a global mean warming of 2°C above pre-industrial levels, India's food water requirements will exceed green water availability. Climate models also predict that droughts will pose a significant risk in the north-western part of India while the southern part of the country will experience an increase in wetness (Shiao et al. 2015).

A mismatch between the demand and supply of water is likely to have far-reaching consequences for the country's food grain production because Indian agriculture continues to be heavily dependent on monsoons and according to the Economic Survey 2017–2018, about 52% of the net sown area (approx. 73.2 million hectares) was unirrigated in 2017. Estimates suggest that extreme rainfall shocks result in a 6.2% and 4.1% decline in *kharif* and *rabi* yields, respectively, in irrigated areas but the decline in yields is much higher in unirrigated areas – 14.7% and 8.6% for kharif and rabi crops, respectively. The states of Rajasthan, Gujarat, Maharashtra, Madhya Pradesh, Karnataka and Uttar Pradesh have been found to be most vulnerable to climate change. Climate change will also increase the likelihood of extreme temperature shocks which have adverse effects on food grain output. The Economic Survey 2017–2018 also estimates that extreme temperature shocks, that is, when a district is significantly hotter than usual (in the top 20 percentiles of district-specific temperature distribution), agricultural yields during rabi and kharif seasons declined by 4% and 4.7%, respectively. Rice and wheat, two crops central to nutrition in India, are particularly sensitive to climate change. According to Lobell et al. (2012), wheat growth in northern India is highly sensitive to temperatures greater than 34°C. However, the impact of water shortage on wheat crops could be limited through elevated carbon dioxide levels but the effect on rice yields is likely to be more pronounced. Water shortage and thermal stress are likely to have a significant impact on rice productivity in India even after considering the positive impact of elevated carbon dioxide levels in the future (Lal et al., 2001).

Impact on access to food

As mentioned earlier, there has been some progress in understanding the impact of climate change on food production but there are relatively few studies which systematically study the impact of climate change on access to food. Given the fact that a large section of the population in India depends on agriculture for its livelihood, any adverse impact on Indian agriculture will affect farm incomes and consequently their ability to access food. According to the latest estimates from the Economic Survey 2017–2018, farm income losses from climate change could range between 15% to 18% on average; in unirrigated areas, farm incomes can fall by 20% to 25%. Landless labourers completely dependent on agricultural wages are the most vulnerable to climate change (Schmidhuber and Tubiello, 2007; Dev, 2012). The adverse effects of climate change will also be felt by fishermen and forest-dependent people.

In regions with high inequality and food insecurity, extreme events like floods and droughts will affect children more, given their vulnerability. A survey of nine villages in the drought-prone districts of Maharashtra revealed that the drought of 2012–2013 had led to a 60% decline in local crop yields and annual incomes of farmers. Such large drops in income are associated with massive long-term consequences for child nutrition. Similar results were found by Rodriguez-Llanes et al. (2011) in another study based on 14 flooded and 18 non-flooded villages of Jagatsinghpur district in Orissa (Rodriguez-Llanes et al., 2011). According to their study, children who are exposed to floods in the first year of their lives suffer from chronic malnutrition.

The impact of climate change on food access is not confined to rural areas. Urban food insecurity is equally critical because poor households from rural and coastal regions migrate to urban areas in search of better livelihood opportunities. Such poor households join the urban informal sector, where there is no security of tenure or legal minimum wage. Undernutrition is rampant among poor urban residents in India. According to figures from the National Family Health Survey 2015–2016, over 30% of children below five years of age in urban Bihar, Madhya Pradesh and Karnataka are underweight. The survey also finds that the proportion of urban children who are wasted and stunted is very high even in prosperous states like Maharashtra and Gujarat. Climate change will exacerbate urban food insecurity, especially for low-income groups living in urban informal settlements, located in areas, that are prone to floods and other extreme events are at the highest risk. In fact, India's largest and most populous cities such as Kolkata, Chennai and Mumbai are at tremendous risk. Climate change is likely to cause frequent flooding in the Hooghly river during the monsoon which will affect the lives of the city's poor who live in low-lying areas or wetlands that are prone to tidal and storm surges (Dasgupta et al., 2012; World Bank, 2013). Food is the single largest expenditure for the poor, as such, loss of livelihood or productive assets due to extreme weather events like floods will have a huge impact on household food security. The urban poor are also extremely affected by increased food prices following the decline in food production due to climate change.

Impact on food utilization

Food utilization refers to an individual or a household's capacity to consume and benefit from the food that is consumed. Physical as well as economic access to food is a necessary condition for food utilization, but by no means all of it. The utilization of food is related to the nutritional aspects of food consumption. Climate change affects food utilization in complex and uncertain ways which is why the impact of climate change on food utilization is least studied. The two key pathways through which climate change affects food utilization are diet and health. The diet pathway relates to the impacts of climate change on the nutrient content of the food that is grown and eaten by the people; whereas the health pathway entails food and water safety and diseases that erode the ability of the human body to absorb nutrients.

Climate change could lead to a reduction in the production and therefore consumption of certain foods, such as fish, fruits, vegetables and wild fruits, which play a critical role in the diets of vulnerable populations (FAO, 2016). Given that most studies focus on the impact of climate change on cereals, its impact on fish, fruits and vegetables is not very well known. Elevated carbon dioxide levels could also lead to a reduction in the quality of foods, as for instance, reduced concentration of proteins and minerals like zinc and iron. According to a study by Myers et al. (2014), rising levels of carbon dioxide will have serious consequences on human health by reducing levels of nutrients in important crops (see Table 10.3). In a country like India where the bulk of the population depends on C_3 grains, the decreased protein content in non-leguminous crops will have serious consequences on public health (Myers et al., 2014). The impact of decreased iron levels on women and child nutrition will be particularly severe, as about 53% of India's female population already suffers from anaemia (National Family Health Survey, India).

Evidence also suggests that climate change will lead to an increase in the incidence of diarrhoeal diseases in children. Diarrhoea is one of the leading causes of child mortality in India, accounting for roughly 13% of all deaths in children under five years of age (Lakshminarayanan and Jayalakshmy, 2015).

Table 10.3 Change in nutrient content at elevated CO_2 compared with ambient CO_2

Grain	*Zinc (%)*	*Iron (%)*	*Protein (%)*
Wheat	−9.3	−5.1	−6.3
Rice	−3.3	−5.2	−7.8
Field peas	−6.8	−4.1	−2.1
Soybeans	−5.1	−4.1	0.5
Maize	−5.2	−5.8	−4.6

Source: Myers et al. (2014)

According to Moors et al. (2013), climate change will lead to a 13% increase in the incidence of diarrhoea in the Ganga basin (Moors et al., 2013). In fact, Ramachandran (2014) asserts that climate change could reverse India's achievements in reducing diarrhoea-related deaths (Ramachandran, 2014). Due to climate change, more people in India will be exposed to vector-borne diseases like malaria, dengue and chikungunya. The entire population of India except for those living 1,700 m above sea level is at risk of contracting malaria (Ramana et al., 2014). By the 2050s, the geographic range of malaria is expected to shift away from central regions towards the southwestern and northern states and the transmission window is likely to widen in northern and western states. The study also finds that while malaria will persist in Orissa, West Bengal and southern parts of Assam, the northern states might also become prone to it. The incidence of arboviral diseases like chikungunya and dengue may also be influenced by climate change as both are transmitted by the common vector *Aedes aegypti*. Prevalence of these diseases is likely to affect food utilization through a reduction in appetite, loss of nutrients and the body's ability to absorb nutrients.

Impact on stability

The stability of a food system is determined by the temporal availability of, and access to food (FAO, 2008). An increase in the frequency of extreme events due to climate change has the potential to disrupt the stability of food systems through adverse impacts on food supply, food prices, agricultural incomes and even social entitlements. For instance, with an increase in the incidence of floods and droughts, maintaining the stability of the local food system becomes very difficult. Extreme events like floods and droughts will also impede the ability of global food systems to respond to food crises because the world is interconnected by trade so a food shock in surplus producing regions of the world will affect food-importing countries.

Similarly, greater price volatility due to climate change can jeopardize the stability of farm incomes and impair the ability of small farmers to access food. Climate change is also likely to lead to an increase in the frequency of food emergencies. Higher temperatures and humidity levels are also likely to increase the costs of storing food grains and limit the ability of countries to provide emergency relief (ibid.). According to the IPCC's fifth assessment report, increased incidence of climate change also reduces incentives to invest in agricultural production (Porter et al., 2014.). This is especially true for small farmers who lack access to institutional credit and insurance facilities.

Domestic policy

Without appropriate measures, climate change will have serious repercussions on India's long-term food insecurity. Therefore, a range of policy actions has to be taken at the national level. First of all, Indian agriculture which is extremely vulnerable to climate change must be climate proofed. Adapting India's agriculture sector to climate change will be a major challenge for policymakers because agriculture continues to be heavily dependent on monsoons, landholdings are very small and a large section of the population is dependent on it. Moreover, the majority of the Indian farmers are poor, less educated, lack access to technology and finance and are debt-ridden. As a consequence, their adaptive capacity is much lower than developed country farmers. Based on information collected from the farmers in eastern Uttar Pradesh, Tripathi and Mishra (2017) found some instances of unintentional adaptation by farmers by changing agricultural practices such as switching to crops of shorter duration, agroforestry, investment in irrigation, intercropping, changing sowing and harvesting time, etc. (Tripathi and Mishra, 2017). But autonomous adaptation by a handful of resourceful farmers will not be sufficient to offset the losses from climate change. Therefore, India needs a planned, co-ordinated and policy-driven adaptive strategy.

India is currently going through an unprecedented agrarian crisis and rural unrest is at its peak. Sadly, most of the current domestic policies have a short-term focus, loan waivers for distressed farmers, for instance. The share of agriculture in India's gross fixed capital formation and the share of irrigation in total outlays to agriculture have declined consistently since the 1980s (De Roy, 2017). This is despite the fact that lack of irrigation facility is one of the main reasons behind low productivity. The bias against government intervention in agriculture needs to be reversed and public investment in irrigation, rural infrastructure, agricultural research and extension services, and climate-smart agricultural practices should be stepped up. To address the ecological crisis in Indian agriculture, the government must actively promote agro-ecological farming which entails a shift away from chemicals and the adoption of renewable sources of nutrients.

The existing adaptation measures under the National Action Plan for Climate Change (NAPCC), State Action Plans for Climate change (SAPCC) and the National Adaptation Fund for Climate Change (NAFCC) have met with some successes but there is an urgent need to step up adaptation efforts in agriculture. The NAFCC has played an important role in creating awareness and a number of works have been initiated which will facilitate India's response under the Paris Agreement. So far, 23 projects worth Rs 483.76 crores have been initiated between 2015–2016 and 2017–2018. According to Prasad and Sud (2019), substantial capacity gaps exist at the state level in India which impairs the successful implementation of adaptation projects in India. Therefore, urgent efforts must be made towards building the capacity of state and local level officials in India and the union government must make efforts to handhold the state governments in the implementation of adaptation projects. Given India's vulnerability, India needs to step up public spending on adaptation measures in its agriculture sector. As a developing country, there are multiple demands on public funds. In this context, mainstreaming of climate change into existing development schemes is likely to be a good solution for India.

As outlined above, climate change will undermine access to food by adversely affecting the livelihoods of the poorest people in both rural and urban India. As a result, the state will have to provide safety nets for the poor and vulnerable sections of the population. The Mahatma Gandhi National Rural Employment Guarantee Act (MGNREGA) and the Food Security Act were designed to provide strong safety nets for the poor in the form of livelihood security and provision of subsidized food grains for the poor, respectively. In addition to the welfare-enhancing effects of MGNREGA through higher incomes and employment to the rural poor, MGNREGA has also played an important role in natural resource management because about 60% of its total expenditure is spent on water harvesting, afforestation, water conservation and land development. Scholars like Hans Nicholai Adam assert that though the scheme is not transformative in nature, conceptually MGNREGA meets the fundamental requirements for mainstreamed adaptation actions (Adam, 2015). As the world's largest public work's programme in which projects are selected by the local village governments and women do most of the work, the scheme has huge welfare benefits, but the adaptation opportunities have not been fully exploited. Therefore, future public works under the programme must be selected carefully so that they contribute to improvement in agricultural productivity and creation of productive assets in rural areas.

Given the scale of urban poverty, undernutrition, unemployment and the poor quality of urban infrastructure which makes the urban poor vulnerable to extreme events, there is a strong need to introduce an employment guarantee act for the urban poor as well. The public works initiated under the urban employment guarantee act should not only provide livelihood support to the urban poor and improve their nutritional standards but also be designed to improve urban infrastructure and make Indian cities more climate-resilient. Similarly, the enactment of the NFSA was a landmark in India's development history because the Act provided subsidized grains to nearly two-thirds of the country's households. The Act also contributes to promoting climate resilience by including millets, sorghum and maize, often known as "coarse grains", within the public distribution system which had earlier only limited itself to "fine grains" like wheat and rice. The coarse grains are not only highly nutritious but also resilient to climate-induced stresses. Stimulating the production of coarse grains would contribute to climate adaptation and food security. Unfortunately, the implementation of the FSA has not been satisfactory. In fact, the implementation of both MGNREGA and FSA has suffered due to fiscal constraints which do not bode well for India. Public spending on climate change adaptation and food security must be prioritized in India.

Global governance

Attaining food security was a matter of prime importance for India since the early days of development planning. The enactment of the National Food Security Act was a turning point because the Act marked a paradigm shift, away from a welfare measure to a rights-based approach. Although India has instituted many measures to ensure food security for its citizens and the country is often regarded as a model for other developing countries, particularly in Africa, the challenges of climate change and food security require a global response. Climate change is essentially a collective action problem that requires policy coordination and multi-level governance. Moreover, in a globalized world, a country's food security is not dependent on its own policies alone. In fact, food security is often regarded as a global public good requiring international action. The interplay between the twin global challenges, as described in previous sections, is complex and uncertain. Therefore, international action is required for addressing the challenges that climate change poses for food security in developing countries like India. The following section discusses the major areas for international action.

Integration of climate change and food security concerns

As discussed above, climate change and food security, the two leading challenges for developing countries like India, are globally interconnected problems that call for a combined response. Therefore, food security considerations must feature more prominently in climate change negotiations. In its report on food security and climate change, the High-Level Panel of Experts on Food Security and Nutrition argued that climate change policies that fail to take into account the challenges confronting food and agriculture sectors in developing countries could prove extremely costly.

Despite the importance of the agriculture sector from the point of food security and the significant impact of climate change on this sector, the sector did not play a prominent role in climate negotiations for a long time. Agriculture became an agenda item under United Nations Framework Convention on Climate Change (UNFCCC) at the Conference of Parties (COP) 17 in Durban in 2011 where the UNFCCC's technical body (Subsidiary Body for Scientific and Technological Advice – SBSTA) was tasked to consider issues related to agriculture. Although negotiations on agriculture have been particularly difficult due to wide differences between countries, there has been some progress in recent years. The Paris Agreement concluded at COP 21 recognized the importance of safeguarding food security and ending hunger, as well as the particular vulnerabilities of food production systems, to the adverse impacts of climate change. Article 2 of the agreement emphasizes the importance of protecting food production while reducing greenhouse gases (UNFCCC, 2015). However, COP 23 in Bonn was the most significant step towards improving the livelihoods of farmers and making the global food supply more resilient while mitigating climate change. The Koronivia Joint Work on Agriculture adopted at Bonn, provides a new opportunity for addressing climate change impacts on agricultural production and addressing key issues like improving soil health, nutrient management and livestock systems, socio-economic issues and food security concerns. A feature of the Koronivia Joint Work on Agriculture is that for the first time the UNFCCC's implementation body (Subsidiary Body for Implementation – SBI) and the technical body, SBSTA, will work together to jointly address the issues facing agriculture. This is undoubtedly a welcome development but given the challenges that climate change poses for food security, transformative changes are required in the next decade.

A well-functioning international trading system as an adaptive strategy

Global food trade can play a significant role in offsetting the negative effects of climate change by allowing food to be supplied from surplus regions to deficient regions. Therefore, the freer movement of affordable food across borders is an essential adaptation strategy. Therefore, agricultural trade negotiations must incorporate the challenges of food security and climate change. The report of the High-Level Panel of Experts on Food Security and Nutrition of the Committee on World Food Security recommends a "transparent, accountable, and rules-based multilateral trading system" which takes into account public policy concerns regarding food security and the special needs of the poor and vulnerable countries and social groups (HLPE, 2012).

Given that food supply is likely to fluctuate in the future due to climate change, grain reserves will play an important adaptive role. Although grain reserves are an old concept, in recent years the subject has been fraught with many controversies. According to Murphy (2009), over the last 20 years, governments all over the world have curtailed their reserve programmes. This is largely because the dominant economic thinking in the globalized world, which favours open markets and is against any form of government intervention, did not subscribe to the idea of public food stockholding. However, grain reserves have served as a food security tool since time immemorial. In her paper on managing grain reserves, Sophia Murphy argues that the idea of a grain reserve is as old as civilisation itself and asserts that grain reserves are an important policy tool (Murphy, 2009).

In recent years, the issue of public food stockholding has proved to be the key stumbling block in WTO negotiations in the Doha Development Round. Under the global trade norms, a country's food subsidy bill should not breach the food subsidy cap of 10% of the value of production based on the reference price of 1986–1988. The full implementation of India's National Food Security Act might result in a breach of the prescribed limit. Therefore, India has been pushing for a revision of rules under the WTO's Agreement on Agriculture. Although the "peace clause" allows India's existing programmes to continue, a permanent solution is important for all developing countries wanting to establish food reserves to address their food security concerns, not just India.

Agricultural support in developed continues, one of the most controversial issues in global trade negotiations, also has important implications for the ability for developing country farmers to adapt to climate change. Hoffman (2011) argues that agricultural subsidies in developed countries act as a disincentive for the transition to sustainable agricultural practices in developing countries. Agricultural subsidies in developed countries as a percentage of the gross value of farm receipts are estimated to be about 30%, that is, about US$ 1 billion per day which costs developing countries about US$ 17 billion per year (Hoffman, 2011). Developing countries in Asia and Africa cannot be expected to implement a paradigm shift towards sustainable agricultural production if the Doha Round fails to address such fundamentally unequal conditions. Phasing out developed country agricultural subsidies must also be accompanied by a reform of the international trade policies that support ecological agriculture. The following measures are thus essential: the augmentation of local food production in developing countries by the adoption of improved technology, improved market access for developing country produce, policy space for developing countries to support their agriculture sector, government support for farmers' livelihoods, rural development and safety nets for the poor.

Higher share of agriculture in international aid

For a successful transition to climate-smart sustainable agriculture, international development cooperation needs to refocus on agriculture. Most studies indicate a consistent decline in the share of agriculture in official development assistance from the mid-1980s. For instance, Islam (2011) finds that the absolute amount of the total aid to agriculture in real terms increased from the early 1970s to the late 1980s and early 1990s but there was a steady decline from the 1990s onwards (Islam, 2011). According to Chimhowu (2013), the share of agriculture and rural development in total official development assistance declined to a mere 7% in 2009 from a high of 43% in the 1980s (Chimhowu, 2013). One of the main reasons for the decline in total aid to agriculture has been the higher prioritization of other sectors such as health, education, general budget support and water supply. But more importantly, the decline in the share of agriculture in total aid can be attributed to the international development community's complacency in terms of food availability since this was a period of relative food abundance and lower commodity prices (Islam, 2011). On the one hand, food production increased rapidly in food-exporting countries like Brazil and Argentina. On the other hand, there was low demand from large food consumers like India and China on account of higher self-sufficiency. As a result, the export interests of developed countries opposed aid for increasing production in developing countries out of fear of a further decrease in prices. Moreover, neo-liberalism gained currency in the mid-1980s. State control and regulation of agricultural markets were regarded as the main causes of structural problems in agriculture. Thus, donors cut back on direct support for agricultural inputs, agricultural extension services, agricultural finance and research (Chimhowu, 2013).

Such a narrow view of aid to agriculture fails to take into account the long-term imbalance in food demand and supply due to climate change. Given the challenges that small farmers in developing countries face, there is an urgent need to step up international aid for agriculture. Higher aid to agriculture had the potential to improve the adaptive capacity of the small-scale farmers in developing countries, help them adopt climate-smart agricultural technologies, and alleviate poverty in rural areas. Kaya et al. (2013) assert that aid given to the agricultural sector is very effective in reducing poverty both directly and indirectly through growth and a policy variable representing pro-poor expenditure. The positive impact on farm incomes and poverty reduction will also lead to an improvement in food access.

Things have changed for the better since the global food crisis in 2008. In 2009, the developed countries approved the L'Aquila Initiative on Global Food Security with the objective of investing USD 20 billion to encourage rural development in developing countries. At the regional level, the Comprehensive Africa Adaptive Development Programme (CAADP) compact committed African countries to spending 10% of government expenditure on agriculture. However, progress has been slow. There is an urgent need to step up investment in agriculture in developing countries.

Need for research

Lastly, it is important to recognize that our understanding of the impact of climate change on the overall food supply and food security is still at a nascent stage. The discourse on food security has mainly centred on its negative impact on cereal production. Less attention has been devoted to the study of the impact of climate change on the access, utilization and stability aspects of food security. Likewise, more research is required on the adaptation side of the problem. Agricultural research often serves the interests of large corporations in developed countries. But for a successful adaptation to climate change, future research needs to take into account the needs of the small producers, fishermen, indigenous people and the urban poor in developing countries.

Conclusion

Despite high rates of economic growth in the liberalized era, India continues to grapple with the issue of undernutrition. Agricultural productivity in India is low and Indian agriculture is in deep crisis. Providing a nutritious diet at affordable prices to its growing population will be a great challenge for India in the coming decades. Climate change poses significant additional stress on India's food security. This chapter highlights India's vulnerability and lists a range of policy recommendations at the national and global levels. At the national level, to ensure food security in a climate constrained world, the Indian state must climate-proof its agriculture sector by expanding its adaptation programmes and providing adequate safety nets for the poor. Climate change adaptation must be mainstreamed into existing successful welfare schemes like the MGNREGA. Given the vulnerability of the poor in urban areas, this chapter recommends an urban employment guarantee scheme which will not only provide livelihood security to the urban poor but also help create climate-resilient urban infrastructure. However, such national actions will be fruitless without some major policy changes at the international level. Firstly, there is a need for closer integration between food security and climate change actions. Secondly, a fair international trade system which keeps in mind the interests of the small producers and the poor in developing countries will play an important role in addressing food insecurity in the face of the climate challenges. Thirdly, developed countries need to step up agricultural aid to developing countries. Lastly, our understanding of the impacts of climate change on food systems and food security is still at a nascent stage and requires more intensive research.

References

Adam, Hans Nicolai, 2015. 'Mainstreaming Adaptation in India – the Mahatma Gandhi National Rural Employment Guarantee Act and Climate Change', *Climate and Development*, 7(2), 2015, pp: 142–152.

Chimhowu, Admos, 2013. 'Aid for Agriculture and Rural Development in the Global South: A Changing Landscape with New Players and Challenges', UNU-WIDER Working Paper No. 2013/014, United Nations University, February 2013. Online at: http://www20.iadb.org/intal/catalogo/PE/2013/11816.pdf

Dasgupta, Susmita, Subhendu Roy and Maria Sarraf, 2012. 'Urban Flooding in a Changing Climate: Case Study of Kolkata, India', *Asian-African Journal of Economics and Econometrics*, 12(1), 2012, pp: 135–158. Online at: http://www.serialsjournals.com/serialjournalmanager/pdf/1436348337.pdf

Deshpande, R.H. and Nagesh Prabhu, 2005. 'Farmer's Distress: Proof Beyond Question', *Economic and Political Weekly*, 40(44/45), 2005, pp: 4663–4665.

Dev, Mahendra S., 2012. 'Small Farmers in India: Challenges and Opportunities', Working Paper, WP-2012-014, Indira Gandhi Institute of Development Research, Mumbai. Online at: http://www.igidr.ac.in/pdf/publication/WP-2012-014.pdf

De Roy, Shantanu, 2017. 'Economic Reforms and Agricultural Growth in India', *Economic and Political Weekly*, 52(9), March 2017, pp. 67–72.

Economic Survey, 2018. 'Climate, Climate Change and Agriculture', in *Economic Survey 2017–18*, Ministry of Finance, Government of India, New Delhi.

FAO, 2008. *Climate Change and Food Security: A Framework Document*, Rome.

FAO, 2016. *Climate Change and Food Security: Risks and Responses*, Food and Agriculture Organisation. Online at: http://www.fao.org/3/a-i5188e.pdf

FAO, 2017. *The State of Food Security and Nutrition in the World. Building Resilience for Peace and Food Security*, Rome.

Ghosh, Jayati, 2014. 'Growth, Industrialisation and Inequality in India', *Journal of the Asia Pacific Economy*, 20, 2015, pp. 42–56.

HLPE, 2012. *Food Security and Climate Change. A Report by the High-Level Panel of Experts on Food Security and Nutrition of the Committee on World Food Security*, Rome.

Hoffmann, Ulrich, 2011. 'Assuring Food Security in Developing Countries under the Challenges of Climate Change: Key Trade and Development Issues of a Fundamental Transformation of Agriculture', UNCTAD Discussion Paper 201, February 2011.

Islam, Nurul, 2011. 'Foreign Aid to Agriculture: Review of Facts and Analysis', IFPRI Discussion Paper 01053, January 2011, Online at: http://cdm15738.contentdm.oclc.org/utils/getfile/collection/p15738coll2/id/124880/filename/124881.pdf

Kaya, Ozgur, Ilker Kaya and L.F. Gunter, 2013. 'Foreign Aid and the Quest for Poverty Reduction: Is Aid to Agriculture Effective?', *Journal of Agricultural Economics,* 64(3), 2013, pp: 583–596. Online at: https://doi.org/10.1111/1477-9552.12023

Kumar, Praduman, P.K. Joshi and Pratap S. Birthal, 2009. 'Demand Projections for Food Grains in India', *Agricultural Economics Research Review*, 22(July-December), 2009, pp: 237–247.

Kumar, Praduman, P.K. Joshi and Surabhi Mittal, 2016. 'Demand vs Supply of Food in India – Futuristic Projection', *Proceedings of the Indian National Science Academy*, 82(5), December 2016, pp: 1579–1586.

Lakshminarayanan, Subitha and Ramakrishnan Jayalakshmy, 2015. 'Diarrheal Diseases Among Children in India: Current Scenario and Future Perspectives', *Journal of Natural Science, Biology and Medicine*, 6(1), 2015, pp: 24–28. Online at: https://www.ncbi.nlm.nih.gov/pmc/articles/PMC4367049/

Lal, M., et al., 2001. 'Asia', in *Climate Change 2001: Impacts, Adaptation and Vulnerability, Contribution of Working Group II to the Third Assessment Report of the Intergovernmental Panel on Climate Change*, Online at: http://www.grida.no/publications/other/ipcc_tar/

Lobell, David B., Adam Sibley and J. Ivan Ortiz-Monasterio, 2012. 'Extreme Heat Effects on Wheat Senescence in India', *Nature Climate Change*, 2, 2012, pp: 186–189. Online at: http://www.nature.com/nclimate/journal/v2 /n3/full/nclimate1356.html

Ministry of Finance, 2018. 'Climate, Climate Change and Agriculture', in *Economic Survey 2017–18*, Ministry of Finance, Government of India, New Delhi.

Ministry of Statistics and Programme Implementation, 2014. *Key Indicators of Situation of Agricultural Households in India, NSS 70th Round*, National Sample Survey Office, Government of India, December 2014.

Mittal, Surbhi, 2006. 'Structural Shift in Demand for Food: Projections for 2020', Working Paper 184, Indian Council for Research on International Economic Research, New Delhi, August 2006. Online at: http://www.icrier.org/pdf/WP_184.pdf

Moors, E. et al., 2013. 'Climate Change and Waterborne Diarrhoea in Northern India: Impacts and Adaptation Strategies', *Science of the Total Environment*, 468–469(Supplement), 2013, pp: S139–151, 2013, Online at: https://www.ncbi.nlm.nih.gov/pubmed/23972324

Myers, Samuel S., et al., 2014. 'Rising CO_2 Threatens Human Nutrition', *Nature*, 510(7503), 2014, pp: 139–142. Online at: http://www.ncbi.nlm.nih.gov/pmc/articles/PMC4810679/

Murphy, Sophia, 2009. 'Strategic Grain Reserves in an Era of Volatility', Institute for Agriculture and Trade Policy, October 2009. Online at: http://www.panna.org/sites/default/files/GrainReserves_IATP.pdf

Porter, J.R., et al., 2014. 'Food Security and Food Production Systems', in: *Climate Change 2014: Impacts, Adaptation, and Vulnerability. Part A: Global and Sectoral Aspects. Contribution of Working Group II to the Fifth Assessment Report of the Intergovernmental Panel on Climate Change* [Field, C.B., V.R. Barros, D.J. Dokken, K.J. Mach, M.D. Mastrandrea, T.E. Bilir, M. Chatterjee, K.L. Ebi, Y.O. Estrada, R.C. Genova, B. Girma, E.S. Kissel, A.N. Levy, S. MacCracken, P.R. Mastrandrea and L.L. White (eds.)]. Cambrdige: Cambridge University Press, pp: 485–533.

Prasad, R.S. and Ridhima Sud, 2019. 'Implementing Climate Change Adaptation: Lessons from India's National Adaptation Fund on Climate Change (NAFCC)', *Climate Policy*, 19:3, 2019, pp: 354–366. Online at: https://doi.org/10.1080/14693062.2018.1515061

Ramachandran, Nira, 2014. *Persisting Undernutrition in India: Causes, Consequences and Possible Solutions*, Springer, New Delhi.

Ramana, V. Dhara, Paul J. Schramm and George Luber, 2014. 'Climate Change & Infectious Diseases in India: Implications for Health Care Providers', *Indian Journal of Medical Research*, 138(6), 2014, pp: 847–852. Online at: http://www.ncbi.nlm.nih.gov/pmc/articles/PMC3978971/

Reddy, V. Ratna and S. Galab, 2006. 'Agrarian Crisis: Looking beyond the Debt Trap', *Economic and Political Weekly*, 41(19), 2006, pp: 1838–1841.

Rodriguez-Llanes, J.M., Ranjan-Dash, S., Degomme, O., et al., 2011. 'Child Malnutrition and Recurrent Flooding in Rural Eastern India: A Community-based Survey', *BMJ Open*, 1, 2011. Online at: http://bmjopen.bmj.com/content/1/2/e000109.full

Schmidhuber, Josef and Francesco N. Tubiello, 2007. 'Global Food Security under Climate Change', *Proceedings of the National Academy of Sciences*, 104(50), 2007, pp: 19703–19708. Online at: http://www.pnas.org/content/104/50/19703.full.pdf

Shiao, Tien, Andrew Maddocks, Chris Carson and Emma Loizeaux, 2015. '3 Maps Explain India's Growing Water Risks'. Online at: http://www.wri.org/blog/2015/02/3-maps-explain-india%E2%80%99s-growing-water-risks

Tripathi, Amarnath and Ashok K. Mishra, 2017. 'Knowledge and Passive Adaptation to Climate Change: An Example from Indian Farmers', *Climate Risk Management*, 16, 2017, pp: 195–207.

UNFCCC, 2015. Adoption of the Paris Agreement, United Nations Framework Convention on Climate Change, Conference of Parties, Twenty-first Session, Paris, 30 November-11 December 2015. Online at: https://unfccc.int/resource/docs/2015/cop21/eng/l09r01.pdf

United Nations, 2015. *Interim Report of the Special Rapporteur on the Right to Food*, United Nations General Assembly, Seventieth Session, Item 73 (b), A/70/287, August 2015.

United Nations, 2017. 'World Population Prospects: The 2017 Revision, Key Findings and Advance Tables', Working Paper No. ESA/P/WP/248. United Nations, Department of Economic and Social Affairs, Population Division, 2017.

World Bank, 2013. *Turn Down the Heat: Climate Extremes, Regional Impacts, and the Case for Resilience*, International Bank for Reconstruction and Development/World Bank, Washington DC, June 2013.

Index

Note: Page numbers in *italic* indicate figures and in **bold** indicate tables.

Aadhaar-Based Biometric Authentication (ABBA) 13, 14
Aadhaar cards xxii, xxv, 30, 32, 56
Accredited Social Health Activist (ASHA) 39
Adam, H. N. 164
agrarian distress, and farmer deaths 33–34
Agreement on Agriculture (AoA) 109
Agricultural Market Information System (AMIS) xxviii, 140
agricultural subsidies 136, 139, 167
agriculture aid, decline in 167–168
Agriculture Produce Market Committees (APMC) Act 112
agriculture prosperity, impact on rural poverty 113
AgriTech exhibition 126
Agri-Tech Infrastructure Fund (ATIF) 40
aid to agriculture 167–168
Akshaya Patra Foundation 50
All India Coordinated Wheat Improvement Project 144
All-India FPS Owners Association (AIFSDF) 59
Anderson, G. 144
Andhra Pradesh 15, 33, 50, 56, 92, 125, 158
Anganwadi (childcare centre) 1–3
Annamitra programme 50
Annapurna Yojana 105–106
Antyodaya Anna Yojana (AAY) 4, 16, 55, 86, 105
arboviral diseases 162

Basu, J. 124
Bengal famine (1943) 68
Bhalla, S. 105
Bharatiya Mazdoor Sangh (BMS) 91
Bharat Nirman Scheme xxi
Bharti Foundation 50
Bihar 62; access to land, in rural households 76, 77; food entitlements in xxvi, 69–71; food production, challenges in 71, 76–77; food security, at household level *see* household food security study, in Bihar and Karnataka; land reform efforts in 70, 81
Bill and Melinda Gates Foundation 107
biofortification 47–48
biometric unique IDs (Aadhaar) *see* Aadhaar cards
bonded labour 99
Borlaug, N. 144
"Bringing the Green Revolution to Eastern India (BGREI)" 22, 33
Britannia 50–51
Britannia Nutrition Foundation 51
Burnett, K. 138

carbon dioxide levels, elevation 159, 161
Centralized Online Real-time Electronic PDS (CORE PDS) 12–13, 61
Centrally Sponsored Schemes (CSSs) 9
Central Research Institute for Dry-land Agriculture 72
Chhattisgarh: CORE PDS, reform programme in 12–13, 61–62; doorstep delivery, to FPS 61–62; GPS tracking, of food trucks 25; issued food coupon 25; offline transactions 64; "portability" of entitlement/FPS 62, 63; self-help groups

(SHGs), handling ration shops 61; success model, of TDPS 58, 61–63; technology interventions, to eliminate corruption 34, 62
chikungunya, and dengue 162
Chimhowu, A. 167
climate change: carbon dioxide levels, elevation 159, 161; collective action problem 165; floods and droughts, occurrence 160, 162; food insecurity and 155, 160; global food trading for 166–167; impact understanding, need for research 168; integration with food security concerns 165–166; international action/aid, need for 165–168; rainfall fluctuation, and extreme heat 158–160; urgent efforts, need for 163–164
climatic changes, impact in India's food security xxviii, 67–69, 155, 156–158, 165; access to food 159–160, 164; challenges for India, agriculture 156–158, **157**; food production and availability xxviii, 68–69, 155, 158–159; and food security, interconnected problems 165–166; food utilization 161–162, **161**; range of policy actions, taken for 162–164
Committee on Food Security (CFS) 139
Comprehensive Africa Adaptive Development Programme (CAADP) 168
Comprehensive Framework for Action (CFA) 107–108, 139
"Core of Core" programs 9–10
COVID-19 pandemic, and economic disruption 129
crop insurance, universalization of 34
cropping systems, in India: crop rotations 42–43; intercropping/mixed cropping 43–44; species of pulse crops 42
Custom Milled Rice (CMR) agencies 28

Dalwai, A. 33
Deaton, A. 79, 82
Department of Agriculture and Co-operation and Farmers' Welfare 20
Department of Fertilizer 20
Deshpande, R. H. 157
Development as Freedom (Sen) 19
diarrhoea-related deaths 161–162
direct benefit transfers (DBT), implementation 15
Doubling Farmers Income (DFIC) 33–34, 145
Drèze, J. 79, 82
drip irrigation technology 122, 128
droughts, and floods xxix, 19, 30, 44, 123, 160, 162
Du Pont 50, 51
DuPont Danisco Soy Protein 51

economic development 70; disaster of 105
Eleventh Five Year Plan (2011–2012) 30
El Niño/La Niña phenomena 155
Emergency Feeding Programme (EFP) 86, 105
employment, key factor 70
e-NAM (National Agricultural Market) 32–33, 40
entitlements: Aadhaar role in accessing 30, 59; among poor households xxvi; *see also* household food security study, in Bihar and Karnataka; defined as 69; direct and indirect food, for vulnerable groups 86–87; *see also* Odisha, food entitlements in; exchange 75, 77–78, 81; to governmental food security programmes *see* National Food Security Act, 2013 (NFSA); Targeted Public Distribution System (TPDS); legal, providing stable access to food 69–71; process of claiming, in beneficiary death case 94–95; Sen's concept of 69; to work *see* Right to Work Act
Essential Commodities (Amendment) Act 34
Essential Foods Act 112
EWA (Extraction of Water from Air) technology 126
Excessive Food Price Variability Early Warning System xxviii
exchange entitlements 75, 77–78, 81

Fair Price Scheme xxii
famines 67, 103
Farmers Agreement on Price Assurance and Farm Services Act 34
Farmers' Field Schools (FFS) 22

farmers' insurance 20, 32, 145; *see also* Doubling Farmers Income (DFIC)
Farmers' Produce Trade and Commerce (Promotion and Facilitation) Act 34
food: aid 118, 136, 149; availability, and access to land 70; business organizations, for supplying nutrition 50–51; choices for urban consumers 47; commodities loss 45; delivery and distribution, gaps in 56; entitlements, in Bihar/Karnataka *see* household food security study, in Bihar and Karnataka; forestry, as source of 44–45; fortification plan 48; grain distribution, subsidized 1, 3; *see also* Public Distribution System (PDS); Targeted Public Distribution System (TPDS); issues, complicated terrain of 138; price crisis, 2008 xxviii; production impetus 39–42; risk assessment and risk management (RARMs) of 46; shortages issue, institutions addressing 136, 137; supply, challenges to 67–68; utilization, refers to 161
Food and Agricultural Organization (FAO), UN 102, 136–138
Food Corporation of India (FCI) 24, 38, 57, 103
food crisis: in 2007–2008 135–136, 139, 147, 168; biofuels production, and food grains diversion for 135, 147, 148; first, in 1970s 134, 137
food processing industry (FPI) 46
Food Safety and Standards Authority of India (FSSAI) 46, 47
Food Safety and Standards Regulation 48
food security: agenda, international trade negotiations xxii; agriculture, mainstay of 39; BRIC countries, action plan on xxix; challenges to 45, 111, 115, 118, 123, 129, 155; complex sociopolitical phenomenon xx, xxiv; crux of, in India 54, 144; ecosystem of xxv, 19; emphasis on, improving policy implementation 111–113, 115; empirical studies on xxv, 71–73; FAO defines 102; FAO's approach to 136; four-pronged approach to 139; G20 addressing issues relating to 133; *see also* Group of Twenty (G20), and governance of food; global, narrative of 134–136; globalization of agricultural markets 110; governance, changes to improve 111–114; at household/local level 67–68; human rights regime, and FAO approach to 138–139; in India, empirical studies xxv, 71; *see also* household food security study, in Bihar and Karnataka; initiatives, by Indian government **104**; international institutions relevant to 106, **107**; issue for developing nations 109; legal frameworks of xxv; "lifecycle approach" to 87; measures, individual xxi; and Multi-Year Plan for Development xxvii; Narayanan's article on 1; narrative on, issues dominating 144; objectives at grassroots level, challenges 54; regulatory interventions 70; schemes addressing issue of xxi–xxii; solutions 67; story in India 144–148; WFP defines 1; World Food Summit, defines (1974/1996) 134
food sovereignty movement xxiii
food systems approach 68
forest biodiversity 47, 52
Freedom from Hunger campaign 147
Fundamental Right to Life, (Article 21) 24

G20 Food Security and Nutrition Framework 140–142
Gal-Mobile 126
General Agreement on Tariffs and Trade (GATT) 106
genetically modified organisms (GMOs) seeds xxiii
Global Crop Diversity Trust, 2004 xxiii
global food governance: complexity, and challenges xxvii, 108–110; food-related issues, governance at global level 136–139; and India's food security xxvii, 108–109, 111–114; India's role in 106–109; institutions and mechanisms, contributing to xxviii, 106, **107**; liberal trade policies, and exports 109
global food reserve 136
global food security complex 138

Global Hunger Index (GHI) 54, 119–120, 129, 133, 156
Global Poverty Index 129
Global Seed Vault, in Svalbard xxiii–xxiv
governance, of food: G20 focus on agriculture and 140–144; history of, in India 103–106; international, India's role in 114–115; local and global significance of xxviii–xxix; research, in India xxiv–xxviii; *see also* global food governance
greenhouse gases, threat 155
"green revolution" xxi, 21–23, 39, 54, 103; cereals, pulses and oilseeds, production of **22**; food production, insufficiency 122–123; semi-dwarf varieties of wheat 144
Group of Twenty (G20), and food governance xxvii–xxviii, 139–144; achievements 141; assistance for 140; countries 133; developmental issues, in agenda 140; events/summits held xxviii–xxix, 140–143; GHI scores of 133; global food security narrative 134–136; important role of 139; shortcomings in action on, food security-related issues 143
Gujarat 112, 123, 125, 156, 159–160
Gulati, A. 70
Gupta, B. K. 143

Harvest Plus 47
Haryana 22, 50, 103, 125, 127
hidden hunger 40, 47–48
High-Level Task Force on the Global Food Security Crisis (HLTF), UN xxviii, 107, 139
High-Value Agriculture (HVA) 21
high yielding varieties (HYVs) 103
Hoffmann, U. 167
Horticulture Mission 21
horticulture policy xxi
household food security study, in Bihar and Karnataka: dhal and staple foods in meal 73–74, **73**, 75; differences between states 71–72; disadvantaged, concentration in 72–73; employment, and source of income **77**, 78; food deficit, reasons for 75, *76*, 81; food production, challenges in 71, 76–**77**; household surveys, and data collection 71–72; illiteracy rate 72–73; implications of poverty 71; interview on, meals day before 73–74, **73**; land access, and sharecropping 76, **77**; meal patterns, questions on eating 72, 80; MGNREGA scheme, implementation 78; migrant workers in 78, 81–83; PDS high dependence on 74, **75**, **79**, 81; procurement of food, forms of 74, **75**, 79; public programmes offering food in 79–80; public services, reach of 78–80; rural districts, surveys in 72; self-employment, among rural households 78; social rights, performance in 78–80, 82; unemployment/low income, factors 75, 78; urban slums of Bangalore/Patna, surveys 72, 75; vulnerability, indicators assessing 72
Human Development Index (HDI) 71, 119, 156
hunger-related issues and deaths 86, 133

identity document, and benefits/entitlements 30, 32
India: access, equity and inclusion (AEI) issue 46–47; active role in FAO 145–146; agrarian crisis in, current 163; agricultural policy in, departments role 20–21; agricultural problems 123; agriculture exports from 108–109; challenges, climatic 156–158, **157**; CoEs list in **125**; components of, food security 118, 129; continuing increase, in national food production 39–42; Covid pandemic, impact in vulnerable states 82–83; cropping systems, spectrum of 42–44; farmer suicides across xxiv, 33–34, 123, 158; food challenges history in 102; food governance history in 103–106; food insecurity in xx–xxi, 37, 67–69, 102, 105, 113–115; *see also* food security; food security challenges, Israel's role in addressing 119–120, 123; food security initiatives, by government **104**; food subsidy bill 109–110; Green Revolution in xxi, 21–23; IFAD strengthening 147; integrated farming system for,

small farms 41–42; interventions in food-related issues 147–148; key role on, global food governance xx, 106–109, 114–115; malnutrition in *see* malnutrition; nutritional security challenges in xxv, 37, 51–52, 156; *see also* nutrition, and security of; population size xxii; ranking in, GHI and GPI 54, 119–120, 129, 133; self-sufficiency, in food production xxi, xxii, 19, 108, 144, 147, 168; small farmer distress in xxiv, 105, 135, 144–146, 149; technological assistance, from Israel to xxvii, 118, 126, 128–129; undernutrition in 38–39, 47, 49, 156, 160, 164, 169; urban poor, rising numbers of 146; WTO Agreement on Agriculture 24, 109–110, 135, 167
India Brazil South Africa (IBSA) dialogue xxix
Indian Council for Agriculture Research (ICAR) 20
Indian Council of Legal Aid and Advice (ICLAA) 88
Indian International Rice Research Institute (IRRI) xxi
Indira Awaas Yojana 92
Indira Gandhi Matritva Sahyog Yojana (IGMSY) 1, 2, 8
Indo-Israeli Agricultural Project (IIPA): Centres of Excellence (CoE), formation 124–**125**, 126, 128; Israel's role in 126; primary objectives of 124
Indo-Israeli relations: de-centralization process 124, 127; food security, core areas in 118; issues relevant in 126–127; opportunities, and challenges of xxvii 119, 128–129; primacy of agriculture 124–127; and security-strategic issues 118; Strategic Partnership in Water and Agriculture 126; water management 126–127
informal labour market 70
Ingram, J. 68
insecurity, of food: agriculture prosperity need for 113; challenge 155; characterized as 67; explanation for 68; Himalayas, case study 68; household, dependence on legal entitlements 69–70; impact of environmental degradation *see* climate change; implications of xxiv; and malnutrition xx, 67; number of conflicts and 155; nutritional challenges with 37; persistence, in India 105; poverty, as main cause of 141; *see also* food security
Integrated Child Development Services (ICDS) 1, 9, 46, 48, 49, 71, 79, 86, 104, 146
International Crops Research Institute for the Semi-Arid Tropics (ICRISAT) xxi, xxiv
International Developmental Cooperation (MASHAV) 124
International Food Policy Research Institute (IFPRI) 136
International Fund of Agricultural Development (IFAD) 137, 147
International Grain Price Agreement 137
international institutions, relevant to food security 106, **107**
ISKCON Food Relief Foundation (IFRF) 50
Islam, N. 167
Israel: accomplishments 121–122; agricultural practices of 127; desalination projects in 122, 126; differences between 119–120; emerged as, leader in water technology 122; FAO reports on 119–120; GHI, ranking in 120; Global Food Security Index, ranking in 120; innovative methods, for self-sufficiency 121; poverty rate in 119; role in assisting India, in agricultural sector xxvii, 118–120, 123–127; socio-economic indicators, in terms of 119; undernourishment in 120; water scarcity issue 120–122; *see also* food security; India
Istanbul Summit, 2015 G20 141

Jakhar, B. 124
Jameel Poverty Action Lab (J-PAL) 15
Janani Suraksha Yojana (JSY) 9
Jharkhand 14, 50, 56, 146, 156, 158

Karnataka: exchange entitlements 77–78; food entitlements in xxvi, 69–71; food security in 73–76, **73**, **75**, 76,

77; *see also* household food security study, in Bihar and Karnataka
Kaya, O. 168
Kerala 56, 112, 114, 123, 146, 158
Khera, R. 15, 82
Kisan Bima Yojana 145
Kisan Credit Card programme 20
Krishi Bhawan (KB), and policies 21
Krishi Karman Awards 28
K.S. Puttaswamy vs. Union of India 32
Kumar, P. 156

La Aquila Summit of 2008 139
land reform legislation 70
L'Aquila initiative 147, 168
"learner" states 89
Lobell, D. B. 159

Madhya Pradesh 11, 32, 33, 125, 156, 158–160
Maharashtra 11, 33, 50, 89, 125, 156, 159–160
Mahatma Gandhi National Rural Employment Guarantee Act (MGNREGA) xxi–xxii, 19, 29; implications for rural economy 30, 78; performance of **31**; role in natural resource management 164
malaria 162
malnutrition, and lack of food: as (SDG)-2 goal 49–50; in India, persistence of xx, 1, 38–39, 106, 112; lack of purchasing power, leading to 82; micronutrient/ due to caloric imbalances 47–48, 67; MNCs working for 51; NFSA preventing malnutrition 87; policy improvements to 105; protein 51; in rural and urban population 47, 67; *see also* undernutrition
Margulis, M. E. 138
maternity benefits, under NFSA 2, 8, 9; *Janani Suraksha Yojana* (JSY) 9
Meeting of Agricultural Chief Scientists (MACS) 143
Mexico Summit, 2012 G20 140, 143
micro, small and medium enterprises (MSMEs) 41, 45, 52
micronutrient malnutrition, and biofortification 47–48, 51
Mid-Day Meal (MDM) scheme xxi, 1, 9, 46, 49–50, 71, 79, 86, 88, 105
Minimum Support Price (MSP) xxi, 103, 110
Ministry of Commerce 20
Mirzapur 57
Mishra, A. K. 163
Mission Mode programmes 21
Mission on Micro Irrigation 21
Mittal, S. 156
Modi, N. 118, 126, 128
monsoon, and agriculture 44, 123, 158
Moors, E. 162
Mousseau, F. 136
Multi-Year Plan for Development xxvii
Murphy, S. 166
Myers, S. S. 161

National Action Plan for Climate Change (NAPCC) 40, 163
National Adaptation Fund for Climate Change (NAFCC) 163
National Agricultural Development Program (NADP) xxv, 39
National Agriculture Research (NAR) system 20
National Electronic Fund Transfer (NEFT) 29
National Farmers Insurance Programme 20
National Food Security Act, 2013 (NFSA) xx, xxv, xxvi, 1–2, 16, 19, 71, 167; Aadhaar card, and fake ration cards removal 32; beneficiaries identification issue 10–11, 71, 112; budgetary allocations for programmes 6, **9**, 10; cash *vs.* kind transfers 14–15; challenges traditional gender norms 87; children, nutrition for 3; delayed implementation, reasons 6, 8, 16; eligible households identification 5; emphasis on, TDPS reforms 5–6, 27, 112; enactment of 1, 2, 24–25, 54–55, 106, 144–145, 164–165; evolution of **25**; extends TPDS coverage 4, 55; fiscal devolution impact on, implementation of 9–10; grievance redressal mechanisms 87; implementation challenges 2, 9–12; maternity benefits under, pivotal role 2, 8–10; Ministry of Law and Justice, defines 86; old TPDS beneficiary database, use 11–12; prices

reduction, food grains 5; promoting climate resilience 164; provision for, food security allowance 6; -related dates, and timeline of implementation 7; rights-based approach, to food entitlements 25, 55, 86–88; rollout, issues related to 2, 6–10; salient features of **23**; shift from welfare to rights-based approach 25, 55, 86; special provisions in 87; subsidized food grains under 3–4, 49, 51, 55, 71; universal maternity benefits, lack of 8–9; use of SECC/old TPDS beneficiary database 10–12; weaknesses, and issues unaddressed 145; *see also* Public Distribution System (PDS); Targeted Public Distribution System (TPDS)
National Food Security Bill, 2013 xxii
National Food Security Mission (NFSM) xxi, xxv, 19, 22, 39
National Health Plan, 2017 39
National Horticultural Mission (NHM) 39
National Human Rights Commission (NHRC) 25
National Initiative of Climate Resilient Agriculture (NICRA) 72
National Institute of Nutrition 47
National Mission on Horticultural Development (NMHD) 39
National Mission on Sustainable Agriculture (NMSA) 40
National Nutrition Mission, 2018 112
National Population Register (NPR) 11
National Rural Employment Guarantee Act (NREGA 2006) xxii
National Rural Health Mission (NRHM) 49
National Water Carrier 122
Nestlé Healthy Kids Programme 50–51
Netanyahu, B. 118, 126
nutrition, and security of: business organizations, supplying 50–51; challenges of 51–52; crop-genetic improvement technologies, enhancing 40–41; deficiency, and biofortification 47–48; food as source of 38–39; forestry and food for 44–45; full spectrum of 38; ICDS role in *see* Integrated Child Development Services (ICDS); implies 37; improving 112; integrated farming system role 40–41; mandatory food fortification for 48–49; requirements for Indians 47; security, government schemes for 49–51; women's empowerment role in 52

Odisha, food entitlements in xxvi–xxvii, 62, 86, 88; accessibility to poor, problems in 90–99; civil society engagement, need for 90, 92; decentralization process, critiquing 89, 96, 97; direct cash transfers, in banks 98; food security and governance in xxvi–xxvii; hunger related measures in, as per SC directives 86, 88–89, 93–94; institutional coordination, lack of 99; Kalahandi–Bolangir–Koraput region in 62, 98, 105; mining corporations, favours to 99; officials/dutybearer's, attitude towards poor xxvii, 92–93; people's unawareness 91–92; political will and commitment, for implementation 86–89, 91, 99–100; rights-based policies, problems relating to 94–96; schemes for disabled 91; shortcomings in schemes 95–96, 99; state preparedness, in terms of resources/actions xxvii, 86, 88, 90, 98, 100; unequal social status impact 92–93

Panchayati Raj Extension Services Act (PESA) of 1996 96
Paris Summit, G20 146
Patel, R. 79, 82
Patenting Act, 1970 xxiii
Pawar, S. 124
People's Union for Civil Liberties (PUCL) 24
Peres, S. 124
pigeon pea crop xxiv
point of sale (PoS) machines 12
poor households, entitlements among xxvi
poor nutrition problem xxv
Popularly Positioned Products (PPPs) 51
poverty: (SDG 1), goal to end 27, 120; above/below line (APL/BPL), categories 3–4, 55, 71, **79**, 145;

agriculture/economic growth, for reducing 105, 109, 113; dispersion in rural areas, and land access link 70, 72, 120, 168; lack of income, and food supplies link 68, 82; main cause of, food insecurity 141; study the implications of *see* household food security study, in Bihar and Karnataka; suicides and 33; *see also* malnutrition, and lack of food
Prabhu, N. 157
Pradhan Mantri Matru Vandana Yojana (PMMVY) 1, 2; IGMSY renamed 1, 2
Prasad, R.S. 163
priority households (PHH) 55, 71, 87, 145
procurement policies, and distribution system xxv
Protection of Human Rights Act, 1993 88
Public Distribution System (PDS) xx, 23–24, 38, 54; based on ration cards 71; beneficiaries of, categories 55, 71, 112; Chhattisgarh, as success model 58, 61–63; digitization of 57; as food security measures xxi; impact of right to food on 27; introduced in 1940s 23, 103; introduction of Aadhaar, impact 56; leakages, concerns about xx, xxii, 24, 34, 56, 59, 104; structure of *26*
Public Evaluation of Entitlement Programmes (PEEP) Survey 89
Pulses and Oilseeds Research Station at Berhampore 20
Punjab 22, 25, 103, 114, 125, 127; *Atta-Dal* scheme 25

Rajasthan 13, 14, 44, 50, 89, 114, 123, 125, 159
Rajiv Gandhi Scheme for Empowerment of Adolescent Girls 50
Ramachandran, N. 162
Rashtriya Krishi Vikas Yojana (RKVY) 20, 39
ration cards: bogus 32; categories of 71
"regime complex" 138
Revamped Public Distribution System (RPDS) 3
Rice Research Institute at Chinsurah 20
rights-based policies xxvi
right to food xx, xxi, xxv, 24, 34; Aadhaar card for 32; fundamental right, NFSA made 86–87; from Green Revolution to xxi–xxiv; procurement and prices, impacts on 27; *see also* National Food Security Act, 2013 (NFSA)
Right to Food social audit (2012) 97
Right to Public Services 2013 94
Right to Work Act 29–30, 34
risk assessment and risk management (RARMs) 46
Rodriguez-Llanes, J.M. 160

salt, iodization of 48
schemes addressing, food security issue xxi–xxii
seed sovereignty xxiii
Sen, A. xxvi, 19, 68, 82, 134
Sen, B. R. 146
Seoul Summit of G20 xxvii
sharecropping 70
Silviculture 42
Singh, M. 115
smart ration cards (SRCs) 62
Socio-Economic Caste Census (SECC) data 8
soil health cards 20, 40
Sonebhadra 57–59
SRI (System of Rice Intensification) 22
staple food prices, stability 19
starvation deaths 56–57, 64, 86, 88, 90, 104
State Horticultural Missions (SHM) 39
State Institute for Rural Development (SIRD) 89
St Petersburg Action Plan 2013 140
Sud, R. 163
suicides, of farmers xxiv, 33–34, 123, 158
Sustainable Agriculture Initiative 135
Sustainable Development Goals (SDGs), UN xvii, 27, 37; to end poverty, (SDG 1) 27, 120; Goal 2 (SDG 2), "Zero Hunger" and malnutrition xvii, xxv–xxvi, 27, 49–51, 120, 133; India's progress in meeting, goals one and two 120; sustainable consumption and production (SDG 12) 27
Swaminathan, M.S. 124

Tamil Nadu 25, 56, 112
Targeted Public Distribution System (TPDS) xxvi, 1, 10, 38, 54, 86, 98, 146; beneficiaries, categories 4, 55; cash transfers, shift to 14–15, 54; charges of "leakages," and complaints 56; Chhattisgarh, as success model 58, 61–63; COREPDS, benefits and issues 12–13; criticisms of 13; digitization of 12, 59; "Doorstep delivery" of food grain 5; food preference over cash 15; grains diversion trends, classifies states 3, 12; increased coverage of 4; internet connectivity issues 13, 14, 60; NFSA emphasis on, TDPS reforms 5–6, 55–56; performance, and corruption 3; pursual in districts of, eastern UP 55, 56; *see also* Uttar Pradesh; states with low leakages 56; technology use in 12–14
tax devolution 9
Technology Mission on Pulses and Oilseeds (TMOP) 39
Tilly, C. 69
Trade-Related Aspects of Intellectual Property Rights (TRIPS) xxiii, 146, 147, 149
Tripathi, A. 163

UN Committee on Food Security (CFS) 106–107
undernutrition 38–39, 47, 49, 155, 156, 160, 164, 169
Union Agriculture Ministry, departments 21
United Nations Human Development Index (HDI) 156
unorganized work 70
urban poor, rising numbers of xxiv, 146, 164, 169
Uttar Pradesh, PDS challenges in 56, 63–65; Aadhaar cards, frauds/misuse 59, 60–61; BPL beneficiaries identification, problematic 57–58; complaints 59; corruption, and diversion practices in 58, 61, 63; digitization process 64; disadvantaged groups in 57; food security in, problematic issue xxvi, 56–57; grievance redressal machinery, ineffective in 60, 62, 65; hunger deaths, cases 56–57, 67; inefficiencies/gaps in TDPS practices 57–61; *Kotedars*, and nexus of elites 59–61, 63; malfunctioning machines, and internet issue 59–60; nomadic tribes in 58; PDS reforms, need for meaningful 63–65; procurement and delivery, problems in 58–61; ration cards portability issue 64; "reviving" state 63, 65; scandal, in August 2018 61; TDPS implementation, challenges of xxvi, 56–61; technology, and internet use 64; vigilance committee role 60

Varanasi 57, 59–61
Village Health Sanitation and Nutrition Committee (VHSNC) 39
virtual reserve, notion 136
Vogel, O. 144

wage employment 29, 30
water-food-energy nexus 146
water-surplus states 127
Weizman, E. 124
West Bengal: Centralized Procurement Centres (CPCs) in 29; e-procurement, and NEFT payments 29; Khadya Sathi (Food Support) programme of 25, 28; Krishi Karman Award, five successive 27–28; MGNREGA, Burdwan district in 20; procurement status in **29**; production figures for **28**; research wings in 20
World Food Council (WFC) 137
World Food Programme (WFP) 1, 137
World Food Summit, 1996/1974 67, 134
World Trade Organization (WTO) 106, 136; Agreement on Agriculture (AoA) 24, 109, 135, 138, 167

Yadav, A. 14

For Product Safety Concerns and Information please contact our EU representative GPSR@taylorandfrancis.com
Taylor & Francis Verlag GmbH, Kaufingerstraße 24, 80331 München, Germany

www.ingramcontent.com/pod-product-compliance
Ingram Content Group UK Ltd.
Pitfield, Milton Keynes, MK11 3LW, UK
UKHW020005200926
475702UK00015B/2493
9781032224596